LAUREL CANYON

LAUREL

THE INSIDE STORY OF ROCK-AND-ROLL'S

CANYON

LEGENDARY NEIGHBORHOOD

MICHAEL WALKER

FABER AND FABER, INC.

AN AFFILIATE OF FARRAR, STRAUS AND GIROUX

NEW YORK

Faber and Faber, Inc.
An affiliate of Farrar, Straus and Giroux
19 Union Square West, New York 10003

Library of Congress Cataloging-in-Publication Data
Walker, Michael, 1957–
    Laurel Canyon : the inside story of rock-and-roll's legendary neighborhood /
Michael Walker.— 1st ed.
        p.   cm.
    Includes index.
    ISBN-13: 978-0-571-21149-4 (hardcover : alk. paper)
    ISBN-10: 0-571-21149-6 (hardcover : alk. paper)
    1. Rock music—California—Los Angeles—History and criticism.   2. Popular
culture—California—Los Angeles.   3. Laurel Canyon (Los Angeles, Calif.)
I. Title.

    ML3534.W285   2006
    781.66'09794'94—dc22

                                                        2005025569

Designed by Jonathan D. Lippincott
Map designed by Joe LeMonnier

www.fsgbooks.com

10   9   8   7   6   5   4   3   2   1

For my mom and dad . . .
and for Hilary

CONTENTS

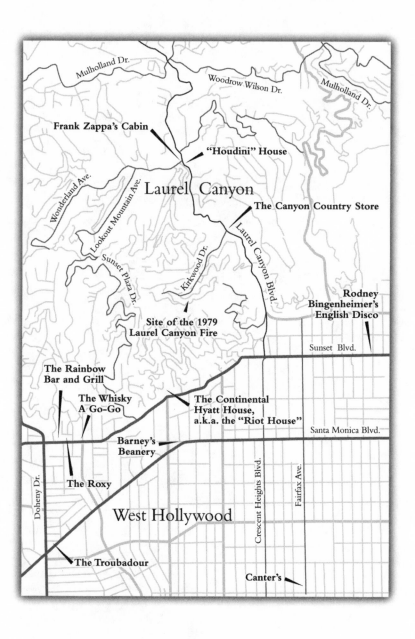

PREFACE

In 1968 a British pop star and the refugees from two seminal Los Angeles bands gathered in a cottage on Lookout Mountain Avenue in Laurel Canyon, the slightly seedy, camp-like neighborhood of serpentine one-lane roads, precipitous hills, fragrant eucalyptus trees, and softly crumbling bungalows set down improbably in the middle of Los Angeles, and sang together for the first time. The occupant of the cottage, which had moldering shake shingles and draft-prone casement windows, was a Canadian painter, poet, and folksinger named Joni Mitchell. The British pop star, sporting a wisp of a goatee and a thick Manchester brogue, was Graham Nash, founding member of the Hollies. The refugees were Stephen Stills, late of the Buffalo Springfield, writer and singer of "For What It's Worth," who had three years before auditioned for the Monkees and, having failed, recommended his friend, a folkie named Peter Torkelson; and David Crosby, late of the Byrds and "Mr. Tambourine Man," possessed of a Buffalo Bill mustache, an immaculate harmony voice, and piercing eyes that Mitchell, with typical literary flourish, likened to star sapphires. (Crosby produced Mitchell's debut album, *Song to a Seagull*.) So it was that Nash, Stills, and Crosby sat in Mitchell's living room on Lookout Mountain, in the heart of Laurel Canyon, in the epicenter of L.A.'s nascent rock music industry, and for the first time, began to sing together.

It is a measure of Laurel Canyon's mythmaking powers that this particular watershed may have actually occurred not at Mitchell's cottage—though that's the way Nash and plenty of others remember it—but a mile away in the living room of Cass Elliot of the Mamas and the Papas, who along with Mitchell briefly co-reigned as unofficial queen of the canyon, one an inscrutable poet-genius, the other a bosomy, meddling mother figure. What is certain is that within the year, Nash, Stills, and Crosby apotheosized into Crosby, Stills & Nash, the third group with Laurel Canyon roots within as many years—after the Byrds and Buffalo Springfield—to score a knockout with their first record. Nash moved into Mitchell's cottage on Lookout, there to write his ode to countercultural domestic bliss, "Our House." Mitchell, in turn, wrote and recorded "Ladies of the Canyon," her paean to the strange bohemian netherland where she and Nash nurtured their affair and where it would soon become evident that some of the twentieth century's most talented and enterprising young men and women had gathered at just the right moment.

Laurel Canyon had been filling up with musicians from Los Angeles, New York, and London since the mid-1960s: Mitchell was a transplant from New York via Saskatoon; Carole King had recently decamped to a place on Appian Way; so had Nico, the Teutonic waif from Andy Warhol's Factory. Up the street from Mitchell's place were John Phillips, Michelle Phillips, and Denny Doherty of the Mamas and the Papas, who, until they moved west and recorded "California Dreamin'" and "Monday, Monday," had busked around as semi-obscure folksingers. British bands touring the States made it a point to stop by Laurel Canyon for a party or two—Beatles, Stones, Animals, Yardbirds, and the rest. Some never left—the British blues legend John Mayall bought a house just over the ridge from Mitchell's place. It was Brigadoon meets the Brill Building, and the repercussions thirty-odd years later continue to pour from radios, iPods, and concert stages around the world.

During Laurel Canyon's golden era, the musicians who lived and worked there scored dozens of landmark hits, from "Suite: Judy Blue Eyes" to "California Dreamin'" to "My Opening Farewell" to "It's Too Late," while selling tens of millions of records and resetting the thermostat of pop culture worldwide. Besides Mitchell, Crosby, Stills, King, Mayall, and the Mamas and the Papas, canyonites permanent and transient included Frank Zappa, Jackson Browne, Chris Hillman and Roger McGuinn of the Byrds, Glenn Frey and Don Henley of the Eagles, Love's Arthur Lee, the songwriter Jimmy Webb, Judy Collins, Nick St. Nicholas of Steppenwolf, Mickey Dolenz of the Monkees, Mark Volman of the Turtles, and John Densmore and Robby Krieger of the Doors.

The musicians flocking to the canyon—at night, caterwauling coyotes and hooting owls made you marvel that you were only five minutes from the noise and neon of the Sunset Strip—constituted an unprecedented breed of incipient celebrity: the rocker-hippie, as much a work in progress as the music they made. As a group, they were nominally countercultural, favoring long hair and thrift-shop apparel, but possessed of ambition as blinding as any junior investment banker in a Brooks Brothers suit. Thanks to this incredible influx of talent, Laurel Canyon and, with it, Los Angeles wrested from New York and London the bragging rights of musical capital of the world and held them through the 1970s. The canyon's musicians took tradional folk, British rock, and savvy pop American songcraft and melded them into a sound that triumphed as thoroughly as the songs of the Beatles and the Rolling Stones. All of this happened without the ocean of hype that launched San Francisco's great paisley coming-out party during 1967's fabled Summer of Love. Although Haight-Ashbury generated some indelible records, it never came close to coalescing into the commercial and cultural juggernaut spearheaded in Laurel Canyon and Los Angeles.

"I felt I had reached Nirvana," Graham Nash told me. "I was in love with Joni, we were living together in Laurel Canyon. I had this new relationship with David and Stephen, and it was producing music that was thrilling me to death. To be part of this boiling pot of music, twelve hours a day, every day? It was an amazing scene." Recalled Jackson Browne, who lived at the time in the laundry room of the music impresario Billy James's Laurel Canyon home, "There was amazing tribal life. There were houses supported by record companies, groups living with an account at the health food store." Ron Stone, Mitchell's former manager, has a clear memory of driving his Alfa Romeo up Laurel Canyon Boulevard and hearing song after song from *Sgt. Pepper* wafting down from the cabins and bungalows all the way home. "It was a magical time," he says.

Laurel Canyon has always attracted blithe free-spirited celebrities—over the years Mary Astor, Tom Mix, Natalie Wood, Orson Welles, and David Niven had lived there—but it never acquired the cachet of Beverly Hills, perhaps because its famous tended to cohabit with infamy. Across the street from Mix's house—a log cabin with a bowling alley in the basement later to be occupied by Frank Zappa—was a large estate, supposedly connected to the Mix cabin via underground tunnel, which later burned under the requisite mysterious circumstances. A three-room cabin on Ridpath Drive—L.A. vice dubbed it "the reefer ranch"—provided a suitably scuzzy mise-en-scène for Robert Mitchum's 1948 marijuana bust. While the rest of Los Angeles and the San Fernando Valley boomed in the 1950s, Laurel Canyon seemed to exist out of time, so much so that by the 1960s its Hansel and Gretel cottages and fraying "mansions" had become embarrassing vestiges of a discredited era, when one could in perfect seriousness name a real estate development Bungalow Land—a subdivision actually built in the canyon in the early 1900s—and advertise its bigoted ownership covenant right on the billboard. Or, as on the west side of the city by the Pacific, not far from where Thomas Mann, Bertolt Brecht, and other literary refugees fleeing the Nazis fetched up in the 1930s, conjure a replica of Venice, Italy, complete with "canals" now clotted with muck.

But just when it seemed the giddy futurism of the New Frontier would eclipse it completely, Laurel Canyon—along with Rush Street in Chicago, Haight-Ashbury in San Francisco, and New York's Greenwich Village—came under siege from young, footloose, self-styled bohemians attracted by cheap rents and the down-market esprit of living among similarly broke brethren. Pointedly rejecting the tired haunts of the Beats like San Francisco's North Beach, the vanguard of the baby boomers, as they'd been dubbed, deliberately distanced themselves from those infrequent outcroppings of hipness to which their parents' generation could lay claim. Not even Lenny Bruce, denizen of "sick" humor and the fading '50s nightclub scene, soon to OD amid gathering irrelevance in a house above the Sunset Strip, was cool enough for their room. Youth would be served, on their terms—and on their turf. (Fittingly, Ciro's, the club on the Strip where Bruce played in his declining years, would become the launching pad for the Byrds.) Of the incredible bounty of rock-and-roll bands soon to emerge in L.A., only the Doors hailed from the former beatnik enclave Venice, and then mostly because the band's organist, Ray Manzarek, happened to live there. It was a time of joyous generational fraternization in Laurel Canyon, marked by hijinks like the morning everyone conspired to open their windows and drop the needle on "Let It Be" at precisely the same moment. Or the night that the singer Barry McGuire, riding high on his hit "Eve of Destruction," set up a bank of enormous speakers at the Mamas and the Papas' house on Lookout Mountain, seized the microphone, and bellowed: "This is God speaking. I have a message for you." At the former Tom Mix cabin a few doors down from Mitchell's house, Zappa hosted a nonstop salon–jam session that raged for the four months he actually lived there before he and his wife, Gail, were driven to saner reaches of the canyon.

Laurel Canyon loves its legends, and subsequent generations of residents have burnished them so adoringly that the truth sometimes seems almost beside the point. The estate across from the Mix/Zappa compound was known then, now, and probably forever as the "Houdini house," although it's almost certain Houdini never lived there. Tiburcio Vasquez, the "Mexican Robin Hood" who went on an extended crime spree during California's first decades of statehood, was said to stash his swag in the caves pockmarking the Mix property. Finally and inevitably, there is Jim Morrison, who among other vagaries held little truck with fixed addresses and so only briefly lived in a house behind the Canyon Country Store, though it must be remembered that alleged Morrison domiciles are to Los Angeles what bars that Hemingway drank in are to Key West. The Morrison house was near a mews that was the probable inspiration for the Doors' "Love Street," "where the creatures meet"—the creatures being hippie canyonites Morrison glimpsed from his window as they sloughed up the steps to the Canyon Store. (During the early 1990s, the graffito MR. MOJO RISIN' graced the front of the derelict property in wobbly black spray paint; a subsequent owner removed the slogan but installed a three-story totem pole within the house that depicted carved likenesses of Morrison, Jimi Hendrix, and Janis Joplin.)

Laurel Canyon's salad days didn't last, of course. As the '60s bled into the '70s, a series of profound psychic earthquakes shook the flowers out of everyone's hair. At the disastrous Altamont festival, held outside San Francisco in 1969, Hells Angels hired as security went berserk and attacked the audience, stabbing to death Meredith Hunter, a young black man carrying a gun in front of the stage while the Rolling Stones played "Under My Thumb." Coming three months after the youth utopia of the Woodstock festival, Altamont was brutal evidence that the peace-and-love generation could just as easily serve up something noxious. Chris Hillman, a founding member of the Byrds who lived in Laurel Canyon during the '60s, opened Altamont with his band the Flying Burrito Brothers. "It was like entering the depths of hell," he told me. "The level of feeling that day was indescribable." Although the Burritos played in brilliant morning sunshine, Altamont, Hillman said, was "just darkness."

Meanwhile, as the records sold and the millions piled up across Los Angeles and the canyon, there was a sense that things were, even by the standards of the late 1960s, getting out of hand; there was a frenzied, grasping, fall-of-Rome desperation to the drugging and drinking and wenching on the Strip and in the ever-more-commodious homes where cocaine—traditional refreshment of decadence—was supplanting marijuana and LSD. The turning point came in 1969, when Charles Manson's hippie girls hacked to death Roman Polanski's wife, Sharon Tate, and three others in nearby Benedict Canyon. One theory for Manson's motive held that he was sending a message to the house's previous occupant, Terry Melcher, the Beach Boys' producer and son of Doris Day who had enraged Manson for allegedly reneging on a deal to record him. The next day, across Laurel Canyon, you could practically hear bolts snapping into place behind doors that for the past five years had gone unlocked day and night.

I've lived in Laurel Canyon since moving to Los Angeles in 1991 and marvel at how little it has changed in all that time. Hazy existentialism, tempered by a work ethic necessary to afford the real estate, is a way of life here—Topanga Canyon after a 12-step program. The 1960s and '70s rock elite are now sparsely represented, most having either moved on years ago or died in harness. John Mayall, my former neighbor on Grandview Drive, finally packed it in for the San Fernando Valley suburb of Woodland Hills in 1996, but not before recording the *Blues from Laurel Canyon* album with its signature "Laurel Canyon Home." Ron Stone took over Mitchell's cottage on Lookout Mountain and lived there for twenty-seven years, raising a family within its hardly expansive walls before reluctantly bailing for larger quarters on the Valley side of the canyon. Celebrities still live here—Ellen DeGeneres, Sally Kellerman, the songwriter Meredith Brooks, the Beatles' recording engineer Geoff Emerick, among them—but they are seldom remarked upon or seen, and when they do turn up at the Canyon Country Store, a '60s throwback decorated with psychedelic art-nouveau exteriors where you can buy bundles of sage incense picked in the canyon, nobody pays them any mind.

Laurel Canyon compels because in an age when genuine contemporary experience has become buried under winking zeitgeist sampling, it neither overindulges its past nor calls much attention to its present. It simply is. The epidemic of trophy houses blighting the ridgelines notwithstanding, the canyon seems pretty much as it was and probably always will be; its ability to have nurtured an incalculable pop-cultural renaissance within its walls in the 1960s and '70s without surrendering its soul to the nostalgia-mongers thirty years later says a lot about its sleepy inertia. Laurel Canyon has what the oenophiles call *terroir*—the theory that the place where the grapes that make a great wine are grown should be evident with every swallow. In that sense, when you hear "Suite: Judy Blue Eyes," you are hearing Laurel Canyon, vintage 1969. Laurel Canyon has great *terroir*. "Laurel Canyon is a consciousness, rather than a physical place," Michael Des Barres, the British singer and actor who lived in the canyon in the 1970s, told me. "Like the Chateau Marmont or Carnaby Street, [it] transcends geographics."

So this book is not about pining for the days when a thousand points of incense dotted the evening sky while a dulcimer's melody wafted on the breeze—though that's not far from what the canyon was like on a good night in 1967. This is the story of how an indelible swath of popular culture was created in a shockingly short time, and how the anomaly of a canyon in the middle of one of America's most unsparing urban landscapes played a part. It's also about serendipity spun into solid gold, of writing a song on a redwood deck on Monday, recording it on Saturday, and having it hit the top of the charts six weeks later and then enter pop culture's permanent collection. It's what it was like to idolize the Beatles and then suddenly find yourself sharing a joint with them backstage. And what it was like, finally and helplessly, to watch it slip away. Nothing remotely approaching the events described here has since come to pass in Laurel Canyon and probably never will again. And that's what makes it all the more essential to understand how a place and time and a handful of history's most willful and self-absorbed young adults made such beautiful music together.

A note about structure: The events covered in this book occur between 1964 and 1981, but it quickly became apparent to me that it would be impossible to place them in their proper context within a rigidly chronological format. Also, I wanted this book to bear some semblance to the shambling nature of the canyon itself. Life in Laurel Canyon, then and now, is seldom tidy or linear, and so the implications of an anecdote taking place in 1969 sometimes don't fully reveal themselves until 1979. For those reasons, although the text is nominally divided into halves covering the 1960s and the 1970s, it is sometimes necessary to leap ahead in time in order not to lose a resonance. "Going with the flow" was a watchword of the canyon, in spirit if not in fact, for much of the time covered here. It is my hope that this book respects as much as possible that well-intentioned if now-antiquated ethic.

PART ONE

JINGLE-JANGLE MORNINGS

ONE

SO YOU WANT TO BE A ROCK-AND-ROLL STAR?

L.A. folkies meet the Beatles, the Byrds take flight, young girls (and everybody else) come to the canyon

In the autumn of 1964, a nineteen-year-old bluegrass adept and virtuoso mandolin player named Chris Hillman stood at the corner of Laurel Canyon Boulevard and Kirkwood Drive contemplating a FOR RENT sign on a telephone pole across from the Canyon Country Store. Hillman's folk-bluegrass group, the Hillmen, had recently disbanded after one album and untold gigs around Southern California—they'd played the Harem Lounge, in Lynwood, the night of November 21, 1963. Now the handsome musician had just joined a trio at loose ends after *their* first record had tanked. The trio—young journeymen singer-guitarists with solid folkie credentials—had recorded as the Jet Set and the Beefeaters and had now decided to reconstitute themselves with electric guitars and drums. Hillman ended up on bass, an instrument he'd never played but one that the Hillmen's manager, who also managed the Beefeaters, figured he could quickly master. The Beefeaters added another handsome young man, Michael Clarke, on drums, who had slim experience but, it was agreed, looked the part. Thus did Jim McGuinn (soon to change his name to Roger), Gene Clark, David Crosby, Michael Clarke, and Chris Hillman—shepherded by a resourceful L.A. jazz producer and man-about-town named Jim Dickson—become the Byrds. Hillman couldn't have known it, but by the time he stood on a corner in the heart of Laurel Canyon in 1964, he was about to participate in the creation of a milestone of twentieth-century popular culture.

With Hillman and Clarke in the lineup and McGuinn and Crosby playing electric guitars, the Byrds married the drive of rock and roll to the harmonies of folk music, then nearing the peak of its popularity with baby boomers in the persons of Joan Baez, Judy Collins, and Bob Dylan. At the time, folk was also still very much the music of left-leaning middle-agers, whom Dylan would famously scandalize at the 1965 Newport Folk Festival by "going electric." "There was a folk scene, but it was yet to be a folk scene of the youth—that wasn't Kingston Trio bullshit," says Judy Raphael, a musician and writer who worked at the Troubadour and the Ash Grove, L.A.'s premier folk clubs, and attended UCLA's film school with Jim Morrison and Ray Manzarek, soon to form the Doors.

All that was about to change. Crosby and every aspiring Southern California folk musician had logged time at the Troubadour's Monday open-mike Hoot nights, which were instrumental in providing a venue where performances could be honed and collaborations struck. A good showing at the Hoot could raise one's stock in town literally overnight. "The first time anybody heard Linda Ronstadt sing would have been in '64 when she did a solo at the Hoot and everybody was just talking about her the whole next day," says Raphael. The Ash Grove, too, was crawling with apple-cheeked folk acolytes in thrall to the music. "There were all these little Jewish boys sitting around in front thinking they could emulate the latest lick by Robert Johnson or Doc Watson. Ry Cooder gave guitar lessons there in '63 at age sixteen. It was really a center where a lot of stuff evolved."

Folk and rock may have made sense as a hybrid musically, but philosophically they could scarcely have been further apart. Though no clear-cut definition exists, folk is generally accepted to comprise music that is populist, lyrically dense, and simple enough to be played by amateurs on whatever instruments are at hand. "In the strictest sense, it's music that is rarely written for profit," Gene Shay, the co-founder of the Philadelphia Folk Festival, said. "It's the people's music." While rock and roll's roots reach deeply into the folk traditions of blues and country, it was from the beginning unabashedly commercial music dependent on, and enhanced immeasurably by, the charisma and dynamism of the musician performing it. Anybody with an Autoharp and a third-grade singing voice can pull off a passable rendition of "Michael, Row the Boat Ashore"; it takes Chuck Berry to sing "Johnny B. Goode."

In the early 1960s folk began launching stars singing the "people's music" in a manner that made the songs inseparable from the singer, as with Elvis Presley's indelible association with "Hound Dog," previously a hit for the blueswoman Big Mama Thornton. Joan Baez and Peter, Paul and Mary sold millions of records and became celebrities of a magnitude that eclipsed pop singers like Connie Francis. Singing hand-sewn songs interpreted as allegories for the civil rights, antiwar, and antinuclear movements, they made a deep impression on millions of young baby boomers raised in the stultifying atmosphere of the American 1950s. Making an equal impression on a generation already showing signs of creeping entitlement was the quality of the folk stars' celebrity, the deference they were shown, and the fact that they, too, were young and sexual. No one could have known it then, but the folk stars of the early 1960s were the first rock stars.

Still, folk had yet to evolve into anything as irresistible and visceral as rock and roll. The Beatles' earliest records, with their Everly Brothers–style harmonies and unapologetic backbeat, hinted at the possibilities—McGuinn and Clark had played Beatles songs in their folk sets, sometimes to the derision of purist coffeehouse audiences. In San Francisco, the Beau Brummels were playing Beatles-influenced rock with intricate folk-style vocal harmonies a year before the Byrds formed. But no one had achieved unambiguous commerical success marrying folk and rock until the Byrds recorded a version of an unreleased Dylan song written in herky-jerky two-four time, which McGuinn slowed to the steady-rolling four-four moderato of rock and roll.

Released on April 12, 1965, "Mr. Tambourine Man"— McGuinn's ringing twelve-string electric guitar sounding the refrain followed by his and Crosby's close-spaced, ethereal harmonies—quickly caught fire and shot all the way to No. 1 on the Billboard charts, becoming a worldwide smash. By spanning the divide between rock and roll and folk music, the Byrds created a hybrid—folk rock—that gentrified American-made rock and roll while putting a commercial sheen on folk only hinted at by Baez, Dylan, and Collins. Dylan would trump the Byrds that summer with "Like a Rolling Stone," a noisy six-minute masterpiece that melded elements of folk, pop, and rock while somehow summing up an entire generation's inchoate longings and paranoia; but before Dylan's breakthrough the Beatles loomed largest in the aspirations of L.A.'s nascent folk rockers.

"I remember the day David Crosby came over with Chris Hillman and knocked on my door when I lived near the Troubadour," says Raphael. "They used to come over to tune up. And [Crosby] turned my radio from FM to AM, to those pop-music stations, which was sacrilege to me. AM had been Frankie Valli and that bullshit, and all of a sudden because of the Beatles it was very, very important, because now all the guys wanted to grow their hair and be pop stars. [Crosby] said: 'Do you mind if I change the station to AM?' And they started playing along. I remember that very distinctly as a turning point. They were listening to all that stuff." Folk rock would prove more popular and remunerative than either genre had separately, and it presaged the truly humongous folk-country-rock "L.A. Sound," perfected by Crosby, Stills & Nash, the Eagles, Jackson Browne, America, Linda Ronstadt, and others, which would dominate from the late 1960s to the late '70s and utterly transform the record industry. But it all started in 1965 with the Byrds. For Hillman and his bandmates, as well as for the eucalyptus-scented Los Angeles canyon where Hillman would soon reside, life would never be the same.

Hillman was raised in northern San Diego County, a largely rural area that had yet to be besieged by veterans perfecting the California dream amid the cosseting climate in subdivisions financed by the G.I. Bill. It was an environment one might expect to foster in a shy young man a consuming passion for arcane country music, less so the primordial rock and roll of L.A.'s chaotic Specialty Records, home of Little Richard. But for the young Chris Hillman, it was everything he could want in the way of excitement. He was captivated by the gritty subgenre of country music associated with Bakersfield, a sunbaked city in California's vast Central Valley. Compared with the mournfully embroidered melodies of Nashville, Bakersfield country was looser, harder-driving, and more apt to swing—perfect for the headlong restlessness of postwar Southern California and, later, as a foundation for the sort of music Hillman would make with and without the Byrds. Bakersfield proponents like Bob Wills, Lefty Frizzell, and Spade Cooley, a singer and fiddler from Pack Saddle Creek, Oklahoma, who led a ten-piece band partial to snazzy matching cowboy outfits, were huge stars in Southern California when Hillman was growing up. Cooley hosted his own TV show, *The Hoffman Hayride*, which at its peak drew 75 percent of the television viewers in Los Angeles. Hillman couldn't get enough of it.

"I would dial in the Spade Cooley live TV show every Saturday night from Los Angeles," he says. "Then I'd watch Cliffie Stone's *Hometown Jamboree*, then the Johnny Otis show, which was R&B. I'm, like, a thirteen-year-old kid and my father was going, 'What's wrong with you?'" Hillman added folk music to his obsessions when his sister returned from college with an armload of albums and his mother drove to Tijuana and bought him a ten-dollar guitar, which he assiduously taught himself to play. Next came the mandolin, whose reedy imprecations he picked out from Flatt and Scruggs records. In 1961 Hillman joined a high-school bluegrass band with the *Mighty Wind*–ish name Scottsville Squirrel Barkers; his next band, the Golden Gate Boys, acknowledged the young mandolin player's burgeoning chops and commanding good looks by renaming themselves the Hillmen.

It was not the sort of résumé that would seem to prefigure worldwide stardom, but Hillman joined the Byrds at what in hindsight was precisely the right moment. Beatlemania, arriving just three months after Kennedy's assassination, had acted like a tonic on the American psyche. "I feel the Beatles actually healed us," Hillman says. "It was almost God-sent that they came over." The Beatles' phenomenal success served as a goad and role model to prospective male American musicians. Crosby always carbon-dated the turning point in the Byrds' folk-to-rock-and-roll conversion to the night he, Clark, and McGuinn saw *A Hard Day's Night* together. "I can remember coming out of that movie so jazzed that I was swinging around stop sign poles at arm's length," Crosby recalled. "[The Beatles] were cool and we said: 'Yeah, that's it. We have to be a band.'"

Like so many other young men of their generation, the Byrds selected their Rickenbacker and Gretsch guitars and Ludwig drums in emulation of John Lennon, George Harrison, and Ringo Starr. Their Beatlesque matching suits were, according to Hillman, another matter. "We *hated* them. I think we wore the suits once, when we worked Ciro's on the Strip the first time. We left them in the dressing room on purpose." The Beatles represented the equivalent of a clean sheet of paper that the largest generation in American history suddenly had license to fill any way it chose. "I felt that there were no boundaries, no rules," says Hillman. "Especially in the music business, which was then a tiny cottage industry. Nothing like it is today. The guys running the companies were music guys, and we didn't have these conglomerate corporate monsters eating up everything. Then it was new, uncharted territory. It was a special time, and for that moment we held the pulse."

Every incipient cultural movement needs its golden nexus. The *New Yorker* crowd of the 1930s had the Algonquin Hotel (and, when in Hollywood, the Garden of Allah at the mouth of Laurel Canyon on the Sunset Strip). So it was in Los Angeles in the mid-1960s that Laurel Canyon, by unconscious lottery of the hip, became the place where every heads-up young musician just knew he had to live. "Laurel Canyon was sort of the mecca," says Hillman. "From '63–'64 up until '69–'70, it was quite the place to be." Billy James, a pioneering artist manager and music publisher who championed some of the brightest lights on the emerging L.A. scene, already lived at 8504 Ridpath Drive, not far from Hillman's FOR RENT sign. "It's all happened within the last year or so," James told Jerry Hopkins, *Rolling Stone*'s first Los Angeles correspondent, in 1968. "If creative artists need to live apart from the community at large, they also have a desire to live among their own kind, and so an artistic community develops." Those selfsame creative artists may also have had an equally consuming desire to live where the rent was dirt cheap. Which is how Hillman found himself in Laurel Canyon looking for a place. It didn't take him long to find one, and, in the canyon's emerging mythos of enchanted serendipity, one presented itself as if by magic.

"This guy drives up and he says, 'You looking for a place to rent?'" Hillman recalls. "I said yeah, and he said, 'Well, follow me up.' It was this young guy who was a dentist. It was his parents' house, a beautiful old wood house down a dirt road—and he lived on the top, and he was renting out the bottom part. I just went, 'Wow, perfect.' The guy ended up being my dentist for a while."

The house was at the top of Magnolia Lane at the summit of the Kirkwood Bowl, a box canyon cut into the west flank of Laurel Canyon. Like many of the roads in the Kirkwood Bowl and on Lookout Mountain, another canyon within the canyon a half mile to the north, Magnolia Lane had been hacked out of the granite by real estate speculators without regard to guardrails or turning clearances. Then as now, the narrow roadways with their incredible pitch dictate that two cars cannot pass without one of them backing up. Protracted horn-blowing standoffs are common, and the unprotected shoulders promise a leisurely plunge, usually through the roof of an unsuspecting house below. There is, of course, an upside to these inconveniences: Hillman's house had a view that stretched from downtown Los Angeles all the way to the Pacific. "It was wonderful up there," Hillman says. "It was the top of the world, a beautiful, beautiful place. I had *the* best place in the canyon." Not to mention that Laurel Canyon's longtime status as a haven for freethinkers could lead to intriguing neighbors. "Right above me was this old Spanish Mediterranean sort of house and [the sculptor] Ed Kienholz lived there," Hillman says. "You'd hear him up there soldering and sawing."

The canyon was meanwhile being colonized by Hillman's bandmates and L.A. contemporaries. McGuinn moved in. Crosby, a headstrong twenty-two-year-old from Santa Barbara with a matchless tenor harmony voice who was already feuding with McGuinn over leadership of the Byrds, was in transient residence all over the canyon before settling in Beverly Glen ten miles west. "At the end of '64, early '65, the folk-rock explosion, that's when the Byrds took their first money and a lot of them moved up to Laurel Canyon," says Kim Fowley, an early L.A. rock producer and entrepreneur. "Everybody else in that folk-rock community decided they'd move up there, too, because you could smoke *dope* and get *laid* and be an asshole with your Porsche convertible out of the prying eyes of the *Man*." The proximity of so many of L.A.'s emerging rock elite had predictable collateral consequences. John Phillips of the Mamas and the Papas, from his perch on Lookout Mountain, would soon famously pen the lyric "young girls are coming to the canyon."

This would turn out to be a colossal understatement. As Fowley recalls: "All these chicks would hitchhike up to the Canyon Store from the Strip, girls from Kansas who'd heard about Laurel Canyon: 'Hi! Folk-rock musicians! I'll clean your house and fuck you and I'm a vegetarian and I can make you macrobiotic stuff as you're shooting heroin.' So those of us who didn't live in Laurel Canyon, we'd go up and grab them and say: 'These guys aren't going to have sex with you, because you're not from New York, so come fuck us.'"

The canyon's gathering folk-rock firmament made an impression on Pamela Des Barres, née Miller, then a seventeen-year-old protogroupie who ran with a gang of like-minded young women that Frank Zappa would dub the Girls Together Outrageously, or GTOs. Pamela frequently hitchhiked over Laurel Canyon Boulevard to Hollywood from her home in the San Fernando Valley suburb of Reseda. "It was perfect—I used to call it God's golden backyard," she says, "just knowing that the people you thought were cool lived up there. The Byrds were my favorite band and they lived there, so that was it for me. It wasn't that hard to find rock-star addresses back then. I went to every single one of their houses and scoped them out."

As with many of the young women who lived in the Valley, Pamela's excursions engendered an awakening to cultural possibilities previously unimaginable. "They went over Laurel Canyon, which was the yellow brick motherfuckin' road into Oz," says Michael Des Barres, at the time a young British actor—he appeared in *To Sir, With Love*—later to become an L.A.-based rock singer whom Pamela would marry. "It was almost like a conduit, a magical bridge from that world and the era of the beehive haircut into Zappa and the revolution of the streets. If it was a film, you would track it from the hot tarmac of Reseda into the luxurious foliage and feathers and flowers of Sunset Boulevard."

Pamela developed an obsessive crush on Hillman after she'd seen the Byrds perform at Ciro's, a 1930s-era Sunset Strip nightclub gamely trying to reinvent itself as a rock-and-roll parlor. "Chris Hillman was my god, my hero, my first true love," she says. "He lived at 5424 Magnolia, at the top of Kirkwood. I used to go there even when he was on the road and just hang out. He had a hammock on the porch, so when he was on the road, I would sleep there at night. I was psycho—I used to sing that song, 'On the Street Where You Live,' when I was up there. I thought, How am I going to get in to meet him? I'd seen him around; I'd met him on the Strip. So I did two different things: Once my Dad gave me a big bag of grapes he brought from Mexico and I was going to give them to Chris but he wasn't home and I remember tripping down his dirt driveway and the grapes spilling and slipping and sliding and oh, my God, it was a nightmare. The next time I got to know his next-door neighbor, Mrs. Matzo, this old, old lady. And her cat had kittens and I thought, Well, I'll bring him a kitten. And that time he *was* home. But he couldn't accept a kitten. Actually, we finally got together. But I would just do anything to be up there, and for that reason alone Laurel Canyon became my mecca." Not to mention that "all my other favorite bands lived there, too."

Hillman saw less and less of the Magnolia house as the Byrds were buffeted by the first disorienting blasts of fame. *Mr. Tambourine Man* was released in June 1965 just as its titular single hit No. 1; barely six months passed before the band's second seminal folk-rock No. 1—a shimmering version of Pete Seeger's "Turn! Turn! Turn!" Two years later the band would record Hillman and McGuinn's withering "So You Want to Be a Rock and Roll Star," but for now the fledgling Byrds were at a loss as to how to go about acting like one.

"The Byrds weren't a rock band," Hillman says. "We didn't know anything from that stuff. We didn't even know how you were supposed to be onstage. I mean, rock-and-roll guys were like show guys, and we had come out of folk music. I was a bluegrass mandolin player, and in bluegrass you've gotta concentrate so much you don't crack a smile and dance around; it's too darned hard to play the music. I was scared to death with the Byrds. I was a little guy in the back row playing the bass." Crosby recalled "standing in front of a mirror with my new Gretsch guitar . . . trying to figure out how to stand up and play. Folkies didn't do that. We were used to sitting on high stools. There I was, alone in front of the mirror, muttering to myself: 'Let's see . . . How do you . . . like this?' Or: 'No, maybe I need to lengthen the strap a little bit . . .'"

Along with sudden fame came sudden, insane money. Crosby had been living in Dickson's basement in Laurel Canyon when "Mr. Tambourine Man" hit; now he owned a green Porsche. Hillman bought a Triumph Bonneville motorcycle, then a Porsche of his own. As the band's chief songwriter, Clark was pulling in tremendous sums from publishing royalties and trumped them all with a Ferrari. "It was like winning a big lottery," he recalled. "We were one of the first American groups to really make money. 'Mr. Tambourine Man' was a hit in twenty-six countries, something like that. The first time we got mobbed by girls screaming at a concert . . . it registered that we actually had pulled it off, that everybody loved us, we were bigger than any of us expected, and we were out there with the Beatles."

The Byrds' first tours were conducted under logistics that now seem impossibly quaint. "That Tom Hanks movie—*That Thing You Do!*—that captures the experience," Hillman says. "It is so like the way we were out on the road in '65, those kind of package shows. We were out with Bo Diddley, Paul Revere and the Raiders." For the first tour, the band invited along a free-form dance troupe led by Vito Paulekas and Carl Franzoni, Los Angeles avant-gardists possessed, for the times, of fearsomely unorthodox dress and coiffure. Franzoni lived in a commune occupying the log cabin at the corner of Laurel Canyon and Lookout Mountain soon to be taken over by Frank Zappa. The Paulekas-Franzoni dancers had by 1965 become the de rigueur, buzz-confirming accoutrement at rock clubs on the Sunset Strip, and Dickson made sure they were in the audience at the Byrds' early shows at Ciro's.

Paulekas, an accomplished sculptor and iconoclast, taught

an hourlong dance class at his studio. The night before the Byrds' first gig at Ciro's, the band played a dance that Vito organized in a church on Melrose Avenue. "The Byrds' management announced at the dance that they had secured Ciro's the next night," says Franzoni, thus ensuring a mob of teenagers outside the club trying to get in. Not that there was any room left inside. "Every young movie star you could think of was there, because the Byrds were involved with Jane Fonda and her group of people, so the word was out and they had a packed house." Fifteen minutes before the band was to go on, Franzoni, dismayed by the crowd's lethargy, shambled onto the empty dance floor and began writhing to the canned discotheque music playing over the house PA. "I'm out there by myself for five minutes. Then Vito and his wife came out, and several other people. It wasn't a full dance floor, but we broke the nut, that it was going to be a dance. Fifteen minutes later the band comes up and from then on it was dance, dance, dance in Hollywood."

It was a signal moment on the Sunset Strip and, by extension, in the culture. Prior to the Byrds' opening night at Ciro's, dancing in L.A.'s clubs tended to be accompanied by Motown hits spun by bored DJs or live R&B bands. "Once the Byrds were invited to Ciro's, the flood hit," says Franzoni. "All the bands started showing up on the Sunset Strip." And playing for audiences whose dancing, thanks to Vito, was as much a performance as the band's. "What we did, we showed them a dance that came out of Vito's classes. We showed them a way to dance they'd never seen before."

"Carl and all those guys were way ahead of everybody on hippiedom fashion," Hillman says. "Carl used to wear tights that looked like a bumblebee, yellow and black. Carl and another dancer named Beatle Bob—these are like rock-and-roll Damon Runyon names—a couple of girls and some other guy, they'd all get out and dance while we played. So you can imagine when we went out on the road in the summer of '65 with those guys, playing in Iowa, it was pretty interesting. Here we are playing these weird places in the Midwest—little dance halls and stuff—and they'd be dancing out there, and sometimes some of those farm boys would get in there and get very upset," says Franzoni; "They were used to lining up and doing that line dance—and here come these crazy people doing this crazy dance. So they would circle us and sometimes there'd be a punch in there."

Forgetting for the moment the calculation of exporting the Sunset Strip experience to the provinces—"It was like a little pre–*Magical Mystery Tour*," Hillman says—the Byrds themselves were earnestly agog at their sudden change of fortune. "Drugs were not dictating. That negative lifestyle wasn't encompassing and smothering everybody. Other than Crosby—who was probably meddling in areas that were going to be his future downfall—the rest of us weren't. Occasionally we'd have a drink or a smoke or something, and that was it. What came along later, the cocaine and all the other garbage, was the downfall for everybody."

Laurel Canyon, meanwhile, was still in its idyllic phase, as for the moment, the nascent peace-and-love aesthetic obscured the mercantile distractions beginning to visit more and more of its inhabitants. The canyon's rugged granite walls and cool, quiet night air sweetened with jasmine and acacia blossoms—only five minutes from the mammon of the Sunset Strip—provided a reassuring physical and psychological barrier for musicians steeped in the egalitarianism of folk music and, lately, the back-to-the-land ethos of the hippies. Hillman has an indelible memory of coming off the road in the winter, most likely after the 1966 tour in support of "Turn! Turn! Turn!," and reacclimating himself to the canyon's rhythms. "It was like January or February and it had just rained in L.A.," he recalls. "The cab stopped and there was a eucalyptus tree down across the road. I literally had to climb over that tree with my bag to get down to the house."

Hillman had moved to the top half of the Magnolia house, the dentist having decided to take the apartment underneath. Pamela's infatuation notwithstanding, Hillman had taken up with a striking British woman, Anya Butler, whom he would later marry. Brian Wilson of the Beach Boys, then entering a phase of increasingly erratic behavior as he struggled with manifold personal demons while trying to keep his band from slipping out of the post-Beatles pop-culture firmament, began appearing unannounced at the top of the dusty driveway, where he would wait, hoping to engage Butler. "I never knew it," Hillman says. "Then she'd tell me: 'Brian came up and parked his car at the top of the driveway.' He just wanted to talk. It was like '66 and he was starting the decline."

Crosby, still a fixture around the canyon, had meanwhile taken to wearing an Oscar Wilde/Frank Lloyd Wright–ish cape wherever he went. It became a bona fide of canyon residency to have seen Crosby roaring down Laurel Canyon Boulevard, cape flying in the wind, on the Triumph motorcycle given to him by Peter Fonda—who along with Jack Nicholson had been part of the house-papering engineered by Dickson at the Byrds' early shows at Ciro's, a shrewd, and correct, inference that hip young Hollywood might find generational solidarity with L.A.'s hippest, newest rock-and-roll band. "You have to remember, this is classic, when [Crosby] was wearing that stupid cape." Hillman fairly snorts at the memory. "He's coming down the canyon real fast with the cape flying, and Jim Dickson says, 'It's Lawrence of Laurel Canyon!' It just fit David perfectly, because he would strut around . . ." Hillman pauses. "He's a funny guy, I really love the guy. He's just one of those people in your life that has a bull's-eye on the front of his shirt."

Crosby wasn't the only one strutting. No one could have adequately prepared in 1966 for the fame that beset the Byrds, least of all maladjusted former folksingers who suddenly were not only being compared to the Beatles but were meeting their heroes as backstage peers. The days of playing for nothing at the Troubadour Hoots and building calluses on slender white fingers outside the Ash Grove must have seemed a million miles away. Now, when a Crosby or a Hillman happened into the Olde Worlde or the Whisky A Go-Go on the Sunset Strip, the few times when they were off the road or not in the studio, enormous deference was paid and, it seemed, expected. Raphael worked as a waitress at Fred C. Dobbs, a coffeehouse on the Strip frequented by scenesters. "They were all hustling, looking for something, and it reeked of egotism to me," she says. "They were all in costumes, with the capes and all that; that's what was so phony. The first time Dylan walked in with his entourage, the idea was: he's one of us, but it's not really cool to acknowledge him. But the buzz went out very quickly—'*THAT"S DYLAN! HE'S STANDING OVER THERE!*' There began to be a feeling that these guys were a cut above the rest of the scene, and that hadn't operated previously."

Given these distractions and the traditional territorialism of young men in close quarters, tensions among the Byrds were already running high. "Gene and Mike and I were the young guys," Hillman says. "David and Roger were three years older than us, which is a huge amount of time at that age, and were vying for leadership and of course always at each other's throats." Clark, meanwhile, developed a phobia about flying and debilitating drug and alcohol habits and left before completing the band's third album, *Fifth Dimension*—though not before recording his triumphant "Eight Miles High," composed with Crosby and McGuinn, widely considered the apogee of the Byrds' flight. "Gene Clark, who came out of Bonner Springs, Kansas, was one of the sweetest guys in the world, and literally [Los Angeles] ate him up and spit him out," says Hillman. "When I met him when the Byrds began, he'd just do anything for you. He was a great-looking guy; he was the focal point onstage. The Byrds would hit that first note and every girl in the audience would look at Gene Clark—there he is: Prince Valiant with a tambourine. The demons got hold of him and never let go."

After endless feuding, Crosby was finally fired from the group during the recording of their fifth album, *The Notorious Byrd Brothers*. The band had been fraying when they'd played the Monterey Pop Festival in 1967; Crosby, between songs, launched into a rodomontade about a government conspiracy to cover up the Kennedy assassination, infuriating McGuinn. "They threw me out," Crosby recalled. "And they were not nice about it. I'm sure I contributed to it as much as anybody. I was *not* an easy guy at that point. I was pretty much of a punk and had an enormous attitude." At loose ends in the year before he would form Crosby, Stills & Nash, Crosby turned up at a house shared by Twice Nicely, a band from Sugarbush, Vermont, memorable only for having as its guitarist Waddy Wachtel, who in the 1970s would provide lead guitar on the signature albums by Jackson Browne and other Laurel Canyon stalwarts. Crosby picked up a guitar and played a song for the assembled musicians. When he finished, he asked them if they'd be interested in recording it. The musicians, through a haze of blue smoke, passed on the song. Its title: "Wooden Ships."

With the departure of Clark and Crosby, Hillman was playing a much larger role in the Byrds, composing and singing while steering McGuinn closer to his own hard-core country and bluegrass roots. After adding Gram Parsons, a Southern-born trust-fund scion, Harvard dropout, and devout student of honky-tonk music and attitude, the Byrds released a flat-out country album, 1968's *Sweetheart of the Rodeo*, now regarded as a classic and a precursor to the country-rock movement of the early 1970s but a thudding commercial failure. In a dismal metaphor for the times, Hillman's Magnolia house burned to the ground one afternoon, nearly killing him.

Fires—house and brush, intentional and accidental—have always shaped Laurel Canyon. A tourist hotel at the pinnacle of Lookout Mountain burned in 1918; the Canyon Country Store in 1929. A large swath just east of Lookout Mountain went up in 1959; twenty-three houses in the Kirkwood Bowl were destroyed in a four-hour wildfire in 1979. For all the Brigadoonian comparisons the canyon inspired among its self-congratulating new residents, the fires cared not at all about pop-cultural pedigree. And so Laurel Canyon would burn and burn again, targeting with uncanny precision the homes of its seemingly enchanted rock demimonde. Hillman's was among the first.

"It was a Santa Ana wind, a very, very hot, dry, windy day," Hillman recalls. "I had a motorcycle—a Bultaco, a Spanish dirt bike—and I pulled it out to take it out and drive it. And it starts leaking gas. So I pull back into the garage, and within a matter of seconds the water heater ignited, exploded, burned my eyelashes. I rolled on the ground instinctively, and the flames just shot up into the house. I lost everything. The fire trucks couldn't get up the dirt road. It was just gone. Roger [McGuinn] was across the canyon and had just gotten a sixteen-millimeter camera because he was always into gadgets, and he filmed the whole thing. I lost everything I owned, including one of the best guitars I ever had—an old [Martin] D-twenty-eight. But here's the twist on it: Crosby was at my house an hour before the blaze. I can't connect it yet—where the Satan factor came into play with David—but I'm working on it."

After the fire Hillman moved out of the canyon and finally left the Byrds in 1968—by then he and McGuinn were the only remaining founding members—and joined Parsons in the Flying Burrito Brothers. It was another star-crossed band whose influence is apprehensible thirty years later but whose tenure was brief, brilliant, underappreciated, and stained with excess—Parsons OD'd at age twenty-six in a motel outside Joshua Tree, California, on September 19, 1973. Hillman is unsparing in hindsight with regard to the era's drinking and drugging and its deleterious effect on the musicians' work ethic, a nonnegotiable prerequisite in the country and bluegrass discipline of his background. "I was no angel," he admits, "and I thank God every day that I survived. Look at all the people I worked with that I lost, by their own choice."

It's been pointed out that the Byrds could have—should have—been bigger; they were hyped to their everlasting embarrassment (and censured by skeptical audiences on early tours in Britain) as "America's Beatles," a preposterous burden that only increased the pressure on the band. Still, the sheer talent of McGuinn, Hillman, Clark, and especially Crosby practically demanded a transcendent career arc. "[The Byrds] could have been bigger, but we needed the discipline and needed to work harder—we were lazy and cocky and it got to us," says Hillman. "We could have been out there probably another five years. The original guys could have all had a really good run into the '70s, if not longer, if we'd had the discipline and structure in place. We didn't have that."

And so Laurel Canyon's first and arguably finest band—in the coinage of both Buddy Holly and the Byrds' spiritual heir Neil Young—faded away, but not before creating the template for so much of the music that would matter to the world for the next twenty years. And when the band was finally inducted into

the Rock and Roll Hall of Fame in 1991, the Byrds came together as they once flew apart, secure in the knowledge of precisely what they had accomplished. All the petty intrigues of the
past, it turned out, paled in comparison. At the induction cere-
mony, Hillman notes with some satisfaction, "The Byrds were
the only inductees in the group category that sat together. And
played together."

TWO

UNCLE FRANK'S CABIN

Freaking out at Zappa's canyon compound, Girls Together Outrageously,
psychedelic bowling, and the final resting place of Tony the Wonder Horse

In 1910, an engineer and speculator named Charles Spencer Mann began selling house lots halfway up Laurel Canyon on a tract of steeply sloped land thick with chaparral, sycamore, and California bay laurel—the latter's jasmine-like flowers had given the canyon its name. Shamelessly emulating a development two canyons to the east whose soon-to-be-indelible logo marched in three-story letters across the summit of Mount Lee, Mann christened his subdivision Bungalow Land and billed it as "a high class restricted park for desirable people only." To lure desirables to a canyon largely populated by coyotes and rattlesnakes, Mann commissioned a trolley from Sunset Boulevard whose cars ran on roads instead of rails. The nation's first "trackless trolley" was soon depositing prospective Babbitts at the intersection of Laurel Canyon Boulevard and a rugged trail that leaped up a cut in the canyon's west wall to the top of Lookout Mountain, a twelve-hundred-foot peak with comely views to the Pacific Ocean and the nascent downtown Los Angeles.

Beneath Bungalow Land's twisting lanes, a log-cabin-style roadhouse was built in 1916 at 2401 Laurel Canyon Boulevard. Among the amenities was a bowling alley in the basement. The tavern later became a private retreat with an unnervingly long, narrow living room dominated by a granite hearth of feudal proportions. Tom Mix, the former rodeo rider turned matinee idol then on his way to earning $17,000 per week prior to the federal income tax, lived there briefly before moving to a seven-acre Beverly Hills compound with front gates emblazoned "T-M" in flowing neon. Mix's journey from Laurel Canyon log cabin (his "wonder horse," Tony, was supposedly buried beneath the bowling alley) to Beverly Hills pleasure dome would uncannily foreshadow the diaspora of a later generation of Laurel Canyon pop culturalists struck by sudden, thunderous wealth.

So it was that in 1968 Frank Zappa, a desperately ambitious twenty-eight-year-old classical-music composer, electric guitarist, and strident pop iconoclast, fresh from a chaotic artist in residency in New York City's Garrick Theater with his band, the Mothers of Invention, installed himself, his wife, Gail, and their baby daughter, Moon Unit, at the Mix cabin. "The rent was seven hundred dollars a month," Zappa later recalled. "It was rustic and decrepit; it really *looked* like an old-time log cabin." On the grounds, Zappa noted, "was a big concrete fish pond full of weeds. Next to that was a hole in the ground filled with stagnant water. I was told it was a secret passageway that went under the street to Harry Houdini's house on the other side of Laurel Canyon Boulevard. I never found out if that was true. Running up the hillside, behind the house, was a collection of man-made caves built out of stucco, with electric wiring and light bulbs inside."

Zappa, his wife and daughter, and an extended family of musicians gifted and aspirant, groupies turned governesses, and unclassified hangers-on would occupy the cabin for only four months before the sheer madness of the place drove them out. But in that brief moment the "log cabin," as it was known to every freak from Sherman Oaks to Hollywood, raged as a rock-and-roll salon and Dionysian playground where groupies were gentrified into recording "artists" and talents as imposing as Mick Jagger and Jeff Beck and as whimsical as Alice Cooper were stabled, jam-sessioned, fed, and fellated while the undisputed master of the house—tolerant of all manner of misbehavior save goldbricking musicians and, perversely for the times, drug use—reigned as the "freak daddy" of the whole show.

"The place was huge and vault-like and cavernous—the living room was like seventy feet long and thirty feet across," says Gail Zappa, Frank's widow. "It was so dark. I think the oldest eucalyptus tree in Southern California overshadowed the whole property. There was no floor in the kitchen, just this sort of platform in one corner that had the stove sitting on it. It was infested constantly with bus groups of rock-and-roll bands looking for a place to crash—they would just show up at all hours of the day and night. It was impossible to keep any food in the place; people were literally eating us out of house and home. There were no locks on any of the doors. It was insanity. *Insanity.*"

It fell largely to Gail to manage the chaos. "For [Frank], it was an interesting social experiment, because we had pretty much most of the band living with us and a lot of the crew. But for me, no; not with a baby. The truth is, that was a temporary stop until we figured out where and how we were going to manage our lives now that we were parents, among other things. That was a house we lived in but it was not our home."

The log cabin nevertheless left indelible memories among those who visited during the Zappa's residency in the summer of 1968. John Mayall bunked there before buying his own place in the Kirkwood Bowl and wrote "2401"—the cabin's address on Laurel Canyon Boulevard—in honor of the Zappas' hospitality: "There's a hero living at 2401 and all around/a family circus in the sun."

Circus, indeed. "It was sort of like being in Las Vegas," Gail says, "in the sense that you have no concept of time. The only thing I can compare it to is living on a battleship—my father was career navy, so was Jim Morrison's. There's a culture that prepares you for this lifestyle, very much like the kind of operation when you're on a battleship in the middle of the sea: you're very isolated from the rest of society and you have a mission." Befitting the unwavering Zappa work ethic, the mission at the log cabin, Gail says, was "defined by your creative output and how much you can manage to get done." Zappa managed quite a bit. "It was one of his most productive periods," she says. "There were so many albums being done at the same time, between the GTOs and the work that he was doing for himself. The building blocks for a lot projects were launched there."

The cabin was part of a compound owned by Fonya Pearson, who lived to the north of the property in a Mediterranean-style villa said to have been built for a state visit to Los Angeles by Edward VIII that evaporated after his abdication. (The record producer Rick Rubin later bought the mansion; the Red Hot Chili Peppers lived there while recording 1991's *Blood Sugar Sex Magik*, and Guns N' Roses shot the wedding scene of the "November Rain" video on its verandas.) The log cabin was already occupied by a fringe-group encampment when Zappa arrived, and the fates of the shaggy tenants and Zappa would be, as in a later Zappa lyric, "intimately entwined." Among the tenants were Sandra Leano and Lucy Offerall, incipient groupies, and Christine Frka, a spectrally thin seamstress from San Pedro, who lived in a large safe next to the basement bowling alley. Finally, there was Carl Franzoni, the fearsomely bedraggled former mail-order salesman of breast-enhancement pumps turned Byrds dancer. Franzoni's brother rented the cabin as a rehearsal space while he put together the Fraternity of Man in 1967; the band ended up writing the epochal "Don't Bogart Me" (soon to be featured in *Easy Rider*) in the cellar. Franzoni and the incipient GTOs moved into the various cubbies and cubicles downstairs, where Franzoni was fond of bowling at two in the morning. Upstairs, the brothers staged dance parties in the cavernous living room. "The room was big enough to hold about four hundred people," Franzoni says. "It had three chandeliers. The bands set up in front of the huge fireplace. We'd feature three bands a night. You could get in for two bucks and you had to bring your own booze. There was no parking—there'd be cars parked all the way down Laurel Canyon—but the police never bothered us." Or at least they stopped trying once they'd met Franzoni.

"It was ten at night, we'd just moved in, and I hadn't washed myself for three days," he says. "The band was rehearsing, and there was a knock on the lower door to the bowling alley—there's a vestibule you come into, the lighting was really dim. So I open this huge door and there's two Los Angeles policemen standing there: 'Your music is too loud, we've gotten too many complaints.' I looked at the cops—the music is blaring behind me—and I said: 'Get the fuck out of here!' And the cops turned around and ran. They were two young cops, and my hair was way high and I'm looking like the Hunchback of Notre Dame answering the door."

Franzoni lived behind the bowling alley in a curtained, tomb-like space lined with egg cartons he had painted in pulsing psychedelic hues. "His bedroom—oh, my God—it was a den where God knows what went on," says Pamela Des Barres. Along with Leano, Offerall, Frka, Linda Sue "Sparky" Parker,

"Mercy" Fontentot, and "Cinderella," Pamela was about to cut a large swath through popular culture as a founding member of the GTOs groupie clique. (Tiny Tim preferred to address each girl as "Miss" followed by her first name; subsequently the GTOs went by Miss Pamela, Miss Christine, Miss Mercy, and so on.) The first time Pamela descended into the cabin's basement she was confronted by the sight of Franzoni bowling naked "except for plastic clip-on curlers in his pubic hair and a big pair of pointy stomping boots. He looked like a nuthouse escapee from someone's wildest nightmare." When Franzoni ventured outside the cabin, he favored a flowing satin cape emblazoned with a large *F*, which Pamela assumed meant Franzoni until he corrected her one evening with "Come meet Captain Fuck!" while flicking his serpentine tongue. "I was always trying to trap her, because she's so good-looking and sexy," Franzoni says. "I think I had one episode in the bathroom downstairs, but she said, No, no, no, so I walked away from her."

Franzoni, Vito, and Vito's wife, Szou (pronounced *soo*), were instrumental in creating the style-and-attitude template for post-Beatles Los Angeles youth. The look was especially influenced by Szou, who ran a boutique downstairs from her husband's studio. Franzoni recalls watching *The Steve Allen Show* and seeing "this guy sculpting Steve Allen, and that was Vito." The sculpture progressed over two or three shows; when it was finished, Franzoni says, "Steve invited Vito's wife to come onstage and show off her clothes, and right in the front row he had all these crazy beatnik girls wearing different clothes of hers."

"[Szou] was the first person in town to sell vintage clothes, to put them in a hip, boutiquey situation and combine them," says Pamela. "She would take them apart and create other pieces of finery. That was real innovative at the time." Says Franzoni: "She started the see-through look. May Co. would come over and buy a dress from her and then you'd see [a copy] on their racks." When subsumed into the media orgy over Ken Kesey's Merry Pranksters and San Francisco's Haight-Ashbury, the Szou look would inevitably be lumped with the all-purpose "hippie" trope. But the prototypical L.A. thrift-shop-clothed longhairs colonizing the Sunset Strip were actually split into several factions, the gnarliest known simply as freaks. (Zappa wrote "Hungry Freaks, Daddy" on the Mothers' first album about Franzoni.)

"A *hippie* was sort of the unwashed, unkempt kid," explains Pamela. "A *freak* was someone who put a lot of care and intention into their appearance, wanting to stand out instead of blend in. I was a combination flower child–freak, because the former was all about love and sharing and adoring each other and having flowers in your hair, literally, and lace and feathers and all that. I never considered myself a hippie. She'd be wearing one of those Indian madras-type skirts with her hair split down the middle, no makeup, sandals, braless—of course, we were all braless. I would have on an old vintage lace tablecloth with ribbons woven through it, feathers in my hair, loads of makeup, sequins stuck all over my face, and spike heels."

Gail Zappa recalls a nightly ritual at the cabin. "Around five all the girls, the GTOs and their friends, would get dressed. They'd bring out *boxes*. I'm not talking about macrame or tie-dye or any of that crap, but things from the turn of the century up to maybe the '30s and '40s. A number of the girls decided they'd call themselves Klondykes, and they would dress like those women from the '40s suddenly smoking on-screen, with their fucking pumps and shoulder pads, kind of a Mae West type. There was a phase of that and then there were all the doilies and feathers. It was constantly evolving. The rule of thumb was: you couldn't wear the same thing twice. Ever."

Vito taught sculpting classes on Tuesday nights at his studio—his pupils included Jonathan Winters and Mickey Rooney as well as feral Beverly Hills matrons more specifically interested in investigating the artist's heroic libido. But Vito's most significant contribution to the budding freak culture was mustering misfits like Franzoni into the wild-dressing, free-form dance troupe that rose to fame with the Byrds and became fixtures at clubs on the Strip, where they would make a mockery of the Brylcreem-and-bouffant straights primly doing the Frug.

Vito and his dancers began their forays in pre-Byrds 1964, at the dawn of L.A.'s folk-to-rock conversion. It was slim pickings at first. L.A. was still in thrall to folk music but the smarter musicians noted that times were, in fact, changing. Henry Diltz, banjo player in the Modern Folk Quartet who would soon become a top rock photographer, credits Vito's dancers as a goad to complacent folkies. "Flower children would come in and they'd be on acid, waving their hands in the air," he recalls. "They didn't want any three-minute song. If you did a three-minute song and it was over, they were just getting into it. So we'd do fifteen-minute songs and play instrumental things—then repeat the whole song—because once they got in the mood they didn't want the music to stop."

Here was a preview, fresh from the streets, of the coming distraction about to shake the music industry and popular culture: young, mainstream audiences would soon embrace albums over hit singles and "progressive" FM radio over Top 40 stations. Music was becoming a journey as opposed to a diversion, a trend that prefigured the extended dance mixes and DJ sets of the hip-hop and rave scenes of the '90s. "You still had your jocks and beehive-hairdo types doing the Mashed Potatoes," says Raphael. "But all of a sudden hip people—these unwashed beatniks—were dancing." And they pointedly were not doing the Swim. "Maybe the freer music inspired the freer movement," Raphael says. "In a partner dance, it was still a guy who led and you were kind of under his thumb; you had to obey the guy. This was wonderful."

Vito's dancers soon became as big a draw as the purported entertainment onstage. "The Whisky didn't want us for a long time until those Italian guys [owners Mario Maglieri and Elmer Valentine] figured out that we were their salvation because it was empty a lot and they had those cage dancers and it was boring, and up the street there were other places you could dance," says Franzoni. John Hartmann, proprietor of the Kaleidoscope, a club at Sunset and Vine in Hollywood, who would later manage Crosby, Stills & Nash, says: "I would let Vito and his dancers into the Kaleidoscope free every week because they attracted people. They were really hippies, and so we had to have them. They got in free pretty much everywhere they went. They blessed your joint. They validated you. If they're the essence of hippiedom and you're trying to be a hippie nightclub, you need hippies."

Says Gail Zappa: "If you had a large enough group you'd probably be allowed in for free to dance, because the people on the Strip knew the value of bringing in the tourists—those are the people paying the cover and buying the drinks, not the [freaks], who didn't have any money to buy alcohol. The customers came to see the freaks dance. Nobody ever talks about that, but that was the case." Eventually, the munificence of the proprietors reached its inevitable limit. "There's a classic event, it was in 1968, where Bernardo [Saldana] or one of the BTOs"— a fashion-conscious male clique that arrived on the scene along with the GTOs—"walked into the Whisky," says Zappa. "And he put up his peace sign in the usual way everyone would to just pass through. And Mario put a peace sign in his face and stopped him and said: 'Two dollars.' And then it became you had to pay to get in. If you were a freak, those days were over."

There was, however, a darker side to Vito's Dionysian celebrations. Miss Pamela recalled an evening's entertainment at Vito's studio that included two barely pubescent girls performing sexually for an alternately rapt and appalled audience. Then there was Vito's son, Godot, soon to fall to his death from a scaffold at the studio. "He was an adorable little boy, two or three, a little blond towhead," says Raphael. One night Raphael was present at Vito's when Godot was produced. "They passed that little boy around, naked, in a circle with their mouths," she says. "That was their thing about 'introducing him to sensuality.' That was well known. It was billed as something you could do. It didn't go over well with people other than that particular pseudo-hip arty crowd. That's why I hated Vito so much. Everybody felt terrible when Godot died, of course, and Vito went into mourning. But, still."

Frank Zappa, meanwhile, had been clawing his way out of obscurity. Born in Baltimore and raised in a litany of dreary Southern California suburbs, he was an adept of the avant-garde composer Edgard Varèse but also a connoisseur of R&B and cheesy doo-wop. An accomplished guitarist with a penchant, decades ahead of its time, for deconstructing popular culture—he'd already appeared on national television playing a duet on spinning bicycle wheels with Steve Allen—Zappa plowed through a succession of bands before joining R&B outfit the Soul Giants in 1964, which he renamed the Mothers.

The Mothers played dense, jarring material that was often an elaborate send-up of prevailing pop pap, made all the more disconcerting by the musicians' aggressively slovenly dress and coiffure, none of which endeared them to the Strip's club owners.

Franzoni met Zappa at Ben Frank's, a *Jetsons*-esque coffee shop on the Strip soon to become one of L.A. freakdom's stations of the cross. "Frank was looking for the key to get into Hollywood," Franzoni says. "He says, 'I want to get into Hollywood. What do I do?' I spent at least three months talking to him in his orange car, his house. I said, Okay, I'm trying to get away from the Byrds. You're next. I'll help you if you want."

With Vito's dancers in tow, the Mothers were soon playing the Whisky and larger venues in all their demented glory. By 1967 Zappa and the Mothers—rechristened the Mothers of Invention by their nervous record label—had released the milestone albums *Freak Out!* and *Absolutely Free*. Meanwhile, Pamela, Christine, Sandra, and Lucy, augmented by new recruits Mercy, Cinderella, and Sparky, split from Vito's troupe and began dancing as the Laurel Canyon Ballet Company. "They were a little ticked off at us for that, but, you know, we were seven girls wanting to do our own little thing," says Pamela. "Then Frank asked us to dance with the Mothers. We were wearing really nutty outfits like diapers and bibs with our hair in pigtails and all of our parts hanging out. We'd dress up in leaves and look like we were trees."

Zappa meanwhile had been introduced to Adelaide Gail Sloatman, a secretary at the Whisky. By the time the Mothers returned from their eighteen-month residency in New York, Zappa and Sloatman were married and the parents of the infant Moon Unit. Gail had come back in advance to house-hunt. Before the move to New York she and Frank had lived together in a house in the Kirkwood Bowl, and now his instructions were explicit. "Frank wanted to live in or near the canyon," Gail says. "Laurel Canyon has historically attracted musicians and people very highly involved in the arts, and usually people that didn't come by who they were with their hands held out or expecting other people to pay the freight." As it happened, Franzoni was about to move out of the cabin. The dance concerts in the living room were petering out as complaints about the noise brought the police to the landlady's door this time. "The police were bugging her more than they were bugging me, and that was the end of that," he says. "We decided to get out of there. Gail was looking for a place, and I said, Y'know, we're moving out of here, so we'll vacate it."

In March 1968, Zappa, Gail, Moon Unit, and various members of the Mothers entourage moved into the cabin. Miss Christine, Franzoni's basement-dwelling roommate, stayed on as baby governess. But the Laurel Canyon Ballet Company spent so much time at the cabin that they were essentially residents, too. "It was just so special when Frank and Gail moved in; it was like it became a holy place for me," says Pamela. "We got to watch Frank create music right on the spot. It was a very communal vibe. He really was a family man but was open to all kinds of humanity and would encourage every strange kind of person to hang out. He would sit us down and make us realize we really did have something to say and had lived interesting lives other people might be curious about."

Pamela and her cohorts intrigued Zappa, and as a first step in their refurbishment he suggested that they ditch the Laurel Canyon Ballet Company name. "He thought of the new name right there in the log cabin," Pamela recalls. "He said, 'Why don't you call yourselves the GTOs, because you're Girls Together Outrageously?' We just freaked and frolicked around the living room, which was *huge*. You could walk into the fireplace and sit in there." Zappa was launching two record labels—Bizarre and Straight—and was considering signing the GTOs. That they had no apprehensible musical talent didn't deter him. "I guess he saw lurking creative potential," Pamela says. "He was always able to spot that in people." "I think that's what Frank's talent really was," says Gail. "He had such respect for people, he created situations for them to be able to realize things they never imagined for themselves."

Zappa instructed the GTOs to write material for an album he would consider upon his return from a tour. The girls descended to the bowling alley to compose for six grueling months. The result, *Permanent Damage*, was recorded with the help of the

Jeff Beck Group, whom the GTOs dragooned backstage at the
Shrine Auditorium and brought to the cabin to meet Zappa.
Before the night was finished, Beck, the pianist Nicky Hopkins,
and Rod Stewart found themselves in a Glendale recording stu-
dio embellishing GTO compositions like "The Eureka Springs
Garbage Lady" and "I'm in Love with the Ooo-Ooo Man,"
Pamela's tribute to Nick St. Nicholas of Steppenwolf, to whom
she'd recently lost her cherry.

The GTOs weren't the only "talent" to audition at the log
cabin for Zappa. From Cortez High School in Phoenix came a
band of former track-and-field lettermen who'd been founder-
ing almost from the moment they hit L.A. They'd performed as
the Earwigs and the Spiders before settling, for reasons never adequately explained, on Alice Cooper, the name also taken by
the lead singer, Vincent Furnier, an otherwise arrow-straight
son of an Arizona pastor. (Cooper would soon become such a
serious boozer that the extravagantly dissipated Morrison considered him a drinking buddy.) Whatever the band lacked in
musicianship was more than made up for in their outré, drag-
femme stage presence, a consequence of being adopted by the
GTOs soon after they hit town, in particular by Christine, with
whom Alice fell in love.

"We really influenced their visuals," says Pamela. "Miss
Christine did Alice's makeup and helped him dress, and the rest
of the guys followed suit, so to speak." Says Gail: "Yes, they had
the name, but they were all like these skinny guys in jeans and
T-shirts. They did not have the makeup or dress. [Christine] was
entirely responsible for that, but Frank was really pushing the
envelope in terms of the image: if you're gonna go, go all the
way. Between Frank's influence and Miss Christine's they became what they are."

Alice Cooper eventually became the house band at the

Cheetah, a rock palace on the pier in Santa Monica. Affairs were at low ebb for the band. When they appeared with the Paul Butterfield Blues Band, Cooper recalled, "there were 6,000 people . . . We started out with the theme from *The Patty Duke Show*. It was as if somebody said, 'There's a bomb in the building.' We cleared the building in three songs." Undaunted, Cooper prevailed upon Christine to set up an audition with Zappa. "He was our hero—knowing him was like knowing the Beatles." Zappa finally relented and told the band to stop by the cabin at seven, which in their exuberance they took to mean 7:00 a.m. At the crack of dawn, Miss Christine let them in and they set up their equipment in the basement and started playing. According to Cooper, Zappa soon thundered downstairs, naked, holding his ears. "All right, all right," he shouted. "I'll sign you! Just stop playing!" (If this version of events sounds too glibly perfect, consider that in other tellings the band played *outside* the cabin.) Gail doesn't recall Cooper's early-morning audition; but she concedes, given the cabin zeitgeist, "it wouldn't surprise me in the least little bit."

Alice Cooper's vaudeville–freak show theatrics were, wittingly or not, a jab at the earnest folk-rock juggernaut beginning to build in the canyon. "Even hippies hated us," said Cooper, "and it's hard to get a hippie to hate anything." Zappa probably saw in the band his own struggles to torment the status quo, but he also clearly relished the delicious joke of putting over a group whose style was several magnitudes more advanced than their substance. Nonetheless, after countless hostile gigs and character-building tours, Alice Cooper was turning into a tough and credible rock-and-roll band, growth that Cooper felt Zappa seemed disinclined to acknowledge. They ended up at Warner Bros. Records, Zappa's distributor, after he sold his Bizarre and Straight labels. Five years after Zappa signed them,

Alice Cooper released *Billion Dollar Babies*, which hit No. 1 on the Billboard album chart.

While Zappa was attempting to make stars out of groupies and inept musicians, rock's budding royalty were pointing their limo drivers up Laurel Canyon Boulevard to the cabin. Or maybe it just seemed that way. "The legend precedes it," says Gail, "because what actually happened was, it was only a very few people that we knew, and yeah, they were incredibly famous. But we were there for such a short time there would have been limos blocking the canyon if you believe the stories you hear constantly." Zappa's absolute intolerance for drugs was perpetually at odds with the proclivities of the cabin's storied guests. "Frank was completely straight," says Pamela. "And you just were not allowed to be high up there. I always felt sort of guilty—because I took a lot of reds then—staggering around the cabin because I knew he hated it. But he didn't ever bust me."

Gail insists the well-traveled story that Zappa booted Mick Jagger and Marianne Faithful from the cabin for inebriation is not true. "What I recall is that [Jagger] came over with Marianne Faithful, and she spent a few minutes demonstrating her ability on the tambourine and then pulled her clothing apart to reveal the bruises it caused on her ass and on her hip. That was very exciting. I also remember that Frank had gotten a splinter in his foot—we were all walking around barefoot, and there were these wood floors that hadn't been taken care of—and Mick Jagger got down on his hands and knees and grabbed Frank's foot in order to see what kind of assistance he could offer. Frank was really taken aback by that. I have very strong feelings about it—it was very genuine and very spontaneous."

Nevertheless, countless hours and joints were consumed in cars parked along Lookout Mountain Avenue by guests getting high before entering the cabin. As to the source of Zappa's virulent antidrug stance, those close to him had little doubt. "It was because he wanted to be in *control*," says Pamela. "It was pretty obvious. He wanted to control everything around him. And that obviously was out of his control when people were crawling around the floor." Although a well-documented martinet when working with musicians in his charge, Zappa "was a very considerate person," Gail says, "extraordinarily kind and very mannered in terms of being considerate. He really respected having good manners. I'm not talking about table manners but regard for another human being. What he was intolerant of was people who worked for him being lazy. He always gave people the benefit of the doubt—not everyone, but people of a naturally artistic persuasion—because they were experimenting with their lives."

Though Zappa relished the notoriety that the cabin bestowed, the round-the-clock parade of personalities great and small was taking its toll. The cabin's awkward location only steps from Laurel Canyon Boulevard, a heavily trafficked route between the Valley and Hollywood, hardly helped matters. One summer afternoon Zappa was sitting in the living room with the GTOs when an intense young man walked through the open front door, introduced himself as "The Raven," and said that he had something for Zappa. "He handed me a bottle of fake blood with a rag in it, and said, 'I have isolated The Specimen!' and pulled out an Army .45," Zappa recalled. Tabulating his options, Zappa led the wretched man outside to the water-filled hole that supposedly led to the Houdini house and persuaded him to toss the gun into the water. And with that, Zappa recalled, he and Gail started looking for another house. The cabin, Gail says, had begun to attract "an unsavory element, and that element became more prevalent than we felt comfortable with." On

September 6 or 7, 1968—Gail can't remember which—she and Frank moved to quieter quarters in the canyon, where he would write and record a staggering fifty-nine albums and father three more children, Dweezil, Ahmet, and Diva, before dying of prostate cancer on December 4, 1993, at age fifty-two.

After Zappa left, the cabin resumed its dreary roundelay of tenants—Eric Burdon of the Animals lived there for a time—while the grounds became seedier, the drugs harder, the parties larger, louder, and darker. Finally, on Halloween night, 1981, the cabin burned to the ground. "It was such a crime when that thing burned down," says Pamela. "It was just a mesmerizing and magical place, knowing right off the bat that it had belonged to Tom Mix and that his horse was buried underneath the bowling alley." Pamela still pictures Zappa "up there with his striped shirts and flowered bell-bottoms, with a cigarette in his hand. Such an amazing, amazing individual."

The day the cabin burned, Pamela says, "I wanted to put the flags at half-mast."

THREE

LADY OF THE CANYON

*Pot and sympathy at Cass Elliot's, Crosby, Stills, and Nash in the living room,
Eric Clapton in the backyard, California dreamin' becomes a reality*

During the American 1920s—a decade of prosperity and social
upheaval unrivaled until the 1960s—the "moderns," as the cultural historian Ann Douglas christened the gadabout young
men and women of the Jazz Age, set about destroying the social
and cultural conventions put in place in the late nineteenth century by the "powerful white middle-class matriarch of the recent Victorian past." Douglas's matriarchs in chief included
Frances E. Willard and her Women's Christian Temperance
Union, proselytizer for prohibition; Mary Baker Eddy, founder
of the Christian Science Church; and the suffragette Carrie
Chapman Catt, midwife of the woman's right to vote. The
moderns, Douglas argued, "aimed to ridicule and overturn
everything the matriarch had championed." Certainly a woman
like Dorothy Parker—promiscuous, atheistic, alcoholic, and unapologetic about her ambition and talent—would have been a
living, breathing affront to the likes of Eddy. By mocking the
conventions of the matriarch in their works and deeds, the male

and especially female cultural stars of the 1920s, the Parkers, Fitzgeralds, Thurbers, Dos Passoses, and Hemingways, ensured that "Christian beliefs and middle-class values would never again be a prerequisite for elite artistic success in America." Not even the matriarch's form, both nurturing and intimidating, was spared. "Plumpness [would] never again be a broadly sanctioned type of female beauty," Douglas noted; "the 1920s put the body type of the stout and full-figured matron decisively out of fashion"—a point driven home by Groucho Marx's relentless humiliation of the stout, full-figured Margaret Dumont, dripping with jewels and self-righteousness, in half a dozen Marx Brothers movies. Once the matriarch and "her notions of middle-class piety, racial superiority and sexual repression were discredited," Douglas concluded, "modern America, led by New York, was free to promote . . . an egalitarian popular and mass culture aggressively appropriating forms and ideas across race, class and gender lines."

The rapidly evolving cultural, social, and sexual conventions of the early 1960s, in Los Angeles as much as in New York, represented a reprisal, though exponentially more far-reaching, of the moderns' revolt of the 1920s. Just as the '20s were a reaction to and rejection of the Victorian past, the 1960s were a bracing slap to the face awakening America from the slumbers of the 1950s. For all the decade's masculine ciphers—the Cold War saber rattling and presence of an actual four-star general in the White House—the zeitgeist of the '50s is indelibly linked to the image of a monolithically white, middle-class suburbia and its nuclear family over which the woman, in conical bra and crino-lined housedress, reigned as mother, housekeeper, and prim sexual helpmate. The Victorian matron, it seemed, had returned, only now she was living in a Levittown split-level with a hus-band named Bud and a brood of Brownies and Cub Scouts. Her comeback would be short-lived; American women themselves would rise up this time to slay her, most famously in the person of Betty Friedan and her book *The Feminine Mystique*. (The matron would nevertheless reappear, gentrified for the post-Reagan age, in the indomitable persona of lifestyle editrix and future felon Martha Stewart.)

At the same time that the ideal of the demure, pure Caucasian female dominated mainstream American imagery, black musical idioms of rhythm and blues and incipient rock and roll struggled—and, late in the decade, briefly succeeded—to slice through the meringue of white popular culture just as jazz had in the 1920s. It was, notably, the daughters as much as the sons of the white American middle class in the 1950s who delivered to stardom Elvis Presley, a white hillbilly singing black-authored or, more typically, black-sounding songs, his courtly country manners betrayed by the unrestrained sexuality of his performance. "[Elvis] won over the children of white people all over the country because the kids instinctively understood how vapid white culture was becoming," the novelist Bobbie Ann Mason recalled of her childhood in 1950s Kentucky. Or, as Janis Joplin told *Rolling Stone*'s David Dalton in 1970, "They were playing that '50s crap on the radio. It seemed so shallow, all oop-boop. It had nothing. Then I heard Leadbelly and it was like a flash. It *mattered* to me."

Just as Parker and her cronies discredited and discarded the lingering culture of the Victorian era, so, too, did the early rock-and-roll scene of Los Angeles in the 1960s set about dismantling the suffocating pop-cultural remnants of the 1950s. In one sense, the Byrds, Buffalo Springfield, and other L.A. rock bands—aided immeasurably by Beatlemania—were simply finishing the job started by Elvis Presley, James Dean, Chuck Berry, Little Richard, Lenny Bruce, Allen Ginsberg, Jack Kerouac, and the early folk-music movement: the relentless, incremental chipping away of postwar America's seemingly bullet-proof self-possession and cultural somnolence. Their advantage, and what now brought their culture, soon to be branded "the counterculture," to critical mass where it had faltered in the '50s, was sheer numbers; not since Fitzgerald's Lost Generation had so many Americans, some seventy-six million of them, arrived in their late teens and early twenties at precisely the same moment. Thanks to network television and other leaps in mass communication, America's baby boom, its vast numbers repeated in England and Europe, could now, on a whim, turn a local trend into an international cultural avalanche. It happened with the Beatles, and by 1965 it was happening to the Byrds, Beach Boys, Turtles, and other L.A. bands.

Rock music—a lot of it initially from England, but more and more of it from Los Angeles—was the glue that bound the generation together. It was at the rock-and-roll ballrooms and clubs of the mid-1960s—the Kinetic Circus in Chicago, the Fillmores in New York and San Francisco, the Whisky A Go-Go in L.A.—and in the quartiers where the musicians lived and commingled, be it Haight-Ashbury or Laurel Canyon, that the far-flung members of the generation first discovered one another and with that discovery the narcotic power of knowing they were in the right place at the right time. As Hunter S. Thompson recalled of his stint living in San Francisco in the 1960s, he could point his motorcycle in any direction and be "absolutely certain that no matter which way I went I would come to a place where people were just as high and wild as I was . . . you could strike sparks anywhere. There was a fantastic universal sense that whatever we were doing was right, that we were winning."

And so the matriarchal culture of the 1950s was dispatched. But where, exactly, women fit into the counterculture, with its intimate ties to music performed by male musicians marketed by male record company executives, booking agents, managers, and concert promoters, and played by male disc jockeys, was not even a matter of debate; it wasn't, in fact, debated at all. Beyond providing comforts creature and carnal, the young women of the 1960s closest to the burgeoning music scene in L.A. were largely excluded.

Judy Raphael has a bell-clear memory of Ray Manzarek at UCLA telling her of his plans to start a rock band with their fellow student, a pudgy Navy brat named Jim Morrison. "I said, 'Can I be in it?' And he said, 'No, there aren't any girls in rock bands. You need to stop running around trying to be somebody all the time.'" (An exception to this breathtaking sexism was the Los Angeles bassist Carol Kaye, a member of the otherwise all-male Wrecking Crew, a confederation of crack session musicians, including the future stars Glen Campbell and Leon Russell, who played on countless hit rock and pop records recorded in L.A. during the 1960s, including the Beach Boys' "Good Vibrations"; except for Roger McGuinn's electric twelve-string guitar, the "band" heard on the Byrds' "Mr. Tambourine Man" was made up of Wrecking Crew hacks.)

The folk movement of the early '60s had been built on the success of sexually integrated bands like the New Christy Minstrels and Peter, Paul and Mary. Joan Baez, Judy Collins, Carolyn Hester, and Judy Henske had achieved success unmatched by solo male folksingers, spectacularly so in Collins's and especially Baez's case. But with the rise of the Beatles and fellow all-male British invaders like the Rolling Stones, Kinks, Yardbirds, and Animals and the American, especially Los Angelean, bands who aped their duende, from haircuts to harmonies, women were held at bay by sheer masculine preemption. "Now all of a sudden you should just be a chick," says Raphael. "Ambition was a downer. You got back into the traditional roles." Observed *Rolling Stone's* David Dalton, "There was a place for women in the 'music biz' all right—as torch chanteuses, teen angels, back-up singers, Mary Quant dollies, song stylists, autoharp/dulcimer-strumming folk madonnas [and] girl groups. Rock Inc.'s experience of women extended for the most part to waitresses, stewies, fans, flacks, groupies or, that most comic condition, rock wives."

But the de facto prohibition on women performers in the rock idiom was tenuous and would soon be breached by Signe Anderson and Grace Slick, the first and second singers of San Francisco's Jefferson Airplane, and most spectacularly by Joplin, an utterly original, ferociously smart, and streetwise phenomenon from Port Arthur, Texas, whose Bessie Smith–influenced, hippie-chick-meets-hooker bravado ultimately overshadowed Big Brother and the Holding Company, the San Francisco group she joined in 1966. But for sheer influence, as much for the way she integrated her personality into the rapidly evolving Los Angeles music scene as for her singing, no one came close to this woman who lived in Laurel Canyon at the moment of its most intense artistic ferment and whose presence there would directly shape the canyon's identity and legacy, and have a profound influence on the music created by other, mostly male, mostly rock-oriented musicians for years to come.

Cass Elliot was one-half of the female half of the Mamas and the Papas, the group's mixed-gender makeup a holdover from its tangled roots in New York and Washington, D.C. Born Ellen Naomi Cohen in Baltimore, Elliot had performed in the Big Three, a folk trio reconstituted as the Mugwumps with the addition of the folkies Denny Doherty, Zal Yanovsky, and John Sebastian, the latter two soon to form the Lovin' Spoonful. After the Mugwumps broke up in 1965, Doherty joined John

Phillips and Phillips's second wife, Holly Michelle Gilliam, a seventeen-year-old aspiring model he'd met in New York, in the New Journeymen. Phillips, a first-rate composer and taskmaster, wanted a fourth, high-harmony voice in the group; Elliot presented herself to Phillips for consideration again and again, eventually following the band to the Virgin Islands. There, in one of the gentler legends associated with her life—the ghastly rumor that she choked to death on a ham sandwich persists, even though she died far more prosaically and plausibly of an apparent heart attack at age thirty-two after a history of drug abuse and binge dieting to tame her obesity—a workman supposedly dropped a length of pipe on her head, knocking her unconscious. Two weeks later, it was claimed, she could miraculously hit the high notes Phillips wanted. "It's true, honest to God," Elliot recalled in 1968. "My range was increased by three notes."

In fact, Elliot left the islands alone and didn't join until the group arrived in L.A. and ended up crashing at the Hollywood apartment she was sharing with her husband and former bandmate, Jim Hendricks (the marriage, never consummated, had been contrived to keep Hendricks from being drafted). Being cooped up in the tiny apartment with the band for weeks worked to Elliot's advantage, as she wore down Phillips's resistance by singing with the group daily. "That's when Harvey showed up," Doherty recalled. "Harvey was an overtone—a fifth voice that was created when the four of us sang together. It wasn't folk music anymore . . . it was really and truly rock and roll." Recalled Elliot: "When I heard us sing together the first time, we knew. We *knew*. This is it." In the first of many acts of networking genius, Elliot contacted her friend Barry McGuire—the former New Christy Minstrel and "Eve of Destruction" singer—who arranged an audition for the band with his producer, Lou Adler.

Kim Fowley, publisher of Hendricks's songs, recalls instead
that Elliot, still not a member of the group, called one day to
invite him to "come down and hear the New Journeymen." After listening to them play "Monday, Monday" and "California
Dreamin,'" Fowley shopped the trio to the producer Nick
Venet, who, upon seeing the four of them together and ascer-
taining that Elliot could indeed sing and knew the fourth harmony, refused to audition them for Mirror Records unless she
was included. "The first time the four of them sang as a four-
piece was in his living room," Fowley says. That was on Saturday. "Monday morning they were looking to get medicated
so they wouldn't blow it at three o'clock at Mirror Records. So
they called up Barry McGuire, according to popular legend, to
bring some refreshments over to bolster their confidence, and
when he heard them sing those songs, he called Lou Adler. So
they all went over in Barry's car and Lou Adler said, 'Sing.'"
Adler immediately offered the foursome a $5,000 advance and
signed them to his Dunhill label. "You figured, who are they going to meet between Saturday and Monday?" Fowley says. "Answer: Dunhill Records. Lou Adler was on the ball on that one."

The Mamas and the Papas' success was as swift and disorienting as the Byrds'. "California Dreamin'," a meditation on the
West Coast utopia written during a dismal winter in New York
City, climbed to No. 4 in 1965. (Although John and Michelle
are credited with co-writing the song, Michelle's contribution
was mostly transcribing the lyrics after John woke her in the
middle of the night.) "California Dreamin'" was followed by a
string of Top 10 hits, including "Monday, Monday" and "I Saw
Her Again," a thinly veiled jab by Phillips at Doherty, who'd had
an affair with Michelle. The Phillipses and Doherty installed
themselves on Lookout Mountain; Elliot bought a rambling estate on Woodrow Wilson Drive on the east side of Laurel
Canyon. Amid the group's incessant television appearances and

tours—and internecine intrigue and escalating drug use—Elliot managed to turn the Woodrow Wilson house into the canyon's de facto salon, a rock-and-roll Bloomsbury whose participants spanned two continents.

Elliot had been active in the musical theater in New York— she competed with Barbra Streisand for the role of Miss Marmelstein in *I Can Get It for You Wholesale*—and she brought with her to Los Angeles a measure of the theater's backstage bonhomie and ebullience. She had a nurturing personality as expansive as her girth, plus a quick mind and highly evolved sense of humor. Inevitably, her obesity kept her from being a sexual object, and that in turn allowed her to become closer to many of the canyon's male musicians than they, or she, might otherwise have allowed. (Michelle Phillips, a lithe, gamine beauty, had the opposite effect; men competed for her sexual attentions inside and outside the band, and her presence became just as inevitably divisive.)

In a scene rapidly filling with priapic young men bursting with talent and ego, Elliot's home was a neutral ground where they could share food, dope, songs, and something approaching real friendship. "My house is a very free house," Elliot said. "It's not a crash pad and people don't come without calling. But on an afternoon, especially on weekends, I always get a lot of delicatessen food in because I know David [Crosby] is going to come over for a swim and things are going to happen." Elliot projected the nonthreatening, nonsexual vibe of an earth mother even as she fell deeply in unrequited love with Doherty. Still, her "Mama" stage name wasn't entirely an act; she had a Jewish mother's compulsion for good-naturedly meddling in the lives of the awkward boys who turned up on her doorstep, and she often really did know what was best for them.

"She was this incredible mother figure," says Graham Nash. "I keep imagining this huge beautiful chicken gathering all her little chicks under her wings and making sure that they're all cool, that this one is talking to that one, and this one knows what that one's doing." Her love of pot stirring launched or enhanced several careers and, in her most celebrated case of matchmaking, changed the course of pop music.

"She had that capacity to be a very good friend, to be there for you and to know what would be good for you even if you didn't," says Gary Burden, who designed album covers for the Mamas and the Papas, Crosby, Stills & Nash, Joni Mitchell, the Eagles, and Jackson Browne. "She was very important not only as an individual artist and a great singer, very underestimated, but also for knowing who would be good with who, who should be working with or singing with who. She had a great instinct for that." Burden himself was one of Elliot's first projects. He had grown up in Laguna Beach, an artists' colony two hours south of Los Angeles, and had taken up architecture as a compromise. "I'd come out of art school going, Shit, I'm going to be Michelangelo," he recalls. "It became very painfully evident I was not." By the time mutual friends introduced him to Elliot, Burden was married with two children and miserable in his job. "I was still wearing three-piece suits and a bow tie and sneaking to smoke pot," he says. "I was looking for a way out. She provided it."

Elliot hired Burden to design a renovation of the Woodrow Wilson house, but it wasn't long before she pulled him aside and wondered why he wasn't designing rock-and-roll album covers. Burden demurred. "I said, 'Cass, I don't know anything about graphic arts.' She said, 'It doesn't matter.' And indeed in those times it didn't matter. You didn't have to be an expert, because it was all new. And because there were no experts, there were opportunities, so a person like myself who knew nothing about graphics could step in and do it." Burden had not yet grasped this essential fact of the '60s; Elliot, having gone from starving folkie to rich rock-and-roll superstar virtually overnight, had. Burden would go on to design hundreds of album covers—several, including Crosby, Stills & Nash's debut, would join Fillmore posters and tie-dye in the iconography of '60s pop culture. But one of his first was a Mamas and Papas album, courtesy of Elliot. "Through her I dropped into this world I'd always wanted to be in," Burden says. "She gave me the life I wound up living, and if for no other reason than that, I would always be indebted to her."

Shooting the photographs for many of Burden's album covers was Henry Diltz, the Modern Folk Quartert banjo player and frequent guest at Elliot's house. "She was an earth mother to the hip and cool," Diltz says. "Very funny, very intelligent." Diltz had come to photography much the way Burden had started designing album covers. Born in Kansas City, Missouri, he went to grade school in Tokyo and high school in Bangkok and logged a couple of years at West Point before fetching up in Hawaii, where he co-founded the MFQ. He'd taken up photography as a hobby, and one day as he walked down the hill from his house on Lookout Mountain to visit his bandmate Cyrus Faryar, he heard music coming from inside a bungalow.

"I walked up to the door and Stephen Stills and the Buffalo Springfield were in there. I knew Stephen real well from New York—we were fellow musicians—and they said, 'Hey, we're going down to Redondo Beach to do a sound check, why don't you come.' I thought, Great, I can walk around the beach and take some pictures. So here was the Buffalo Springfield doing their sound check and I could have been in there shooting thousands of photos but I was shooting people walking down the beach. When they walked out, I said, 'Why don't you stand in front of that mural and I'll take a shot of you.' And that was my first rock-and-roll shot. I wasn't even thinking; I just took it because it would be a nice picture. Then a magazine called me and said, 'We hear you have a picture of the Buffalo Springfield; we'll give you a hundred bucks.' And that started my career that day, and it was just because I walked down the hill and happened to bump into Stephen Stills."

There was no shortage of such serendipitous encounters in the canyon, but Elliot couldn't resist helping them along. "She just loved getting people together," says Diltz. "She was forever meeting English musicians on TV shows who didn't know anybody, and she'd tell them, 'Well, come over.' One day she had a picnic in her backyard for Eric Clapton, who was in town and didn't know anybody, and she invited David Crosby, who brought Joni Mitchell, who he had just discovered—Mickey Dolenz [of the Monkees] was there, Gary Burden was there—just so Eric could meet some people." In one of Diltz's photos from that day, Crosby reposes against a sycamore tree—he's wearing a Borsalino flattop hat and what John Prine would immortalize as an illegal smile. Next to him Mitchell sits Indian style, a Martin dreadnought guitar in her lap, picking out a melody, blond bangs spilling over her brow. Clapton sits on the grass opposite Mitchell, a cigarette clamped in his right hand, staring at her with an intense, inscrutable expression. Such were the afternoons at Chez Elliot. "Music happens in my house," she said, "and that pleases me."

Elliot's greatest feat of matchmaking unfolded in 1968. Stills had met Elliot in their folkie days in Greenwich Village, "before any of us were anybody," he recalled. Diltz, playing New York with the MFQ, would run into Stills on the circuit. "Stephen was playing at a little coffeehouse called a basket house—they would pass the basket around, and that would be his only pay. Between sets he would come down to the Village Gate and stand in the wings and watch us. I know we were a huge influence on him because we did four-part harmony, which was very sophisticated. Most groups had three-part harmony—Peter, Paul and Mary, the Kingston Trio—but we did four-part and that's why he admired us." Stills had harmony on his mind after he'd moved to L.A. and the Buffalo Springfield formed and swiftly imploded. He and Crosby—recently booted from the Byrds—had begun a desultory collaboration. Elliot, as ever, took notice. "David and I were messing around, talking about doing something," Stills said, "and [Cass] comes up to me and says, 'Do you think you need a third voice?' And I said, 'Yeah.' She said, 'Okay, don't say anything, especially to Crosby. And when I call, *come*.'"

Graham Nash was at the time a member of the Hollies, one of the more endearing British Invasion bands, partial to rich harmony singing on winsome hits like "Bus Stop" and "Carrie Anne," many of them co-written by Nash. Diltz was in New York shooting the Lovin' Spoonful, Elliot's old bandmates from the Mugwumps, then cresting on a string of Top 10 hits like "You Didn't Have to Be So Nice," when Elliot appeared unannounced at his studio one afternoon with all five Hollies in tow. "We spent the afternoon drinking margaritas and hanging out and getting to know each other," Diltz recalls. Elliot's networking instincts were just as pervasive on the East Coast; the following day the Hollies asked Diltz to take some publicity pictures of the band, and he ended up shooting their next album cover.

Nash, meanwhile, was growing increasingly frustrated with the Hollies, who resisted recording his more challenging material. "The Hollies didn't want to record my songs," says Nash. "They thought they were shit; they thought *I* was shit. It was a sad time for me personally, artistically." On tour with the band in 1967, he was ensconced at the Knickerbocker Hotel in downtown Los Angeles when the phone rang. "Cass called me and said, 'I'm going to pick you up in ten minutes.' So I got ready and was waiting in the lobby of the hotel, and she pulls up in this convertible Porsche. I got in and she drove me up Laurel Canyon to this house." Waiting there were Stills and Crosby, who sang for Nash the Stills composition "You Don't Have to Cry."

"That was a moment that is indelibly etched on my soul," Nash recalled. "David and Stephen sang it first. I asked them to do it again. I listened very carefully. I asked them to do it one more time. And they looked at each other and went, 'Well, okay.' They sang it a third time and I put my harmony in." It was, by all accounts, an electrifying moment. "When David and Stephen and I were halfway through 'You Don't Have to Cry,' we had to stop and start laughing," says Nash. "Each of us just had terrible experiences with our bands and had left or been thrown out. And all of a sudden we realized we'd have to be a fucking band again. Because how could you deny what you were listening to?"

Burden was there that day. "David and Stephen sang their parts and Graham listened and listened again," he says. "And then suddenly out of nowhere came this razor voice that was, like, perfect. It wasn't like anything had been missing; it was just that suddenly this thing was elevated beyond belief. It was chilling, man, because nobody had heard anything like that before. Everybody was completely knocked out."

What was more stupendous to the musicians was Elliot's clairvoyance, that she could have anticipated the now instantly apprehensible alchemy of Stills's raspy delivery mixed with Nash's reedy tenor and Crosby's gorgeous, transparent harmony. Individually, their voices, especially Stills's, were distinctive; together they were unforgettable. "Cass, somehow or other, heard that in her head because she knew about three-part harmony from her own experience," Burden says. As Nash would marvel thirty-five years later: "Just think about that. What an incredible thing to first of all envision, and secondly to pull off. It's as if it was already a predetermined future to her, in terms of how she viewed me and David and Stephen. I mean, she knew what we had to do. But how do you know that when we haven't even sung together?"

By the time the Mamas and the Papas played the Monterey Pop Festival in 1967—organized in part by Phillips—the band was fraying. Doherty's affair with Michelle Phillips, begun before Elliot had joined the group, provoked a him-or-me showdown when John Phillips caught the two in flagrante. Michelle chose John. Elliot, meanwhile, still in love with Doherty, felt betrayed when she learned of the affair. The intrigue eventually metastasized to include Gene Clark of the Byrds; when Phillips saw Michelle blowing kisses to Clark from the stage during a Mamas and Papas concert, he fired her from the band, with Doherty's and Elliot's approval, and replaced her with Adler's girlfriend, Jill Gibson (the record label actually superimposed Gibson's photo over Michelle's on an album cover before Phillips was allowed to return). Doherty, meanwhile, lovesick over Michelle's rejection, was drinking heavily. The end came at a party in London when Elliot, recounting to Mick Jagger the details of her jailing over an unpaid hotel bill, was mocked by John Phillips and quit on the spot. The band limped through a subsequent contractual-obligation album, which sold poorly, before finally expiring in 1968.

Freed from the ongoing drama of the band, Elliot launched a solo career and had a hit with "Dream a Little Dream of Me," recorded during the band's final hours but released as a solo single. "My role in the Mamas and Papas was basically just to sing," she said after the band's breakup in 1968. "I will admit in all honesty there are a very few songs on all the Mamas and Papas albums that I'm really proud to listen to. I don't have the records in my house." She'd given birth to a daughter, Owen Vanessa Elliot, but wouldn't identify the father and unabashedly admitted to dropping acid while pregnant. "I was told all the things I couldn't do when I was pregnant, and I did them all," she said.

Breaking with the prejudices of her peer group, she launched a Las Vegas solo show at a time when playing Vegas—where the finger-snapping "entertainers" of her parents' generation fled when the folk rockers chased them off the Strip in L.A.—was to commit hipness hari-kari. "They're paying me an outrageous amount of money—$40,000 a week, which is totally silly," she said. "If Emmett Grogan"—founder of San Francisco's Diggers, the hippie charity collective—"ever heard about it, I'd really be in deep trouble." Though the shows were disastrous, appearances on television variety shows and return trips to Vegas followed. Having proposed to Doherty after the band broke up (he rejected her), she married the journalist Baron Donald von Wiedenman in 1971. She had just completed a well-received two-week engagement at the London Palladium when she died in 1974.

Her death was devastating to those she had nurtured in the L.A. rock scene. In a canyon filled with footloose, emotionally dysfunctional young men and women, she had fulfilled, wittingly or not, the role of indulgent matriarch—albeit a hip and acid-tested one. Laurel Canyon, says Burden, was "a place in the middle of this big city that people escaped to. Many of these people didn't really have family scenes of their own—they'd never had the experience of a family. I think people found in those early days the family they'd always wanted." Now the bosomy mother who'd tended to them all was gone.

"It's very interesting," says Nash, "that she really didn't take care of her own relationships with the same kind of care she took of other people's relationships. Whenever things were not going right, or when they were, we'd go over to Cass's house. I was just drawn to this woman; she was a magnificent creature. She knew how artists were, how crazy and fragile they were." Even the most hardened Hollywood types who knew her well were stunned she was no longer around. "Cass Elliot is the only fat person I ever loved," recalled Julia Phillips (no relation to John), the acerbic producer of *Taxi Driver, The Sting,* and *Close Encounters of the Third Kind.* "She'd come over to my house on Nicholas Beach with an eighth [of an ounce of cocaine], a suitcase and a couple of decks of cards and we would get into killer canasta that could last for days—or at least until the blow ran out."

Phillips was as petite as Elliot was obese. One foggy day in Malibu they were walking down the beach to visit the actresses Jennifer Salt and Margot Kidder. When they were two hundred yards away, Kidder and Salt could be seen waving wildly to them. "I wonder," Cass said, "how they knew it was us." At the Woodrow Wilson house, Elliot designated a blank wall in the living room for guests to fill with quips and tropes. "Cass had started it all one night by writing, 'Who is Chuck Barris and why is he saying those things about me?'" Phillips recalled. Before long the wall was black with contributions from Jack Nicholson, Michelle Phillips, Robert Towne—everyone, in other words, who was anyone in L.A. and Laurel Canyon in the 1960s and early '70s. After Elliot's funeral and sodden wake at the Polo Lounge of the Beverly Hills Hotel, Phillips went through her Rolodex, found Elliot's card, and framed the edges in black Magic Marker. "I'm not," she thought to herself, "throwing this one out."

Thirty-one years after Elliot died, just mentioning her name to Graham Nash causes him to sigh deeply and murmur, "Oh, dear." Evidence of her impact on his life confronts him every day. "My daughter Nile was born on the day Cass died, which was July 29," he says. "My daughter's best friend is named Cass." Referring not only to Crosby, Stills & Nash but to the whole of his experiences since driving up Laurel Canyon in her Porsche that afternoon so long ago, he says: "I mean, holy shit, look what happened. And look at what might *not* have happened. If it hadn't been for Cass I would have never met my wife, Susan, and never been married and had children.

"I don't know," he declares, "what my life would have been like if I had not befriended Cass."

FOUR

EVERYDAY PEOPLE

Southern Comfort duty with Janis Joplin, Brian Wilson wants to shave your legs, a lecture from Mickey Dolenz, sleeping with bats and tripping out at the love-ins

By 1968, to paraphrase the increasingly dyspeptic voice of Dylan's generation, it wasn't altogether clear whether quotidian life in America's hippie quarters was busy being born or busy dying. Even as the counterculture was ever more breathlessly parsed by interlopers from the straight media as earnest as *Look* magazine or as absurd as Diana Vreeland, there were stirrings among the brethren in the cities where the hippie-counterculture-call-it-what-you-will had burned brightest that the moment might be passing. The final curtain was still a year away—in the yin and yang of the muddy fields of Yasgur's farm and the killing fields of the Rolling Stones' stage front at Altamont. But already, everyday imagery was more apt to bludgeon than caress: the brutalities visited upon longhairs at the Democratic National Convention in Chicago, the relentless drumbeat of the war in Vietnam, the appalling assassinations of Robert Kennedy and Martin Luther King, Jr., with accompanying full-scale riots. It was becoming increasingly problematic to embrace a philosophy of peace, love, sex, drugs, and rock and roll while Rome, or more to the point, Washington, D.C.'s ghetto, heartbroken and furious after King's killing, burned. (L.A.'s ferocious Watts riots in 1965 had already demonstrated the consequences of allowing a vast underclass to fester in the middle of one of the world's richest cities.) "In '68 everything went south," Chris Hillman recalls. "The climate in the country changed. We were very close to anarchy. Very close. With Vietnam, riots on campus, the assassinations, we were close to collapse."

The denizens of Laurel Canyon, if not oblivious to these steadily more ominous developments, had for the moment settled into something resembling retreat, physical and spiritual, from an ever more troublesome world. A hypothetical map of Los Angeles drawn by a canyonite in the fashion of ancient mariners might have noted "here be dragons" almost anywhere but the canyon. By now the canyon's vast tribe of musicians was being silently culled into successes and failures, though the bona fides of the former and the obviousness of the latter could be, and were, buried in self-delusion. For Kim Fowley the ennui was as thick as the eucalyptus (which, canyonites began to notice, they could no longer smell now that they were acclimated).

"By then a lot of people had been cheated by record companies and managers, so they had to retreat to some kind of pastoral backdrop where they could lick their wounds without looking like they'd totally blown it financially," Fowley says. "Laurel Canyon was kind of a refuge for people who were incapable of eyeball-to-eyeball hustling on Sunset Boulevard. You'd look out the window and write songs in a flannel shirt about *timber* and *chrome* and guys would come by and sit and listen and whenever they'd do a line that meant it was a good song. So you retreated to the country charm of your little ticky-tack place, and like a bulldog on the enamel of a bathtub on a hot summer day you just lay there and panted and hoped that no-body discovered that you were scared to death."

Grappling with the implications of a lifestyle that only two years earlier had seemed practically utopian was not popular sport and may have encouraged the premature mythologizing of the places where it was invented. Says Fowley: "Laurel Canyon was affordable and charming and pleasant. But it was preten-tious. It was a place to pretend you were trendy or eclectic, and if you took away their tumbleweeds and eucalyptus, they were fucking boring."

Crystal Brelsford moved to Los Angeles in 1968 from Sugar-bush, Vermont, in the company of her boyfriend, Waddy Wach-tel, and his band, Twice Nicely. The rock-and-roll business had by then evolved to the point that the money made by cranking out pop pap could now be reinvested in a legitimate rock band, no matter how obscure, which had the effect of cleansing the funds and, as often as not, providing a handsome return. Thus was Twice Nicely taken under the wing of William "Bud" Cowsill, patriarch of the redoubtable family singing ensemble then cresting with an excruciating hit version of "Hair," from the Broadway "hippie" musical. Cowsill installed the band in a house in Benedict Canyon, and Brelsford was given a job in the Cowsills' offices. Twice Nicely turned out to be one of the many bands of the '60s that, given one more piece of luck, might have thrived; instead, they disintegrated after Bud Cowsill moved them to L.A. (Wachtel would go on to become the com-pleat L.A. rock session guitarist and a mainstay on records and tours by Linda Ronstadt and Warren Zevon, whom Brelsford would marry in 1974 and divorce in 1979.)

Having tenuously separated from Wachtel after the band's

demise, Brelsford relocated to a house near the top of Lookout
Mountain that she shared with an airline stewardess and another
woman, both utterly straight. It was a measure of the times that
when Wachtel's brother Jimmy, an aspiring graphic artist, and
Twice Nicely's rhythm guitarist found themselves at loose ends,
they simply moved into Brelsford's not overly large room, which
was furnished with a double bed and a twin. The latter was so
uncomfortable that on alternating nights Wachtel or the guitarist would share the double with Brelsford. Though she was
having sex with neither, the apparent ménage scandalized her
housemates. Their horror deepened when Wachtel and the guitarist began bringing home emphatic young women picked up
in their nightly trawls at the Whisky—"go-go girls, Plaster
Casters, and all that," Brelsford recalls, "these strange people
with tutus and feathers"—and bedding down with them in her
already crowded billet. When Brelsford's mother arrived for a
visit, "I had to get everybody out in the nick of time." She was
nineteen.

Brelsford was raised in Aspen, Colorado. "I came from the
straightest possible background, with these wonderful, almost
Steinbeckian parents," she says. The '60s arrived in Aspen, as
they did in most American towns, via the radio and record store.
"I remember a guy named Mark Selzer walking into the
Matthew's drugstore back room and he had Dylan's first album.
So I invited him home with me because I had a hi-fi." Aspen
was hardly Dubuque; the Aspen Institute, founded in 1950 by a
high-minded Chicago businessman named Walter Paepcke as a
retreat for leading lights of the humanities, had given the town
gobs of international cachet. By the time Brelsford met her
Dylan-toting hobo, Aspen had been overrun with longhairs and
a new generation of literary stars like Hunter S. Thompson and
the novelist and screenwriter James Salter. So Brelsford wasn't

entirely unprepared for life on Lookout Mountain. "I'd grown up in a town where it was pretty bizarre all the time. I always thought I was from the only 'normal' family in town and I hated it. My life just wasn't exciting."

Brelsford began to understand the implications of Los Angeles when she walked into a supermarket and saw Jack Lemmon buying lightbulbs. "Everywhere you looked it felt like someone famous was there," she recalls. "And it seemed attainable." Indeed, less than a week after hitting town, she and Wachtel found themselves sitting three tables away from David Crosby at the Olde Worlde restaurant on Sunset Boulevard. Wachtel screwed up his courage, introduced himself, and invited Crosby to come see the band. In those days in Los Angeles it was still possible for an unknown to commingle with and be taken seriously by someone like Crosby—who had already burned through one seminal band and was about to form another in Crosby, Stills & Nash—because the scene was still evolving around fresh recruits like Wachtel. L.A. in the late 1960s represented one of those periodic cracks in the pop-cultural fortress when frustrated geniuses from the hinterland are not only tolerated but welcomed.

"You had Paris in the '20s, Hollywood in the '60s," says Fowley. "And you really wanted to be there because those places had hope. If you could get the bus ticket to get to paradise, even if you were a waiter, at least you were there." And L.A., Fowley stresses, "was wide-open. Anybody who had charisma or a line of bullshit could walk into any record label and get a deal— maybe just one record, but that's how it worked."

Wachtel had the chops and, more important, an advocate in Crosby, who had great ears for talent—he'd "discovered" Joni Mitchell playing in gaslight clubs in Coconut Grove, Florida, following his dismissal from the Byrds. Now he was back in L.A.

bucking up another unknown. "Crosby really mentored Waddy's band, like telling them about not selling their publishing, which he had learned the hard way," says Brelsford. "We became friends with him. I drove to Aspen and got this great dope and sold it to him and Stills. There was a sense that you could touch fame." Wachtel and Brelsford became friends with Brian and Marilyn Wilson and were invited to the Beach Boy's house on Laurel Way in Beverly Hills. Wilson had by then reached near-mythical status in the music industry but was also close to a breakdown abetted by his drug intake. "I remember sitting next to him on the couch and all of a sudden he's rubbing my leg and asking if he could shave my leg," says Brelsford. "And I was on acid. I was like, Oh, my God, I have to get out of here. Somehow the image of Brian Wilson shaving my leg . . ."

A more typical consequence of the rampant consumption of psychedelics in the canyon—"We were dropping acid at least once a week," Brelsford marvels—was a gentrified laissez-faire known as "going with the flow," from the koan by Zen master Hsu Yun: "Going with the flow, everywhere and always." Henry Diltz explains: "I'd been to [Richard] Alpert [and Timothy] Leary's lecture at the Cooper Union in New York before I ever took acid, so I knew about imprinting and the first bardo and all that stuff. We used it very much as a tool to explore the outer realms—or inner realms—that you couldn't get to otherwise. At the same time, I was reading the autobiography of Paramahansa Yogananda, which gives you a whole new outlook, not hocus-pocus spiritualism but the wonder of everyday life and how beautiful it all is. Each day would kind of take off on its own. Everything would lead to something else. You'd go down to the Canyon Store and bump into somebody, and they'd say, 'I'm up on Kirkwood, we're writing a song, why don't you come over and smoke a joint,' and someone else would

come by and say, 'Hey, we're going down to this club later' . . .
It was like anything could happen, and you just kind of followed
your nose."

One night in 1966, Diltz dropped acid with friends at his
place on Lookout Mountain. (He had impulsively bought the
house after receiving an unexpected $2,000 check from Warner
Bros. Records; Yogananda would have been pleased.) Says Diltz:
"I was still working on this Alpert-Leary thing: you take [acid]
and it's going to interrupt your imprinting and so you want to
go with the flow and I couldn't do that carrying on with a
roomful of friends so I went up the hillside and just sort of sat
there under the trees. There was this bzzzzz bzzzzz of mosqui-
toes, and I remember thinking: Okay, little brothers, I grant you
being, you have every right to be here, but you may *not* bite me,
just you go your way, I'll go mine." All at once Diltz heard "this
amazing music" wafting through the air. "It just grabbed my
ears and pulled me up and I followed this physical wave down
the hill and across the road and up to another house." Diltz
looked inside and beheld a ring of candles on the floor. "This
beautiful black girl Cynthia was sitting there—I knew her, she
was a go-go dancer at the Whisky." He knocked on the window
and she invited him in. "And I remember—I was totally peak-
ing on this psychedelic—she showed me this album cover, and
it was *Rubber Soul*, and then hearing the music—'turn off your
mind, relax and float downstream'—and I'm like, Oh, my *God*!"

Still, behind the canyon's woozy serendipity lay the reality
that money and fame would be made available to only a handful of aspirants, no matter how much or how little they cared
about "making it" or how often they bonded on someone's redwood deck over guitars and Maui Wowee. "There was an underlying competitiveness that was going on that nobody talked
about because it was peace and love and everyone was brothers

and sisters," Brelsford says. "But the 'big break' was always coming. And you were always seeking the bigger one. It was like:
'Well, *they've* got this record deal and *our* music is better, so why
aren't *we* . . .'"

The big break never came for Wachtel's band. The first time
he heard them play, Crosby pulled the young guitarist aside and
told him, "The band sounds really good, but you are the only
one in it. You know that, right? You're the only musician in
here." Diltz's Modern Folk Quartet, with its embarrassment of
musicianship, never managed to make the transition that blasted
the Byrds to fame. Diltz insists it didn't matter, that he was more
interested in "the thrill of making really cool music and trying
to blow somebody's mind. I wasn't thinking: I gotta make it; I
gotta get a bigger house and a bigger car. Not at all."

The odds, in any event, seemed to favor serendipity. "I remember David Crosby in the dressing room at the Troubadour,
before the Byrds, saying to me, 'Man, you're so lucky, you've got
a group, you get to sing harmony, I wish I had that kind of a
thing,'" says Diltz. "And it seemed like just months later I was
sitting at a table there and he said, 'This is Gene Clark, he just
got to town, we're thinking of forming a group'—McGuinn
and Crosby and Clark—and that was the seed of the Byrds." On
the other hand, when Ray Manzarek heard Jim Morrison recite
to him the opening lines of "Moonlight Drive" on the beach at
Venice, the future Doors keyboardist blurted: "That's incredible!
Let's get a rock-and-roll band together and make a million dollars!" Manzarek had been cameraman on one of Judy Raphael's
student films at UCLA. "I ran into Ray one time at Barney's
Beanery"—a hippie-boozer hangout off Santa Monica Boulevard not far from the Troubadour—"and he told me that one
day I'd be coming and licking his shoes because he was going to
be so rich. He said, 'You'll be kneeling down, Judy.'"

"I don't know if they wanted to make the big time in terms of making a lot of money," says Ron Stone, then an apprentice at Lookout Management, which guided the careers of Joni Mitchell, Crosby, Stills & Nash, Neil Young, and, later, Jackson Browne, America, and the Eagles. "It had more to do with power and connections to the political situation, Crosby in particular. The whole thing was about the change that was going on in America. The bigger we were and the more influence we had, the more we could change radio, the more we could change the politics. It was later on the money became a big issue."

In the canyon's supposedly casteless society being stitched together by young baby boomers outside the cultural mainstream, talent for the moment replaced money and station as the key to accessing an inner sanctum that supposedly did not exist. But it did. "There was a certain elitism that went on," Brelsford says. "There were cliques, and I don't think anybody would have said that that was the case then, but you definitely sussed out what was the best thing happening, who was going to be the best group of people congregating where. No one was going to let anyone too far in until they were sure you were okay. Even [Turtles singer] Mark Volman, who was my neighbor, we'd chat and we were friendly, but he was cautious." Wachtel was okay. All it took was talent, knowing someone who was talented, being a beautiful young woman, or, if all else failed, Brelsford says, "dealing really good dope."

Volman moved to Laurel Canyon in 1965 from the Los Angeles beach town of Westchester, where he'd been a founding member of the Crossfires, a surf band firmly in the Vitalis-and-"Miserlou" camp. The Beatles inspired the Crossfires to grow their hair and start singing; Volman and bandmate Howard Kaylan, former tenors in Westchester High's a cappella choir, were amply qualified. A name change ("Turtles," in smirking emulation of "Byrds") and record contract were followed almost immediately by "It Ain't Me Babe," a Top 10 smash in 1965 culled, like "Mr. Tambourine Man," from the apparently bottomless Bob Dylan songwriting catalog. "When 'It Ain't Me Babe' hit, it just changed everything about our lives," says Volman, "and so moving up into [Laurel Canyon] was the natural step."

Volman's house, on Lookout Mountain, purchased for $40,000 in 1967, included a half acre of property and the de rigueur legion of musician neighbors. "Jim Pons of the Leaves was right next door to me. Down the street was Joni Mitchell, Frank Zappa. As you went up Lookout, you had Paul Williams, Joe Schermie of Three Dog Night, John Mayall. Robby Krieger and his wife were very good friends; Danny Hutton of Three Dog Night was probably our closest family friend—he was best man at my first wedding. Henry [Diltz] lived right across the street. I remember several nights that Joni Mitchell held a kind of court at her house with many of the young writers that were coming through—Jackson Browne, J. D. Souther—a plethora of songwriters passing the guitar around and singing the things they were working on."

The Turtles had already been through the pop-star wringer by the time Volman and Brelsford became neighbors on Lookout Mountain. Their enormous hit "Happy Together" was one of the great pop-rock songs, but it undermined the band's tenuous folk rock–psychedelic cred. Disgusted by their record label's demand for more cheery pop hits, Kaylan wrote the treacly "Elenore" ("El-e-nore, *gee*, I think you're *swell!*"), a bald-faced parody of "Happy Together" performed so flawlessly that the song's subversiveness was completely lost on the band's handlers as well as nearly everyone else—it was almost as big a hit as "Happy Together." (This sort of thing—plus their sheer talent as singers and musicians—endeared Volman and Kaylan to the occupant of the log cabin down the road from Volman's house;

after the Turtles' demise they were invited to join one of the innumerable versions of Zappa's Mothers.)

"Happy Together" notwithstanding, the L.A. rock scene was exploding so quickly that fame had not yet been bifurcated into cool and uncool—although those days were coming, and soon. For the moment, there was no stigma attached to hanging out with Mickey Dolenz, of the Monkees, at his Lookout Mountain house. "The Doors were very good friends," Volman says. "We didn't have that: 'Oh, we shouldn't be hanging out, because you're in the Turtles and we're in the Doors.' Everybody was maneuvering toward the same goal and the commonality brought everybody to an equal place, and whoever was successful that week was sort of the lucky one," says Graham Nash. "It was very egalitarian. Everybody would hang out with everybody: 'Oh, you're the drummer from the Monkees? Here, have a hit of this.' There wasn't a star thing going on even with the stars." On the other hand, Volman notes, "I think that people—I don't know if 'envy' would be the word—really looked up to us. We were having all these hits. The Turtles were a hit-making pop band. We were doing what all of them were trying to do: get a record deal, sell records, tour. We were already doing that. I was twenty years old when 'Happy Together' came out. When that record exploded, it lifted us out of any 'scene'—we were sort of in our own scene." Or, as Nash puts it, "I never felt any competitiveness, because how the fuck do you compete with Crosby, Stills & Nash? What do you do to top that?"

These subterranean currents, impossible to articulate and therefore never acknowledged, barely made a ripple in the canyon. "There was a community there, but I don't know how real it was," Brelsford says. "In spite of the times being about peace and love and openness, the less emotionally available you were, the cooler you would be. Celebrity of course lends itself to that, which was a contradiction to what people were espousing: we're all equal, you're my brother, together we can change the world. There were places where that was the sense, but I don't think it was in Laurel Canyon."

As these discomfiting social agendas evolved, the canyon still offered the compelling daily pleasures of leafy surroundings, unstructured lives, and the omnipresent fog of marijuana. "Everybody would be in the living room with the stereo turned up full blast and the wine-bottle candle burning over the spool coffee table," says Brelsford. "Every now and then someone would try to get the candle to drip where it needed more wax. We'd pass around the joint. Someone would say, '*Wowwww.*' Or somebody'd say they were hungry, and we'd drive downtown where they made bagels and you could go at five in the morning and get them hot." Fowley sneers at the hindsight of "beautiful sunsets, lovely mornings with the succulent smell of jasmine, the meadows golden, the dreams never ending . . ." But even he turns wistful at how seriously the average canyon stoner took what Crosby made a fetish of calling The Music.

"In those days when certain songs would come out, people would actually have listening parties, and they'd sit around the record player and smoke dope," Fowley says. "When 'What a Day for a Daydream' came out, there was a party at somebody's house. People would dress up in their bangles and leather and buckskin and bring food and you'd sit there like it was a religious experience—like Howard Dean was coming to your living room in New Hampshire—and they'd play the damn thing for five hours. Then they'd have discussions about it."

As the canyon lurched toward the end of the 1960s, another wrinkle appeared in the social fabric: families. Volman was married in 1967 and had a child the same year. His house was conveniently situated across the street from Wonderland School—a quirk of the ever quirky canyon was to have its own grade school pitched up high in the hills of Lookout Mountain. (Stranger still was a secret fortified redoubt nearby where the Atomic Energy Commission processed movie footage of nuclear bomb tests fresh from the Nevada proving range.) "Most of the pop friends I had in '67 were people who did have family," Volman says. "The Zappa family, the John Phillips family. I was a family man, raising kids. Once I got married, I became much more of a homebody." Ron Stone's and Carole King's children— she lived nearby on Appian Way—attended the hippie-dippy Center for Early Education off Melrose Avenue. A carpool manifested itself, although Stone ended up doing most of the driving. "Carole knocked down my gate at least three times, so I volunteered to drive," he says. "I was worried about my kids getting in the car with her. She's a delightful human being but not the greatest driver in the world."

Brelsford soon acquired a family herself, though in the custom of the canyon it was hardly traditional. She and Wachtel had split—he had moved in with Twice Nicely's singer, Judy Pulver, in a house just up Lookout—though Brelsford continued to have sex with him. Their nebulous "open" relationship, the acid trips, the careening lifestyle, were beginning to wear— although she couldn't bring herself, in the argot of her peer group, to cop to it. "I got scared sometimes by what I was doing," she says. "It was intimidating and a little overwhelming. I look at it now and say, 'What I really wanted was a monogamous traditional relationship.' But I couldn't say that. I've talked to a lot of women my age who were in their early twenties in those years, and the truth is what we all wanted was the same thing: we wanted him, the right man, we wanted children, we wanted marriage. That's not how we were behaving and that's not what we were saying in front of our boyfriends, but that's what we wanted. We were far from being liberated women; we had hidden agendas. I didn't want to be doing the stuff that I was doing, but I wouldn't admit that even to myself at the time. There'd be moments—rare moments—when I'd actually have time alone, and I'd cry into my pillow."

As the prominence of the young male musicians escalated, their preference for unlimited sexual options and open relationships was codified into countercultural fiats that women were loath to challenge out of fear of seeming uncool. "I really did get snookered by that one," says Raphael. "The Pill, free love, the whole thing of 'Hey, man, you should be cool about this, it doesn't matter if I don't come back.'" Still fresh in Raphael's memory was an afternoon encounter with Stephen Stills, pre–Buffalo Springfield. "We were both sitting at the counter at Barney's, both of us too poor to sit at a table. I was having a bowl of chili and so was he, the cheapest thing on the menu, like sixty-five cents. He didn't talk to anybody; he seemed very quiet, and that impressed me. I had gotten very sick of the plastic things that were going on on the Strip, the egos and star trips." It developed that Stills was staying at a nearby hotel, and he invited Raphael to his room to hear his songs after they had taken in a matinee of the Beatles' *Help!* "He played me this fantastic stuff. I couldn't believe how good that guy was. He made the pass, right there, after the guitar."

Afterward, Stills suggested they repair to Fred C. Dobbs, where Raphael had waitressed and been repelled by Dylan and his coterie of supplicants. As they sat there, Stills apparently spotted Crosby's unmistakable Buffalo Bill visage through the restaurant's front window. "He got up. He said, 'Excuse me. I want to go see somebody. I'll be back.' He never came back." Raphael spotted Stills and Crosby, deep in conversation, walking back and forth on the Strip the rest of the night. Though her expectations of what she might hope for from such an encounter had been steadily lowered, nevertheless, she says, "I felt shitty."

Despite the atmosphere of fey liberation wafting through the canyon, women were reminded daily of their place on the sexual-power continuum. "Anybody, including myself, got offered money for all kinds of sexual favors constantly," says Gail Zappa. "Those were the days you got fired if you didn't give your boss a blow job; you kept your job by returning sexual favors that were completely unwarranted. So everybody was always suspicious of anybody who had a real job and was halfway decent-looking." Some young women on the scene—dubbed Organ Grinders—practiced a form of low-grade prostitution by simply sticking their thumbs out on the Strip, where it was well known that men trawled for female hippie hitchhikers who would sexually service them in exchange for cash.

Brelsford moved to another house on Lookout Mountain, this one recently vacated by Paul Williams, then raking in his first serious money as a songwriter and taking his leave in a diaspora that would accelerate as success bled the canyon of its first wave of stars. Brelsford babysat a young boy and girl whose mother had committed suicide. Their father was about to put them in an orphanage when she stepped forward and said she would raise them. It is a measure of the times that she was allowed to keep the children without any legal formalities; she simply moved them in with her at Williams's house and enrolled them in Wonderland School. "So I'm like twenty-one with a six- and an eight-year-old child all of a sudden," she says.

It was an act of naked, unambiguous selflessness, and it inspired an outpouring of support from the canyon that Brelsford recognizes in hindsight was colored with generational self-congratulation. "They liked that—I was the perfect hippie then," she says. "I was this skinny little waifish hippie girl with two orphaned children." Brelsford cobbled together part-time jobs while her parents—who weren't wealthy—sent money. Her first Christmas with the children, she says, "I was absolutely broke.

Cindy, the eight-year-old, wanted to play guitar, and all these people from Laurel Canyon started bringing presents, and we got together the money to get a guitar. We covered up the guitar with all these presents, and in the morning these kids get up—they had come from a nightmare situation before they came to me—and to this day they remember that Christmas."

For Brelsford, the canyon's support was casual evidence that hippie ideals could sometimes transcend the narcissism she shrewdly glimpsed behind the love beads and tie-dye—"The thing that sometimes seemed superficial," she says, "was at times very real." Brelsford allows that some of her skepticism about the canyon's idyllic mythmaking benefits from thirty-five years of perspective. "It's more in hindsight that I have some cynicism," she says. After she could no longer afford to live in the canyon and had moved herself and the children to an apartment in the flats of Hollywood, her neighbors, some no doubt stubbing out a roach before they made the necessary calls, fixed it so the children could continue attending Wonderland School. It was an affirmation that people in the canyon cared for one of their own who had sampled the hedonistic and altruistic possibilities of the counterculture and found the latter just as compelling. It's instructive to remember, as Brelsford does, that in a canyon so steeped in self-styled mystique "there were those people there, too."

The canyon had been accommodating unconventional lifestyles well before the arrival of its free-loving, pot-smoking outlanders, who had the annoying habit of acting as if they'd invented bohemia. Tiger Michiels was raised on the lee side of Laurel Canyon and recalls a boyhood filled with the sorts of adventures Spin and Marty might have invented if they'd lived in L.A. In the '60s there were still huge swaths of the canyon uncolonized by housing developments, which Michiels and his pals claimed as their fiefdom. "We had this Shangri-la of streams, waterfalls, and caves all to ourselves," he says. "We built eight-story tree houses with adjoining rope bridges—you could swing from one tree house to another. You could walk around naked if you wanted to, which I did." When a toddler, Michiels wandered away from the family home on Jaimia Way. "These people found me down by where they were building the Hollywood Freeway"—a not inconsiderable distance—"and put me in the backseat of a Cadillac convertible and drove me around the hills on dirt roads trying to find where I lived. They finally drove by my house and I pointed at it."

Later, the lads would block off Mulholland Drive at Laurel Canyon and Coldwater Canyon and stage drag races along the serpentine road notable for its spectacular views and lack of guardrails. Or they would repair to the Van Nuys Airport—several had already earned pilot's licenses—check out a helicopter or two, and buzz their parents' houses. "You'd lean out the window and there'd be your mother at the neighbor's pool swimming, and she'd shake her finger up at you and scream, 'You're supposed to be home studying!'" When they weren't barnstorming the canyon and reenacting the climax to *Rebel Without a Cause*, there was always the Zappa cabin, the grounds of which were dependable for taking in "music playing, people dancing, people lying in circles with their heads together doing some kind of chant. You could wander in just about any time."

While Michiels was good-naturedly terrorizing Laurel Canyon from the air and ground, Stephanie Spring was growing up on the Valley side just below Mulholland, when the area, like Michaelis's personal Ponderosa, was still wild enough for her family to own horses, which she rode, dressed as an Indian, through scrub and manzanita soon to fall to developers. (She and her friends pulled up the surveyors' stakes for a canyon sub-

division known locally as the Doñas for its maddening gimmick
of beginning all street names with the prefix "Doña.") Whereas
Michaelis's family operated a successful liquor store, Spring's father ran a beauty salon in Beverly Hills frequented by Natalie
Wood; her mother managed a local band, the MC-Squared,
which opened for Janis Joplin. It fell to twelve-year-old
Stephanie to lie behind the drum kit and hand Joplin her bottle
of Southern Comfort during the performance. "I never thought
that this wasn't normal behavior," she says.

Spring's mother produced a short-lived talk show on local
public television with the provocative title *Head Shop*—the host
was Elliot Mintz, later to become John Lennon and Yoko Ono's
publicist—whose guests like Baba Ram Dass and Kris Kristofferson were apt to stop by the Spring residence after the show.
"Our house was like a salon," she says. "Joplin was hanging
out—anybody who was anybody. My mother was one of the
first people to take acid with Leary, when they were doing re-
search." By the time she was thirteen, Spring was loitering
around the Whisky in the afternoons watching bands like Love
do their sound checks. Sunday afternoons she and her friends
would take acid—"it was real acid then, Sandoz, dropped on
sugar cubes"—and make their way to the love-ins in Griffith
Park to work the food banks.

In the back room of a market at Santa Monica Boulevard
and Vine, Spring purchased a fake I.D. for fifty dollars and was
soon frequenting all the big clubs on the Strip. "I was out late at
night playing music, hitting Hollywood Boulevard, and coming
home to go to school." Dressed in her standard uniform of bell-
bottoms, peasant shirt, floppy hat, and moccasins, she crashed
the self-consciously naughty Fig Parties held weekly at a house
in Beverly Hills–adjacent Trousdale Estates—"a sort of a low-
level Playboy Mansion–type thing," she recalls. When she was

eighteen, she danced in a cage at Gazzari's, emulating the go-go dancers at the Whisky; offstage she blackened her teeth and dressed in a coat from the Salvation Army "so I could wander the streets and nobody bothered me. Underneath I had on go-go boots and hot pants." Spring moved in and out of Laurel Canyon over the years after she left home and found the extended family she'd been seeking since she was thirteen. She eventually worked all over the music industry, including Elektra Records, home of the Doors and some of the most progressive acts on the L.A scene. "In 1970 you could still hang out at the Canyon Store, sit on the wall, smoke cigarettes, and talk: 'Hi, I'm going to be jamming tonight.' You'd show up and know who they were or not know who they were. There was always a guitar. Always an all-night jam."

Marlowe Brien West arrived in Los Angeles in the summer of 1968, having driven across the country from New York as a roadie for the Rich Kids, a Long Island band that performed in matching getups meant to evoke Richie Rich—"little velvet short pants with suspenders and velvet jackets with those ruffly shirts and collars," West says—this being the last gasp of rock's mercifully brief punning-costume phase, when Paul Revere and the Raiders appeared onstage in tricorner hats and breeches. (Angus Young of AC/DC would revive the schoolboy look in the 1970s.) West and the Rich Kids traveled to Los Angeles in a secondhand limousine and a van emblazoned with the band's name. Their gig at the Whisky must have been daunting—opening for the Byrds and Cream, Eric Clapton's towering blues-rock powerhouse. Midway through Cream's set Ginger Baker, the band's peripatetic drummer, so bludgeoned his drum kit that it was sliding offstage, and West was deputized to hold the legs of the bass drum while Baker blasted away. "He sweated all over me, but it was fantastic," he insists. When West stepped outside to dry off, a young woman appeared out of the Strip's nightly street carnival. "She just took my breath away," West recalls. "She was the most beautiful girl you had ever seen in your life, flowers in her hair, gorgeous and sweet." It was Miss Pamela.

Earlier that afternoon, as West and the band drove the Sunset Strip in their pathetic limo, a Volkswagen Beetle harboring identical blondes pulled a U-turn and followed them back to their lodgings at the Royal Hawaiian Motel. "They were dressed in black leotards with extra-big black shirts," says West. "Just beautiful Swedish girls with long blond hair, giant blue eyes. Everything like 'I wish they all could be California girls' and all that." West had an epiphany. "I was like, 'I ain't giving this up.'" He returned to New York, where he was scheduled to attend Parsons School of Design on scholarship in the fall. Instead, two weeks before the start of the semester, a friend invited West to accompany him back to Hollywood. "I said, 'I'm going.' My mother said, 'No, you're not,' and I said, 'Yes, I am,'" West says. "So I went and never came back."

Soon after West arrived, his friend's money ran out and he went to live with an aunt in the Valley. Broke and homeless, West wandered into Laurel Canyon one night and stole onto the derelict Houdini estate across from the Zappa cabin. There, amid the elaborate grottoes, he spotted one of the property's man-made caves. "I had no idea what it was but at least it was a place for me to sleep," he says. As he lay inside, he could see "little bonfires up in the hills. It was like the stars melded with the fireflies, and you could hear this music, and I was like, this is definitely beautiful. I was digging it like crazy. I hadn't made up my mind I wasn't going back home, but it was soon made up." West awoke the next morning to a bat hanging from the ceiling of the cave.

As he squeezed himself through the crack in the stone wall that surrounded the estate, someone called to him from across Laurel Canyon Boulevard. It was Miss Lucy of the GTOs, whom West had met at the Whisky with the Rich Kids the summer before. "They had a case of champagne left over from some party, and they were partying already and it was only eight o'clock in the morning." West made his way to the cabin and the champagne. He was eighteen. "Slowly it came into focus what I'd stepped into. It was pretty awesome." Among the revelers on the cabin grounds that morning were the so-called Gypsy boys, Bernardo Saldana and Carlos Lozano, two style-conscious Hispanics and male equivalents to the GTOs, known as the BTOs. "Bernardo and Carlos were legendary in Laurel Canyon," says West. "They were as outrageous as you could ever imagine guys to be: long black hair, colors that would blind you, just the epitome of the flower-child hippie thing. They didn't come off as hippies, though. They were more like glam rock before glam rock. I ended up borrowing their clothes. I became one of them."

Thus began West's transformation from reluctant Parsons student to itinerant Los Angeles BTO. He soon acquired the nom de canyon "Obie." "Miss Lucy and the GTOs just took me right under their wing," he says. Walking out of Ben Frank's on the Strip, BTO Bernardo introduced him to a gaggle of transplanted San Francisco freaks before roaring off with a motorcycle gang. "They had a house down by the Paramount Studios, so I went with them and they were having a party and it turned out to be an orgy and I didn't even know what an orgy was. I was talking to this girl, very beautiful, in the kitchen. She was dressed in a full-length woman's satin slip, very Harlow-style, and this guy came in and got a big can of Crisco out of the cupboard and said he was greasing up the back bedroom floor. Then she told me what an orgy was and he's in the back calling,

'HEY! GET BACK HERE!' So she went back there and I started heading out the door."

As West picked his way through the crashed-out bodies in the front room of the house, a young woman roused herself and refused to let him leave. "She says, 'If you go out there, the cops are gonna get you, there's curfew. Come here, crawl in with me.' West's benefactor was yet another GTO, Miss Mercy, as he discovered the next morning. "The sheets and everything I was lying on were Mercy's clothes that she was *wearing*. She used to wear about ten dresses at the same time, so when she got up, the whole bed went with her." West observed Mercy as she prepared to meet her public. "She had all these bracelets up both her arms and a big knitwork of coins that she was wrapping around her waist, like a gypsy. She was waking up all the hippies—they were cursing her out—'cause it was all 'jingle-jangle.'"

So began a period when West lived from crash pad to crash pad. "It sounds terrible," he says, "but it was really fun." For a time he lived with two girls in the Kirkwood Bowl. "They had LSD in the sugar bowl, people fighting over the couch, that kind of atmosphere." One afternoon West swallowed one too many Seconals and found himself in the middle of the street smashing a case of empty soda bottles. "Mickey Dolenz made a personal appearance and made me sweep it up. He said, 'How am I supposed to get by on my motorcycle?'"

As his friendships with the GTOs deepened, West noticed that their worldview differed considerably from that of the crash-pad wastrels. "Miss Lucy was not really a hippie; she was really like a little movie star wannabe. All the Zappa people were more ambitious," a likely influence of Zappa's ferocious work ethic and intolerance for inebriation. Also like Zappa, they considered themselves freelance provocateurs and iconoclasts. "Lucy used to always take her shirt off—she thought if boys could do it, she could. One time we're walking up Kirkwood with this other girl and they both had their shirts off and this motorcycle guy was coming down the hill and he was like, whoa!, and he came back up the hill. They made believe they were lesbians to try to turn him off, but that got him even more hot." Then, in a moment even Zappa couldn't have better choreographed, a Rolls-Royce pulled to a stop and ejected a motion-picture crew. "They were doing a documentary on Laurel Canyon and filmed the whole thing," says West.

As was inevitable in the canyon, West brushed up against the musicians banking fame and occasionally fortune. One afternoon, thrashed on LSD, he set out barefoot in the Kirkwood Bowl, picking wildflowers. From a hilltop, Arthur Lee of Love watched his relentless progress with amusement and a little awe. West reached the summit and encountered Lee. "He was on LSD, too. He says, 'I've been watching you.' When I ran into him, it was funny because I had to acknowledge how spaced-out I was. I had my arms filled with this gigantic bouquet." West retreated down the hillside and had started up Laurel Canyon Boulevard when Mama Cass pulled over and picked him up. "She had a red nose and talked stuffy—she said she was coming from the doctor's. I gave her my bouquet." On another occasion he glimpsed Eric Burdon being dropped off in front of the Canyon Store. "He crosses the street and hitches down the road, and he's not getting a ride for nothing," West recalls. "I was like, Look at this! Because he was living the same kind of life as I was and he was famous."

Thanks to the GTOs, West had been accepted into the extended Zappa family. Frank and Gail, now parents to a second child, Dweezil, had by then moved to a more secluded location in the canyon. West recalls, though Gail does not, driving Moon Unit and Dweezil to their swimming lessons in Beverly Hills.

The factotums at the pool were deferential, calling him "Mr. Zappa." "I remember helping fix up Moon's dollhouse," says West. She was the coolest kid. She started putting Frank Zappa mustaches on everything. He had a famous painting he was using for one of his album covers—it was very large, with a blond girl—and Moon put a Frank Zappa mustache on her. They all flipped out.

Beyond the Zappas' munificence and tolerance for freaks, so long as they pulled their oar, the canyon itself offered to some the extended family of hippiedom, though the window was closing fast. It was the custom in those fading days of the '60s for the canyon's freaks to gather across from the Canyon Store on a triangular concrete traffic island formed by the intersection of Kirkwood Drive and Laurel Canyon Boulevard. This was a strange choice, if for no other reason than that the traffic noise must have been deafening and that in an area overrun with glades, swales, culverts, stands of eucalyptus, and ridgelines with Olympian views to the ocean, metropolis, and mountains, why gather on a slab of cruel, unshaded concrete, poisoned by auto emissions and the constant threat of being mowed down by a Microbus? The answer was that it was a way to see and be seen in a place where hiding out was turning into an art. The Kirkwood–Laurel Canyon intersection was the L.A. equivalent of Haight and Ashbury streets, a stronghold from which to proclaim to the straight world roaring by on their way to and from the Valley: Behold the hippie. It was also confirmation for the brethren that the tribes still gathered, a stage and staging area for subsequent adventures. "That was the meeting place," says West. "If I went down there, I was bound to end up running off on some kind of rendezvous. Or we'd just hang, have some apple wine."

And it was there, on West's twentieth birthday, that the canyon's family, soon to scatter, offered him its benediction. "I went down there and little by little all these girls came. Teenagers. Little ones. Grown ones. And they all had presents for me. They were all purple because purple was my favorite color. My feet were purple from walking in the berries with no shoes, and sometimes I'd squeeze the juice in my hair. One of the girls made me a cake. It was made in little-girl cake pans, little four-by-six-inch rectangles with purple icing that oozed. They were trying to make a castle for me out of these little squares of cake. It was just totally, totally beautiful." That afternoon, on a pinched piece of concrete, the canyon brought forth for West a moment that would make the ugliness that waited just around the corner seem unthinkable. "In my mind I see it like that," he says. "The way the trees would hang down with their big, long leaves, and it would be hazy-smoggy with the golden light coming through the branches that hovered over the whole thing. It was just as magic as it could be.

"I swear I saw fairies flying around Laurel Canyon," West says. "Because everybody had wings."

FIVE

BUSINESSMEN, THEY DRINK MY WINE

★

The canyon's hippie managers take charge, Neil Young grosses out the money men, David Geffen opens his Asylum, two cats in the yard and an elephant onstage

One of the great miscalculations of the music industry was to treat rock and roll as if it were a demented teenage fad. Shunned by established record labels in thrall to Rosemary Clooney and Perry Como, rock and roll was borne up instead by entrepreneurs like Sam Phillips, founder of Sun Records in Memphis, home of Elvis Presley, and by Leonard and Phil Chess's Chicago-based Chess Records, which boasted the unbelievable stable of Chuck Berry, Howlin' Wolf, Bo Diddley, Muddy Waters, Sonny Boy Williamson, and Willie Dixon, the label's house composer. (The Dixon songwriting catalog would provide hits well into the '70s for blues-rock warhorses from Led Zeppelin to Foghat.) Of course, once the independents established rock as a viable business model, the majors swooped in—RCA bought Presley's contract from Phillips in 1955 for $40,000—and just as quickly cashed out. By decade's end Elvis was in the Army, Chuck Berry was about to be jailed on a Mann Act conviction, and rock and roll was supposedly finished as a commercial and cultural proposition.

The record business turned to flogging teen sensations like Shelley Fabares and Lesley Gore—just as it would turn, in the '90s, to Britney Spears and Christina Aguilera—who sang material ground out production-line-style in New York's Brill Building. "In the early '60s rock and roll had gone to sleep," says Chris Hillman. "We had Bobby Vinton. We had Fabian. We had a lot of stuff that really wasn't doing much." Elvis, finally mustered out of the Army in 1960, continued having hits, but his wholesome-greaser image was becoming embarrassingly retrograde, a situation hardly helped by his rapacious manager, Colonel Tom Parker, who consigned him to a string of increasingly indefensible movies—by 1964 he had starred in no fewer than seventeen. Elvis was rendered superfluous the moment the Beatles struck the opening chords of "All My Loving" on *The Ed Sullivan Show* on February 9, 1964, from the same stage where he had been televised—famously, from the waist up—just eight years before.

While the lull between the end of the '50s and the arrival of the Beatles seemed to herald the death of rock and roll, the hunger among baby boomers for popular culture that was not relentlessly vacuous hadn't gone away. The mania for folk music, a vernacular that reminded the boomers' parents of nothing so much as the Great Depression, was proof that there was a huge, predominately white audience under twenty-five that longed for something different, rootsy, exciting, and most of all young. As it happened, Los Angeles was at that moment harboring entrepreneurs who never got over the rush of first hearing "Twenty Flight Rock" and who had more in common with Sam Phillips than the self-styled executives who then ruled the record industry from New York. Young and hungry, with prodigious reserves of energy and shamelessness, some were refugees from talent agencies and record labels for whom booking Eydie

Gorme had become unbearable. They looked to the street for trends and grasped intuitively what their elders at the William Morris Agency and at Capitol Records (which rejected the Beatles' first singles) could not: that the great wheel of popular culture was turning. Although they couldn't have guessed at the scope, they knew something was coming for the simple reason that they also happened to be the audience. In these revelations they recognized a once-in-a-lifetime chance: for power, influence, and, though it was and remains bad form to admit it, money.

The men who guided rock and roll in the 1950s had been mostly middle-aged hucksters like Parker, a former carny sharp, with little affinity for the music or musicians making them rich. The young hustlers of L.A. instinctively understood what rock was and, more important, what it could be: the glue binding together the unprecedented number of Americans then simultaneously entering young adulthood. By the mid-1960s these young men, none of them over thirty, would remake the music industry in their image and rewrite many of its rules and customs. (An exception was the New York–based Albert Grossman, Bob Dylan's manager, a fortyish eccentric who represented the cream of the folk movement as well as proto–rock stars like Janis Joplin.)

As managers, they eschewed a patronizing attitude toward the "talent," bonding instead in generational solidarity with the musicians they represented against the clueless suits running the labels. Some would start labels of their own and earn fortunes unprecedented in the entertainment industry—as well as the enmity of the artists who had put them there. The empire building of L.A.'s young record men would be accomplished virtually overnight, but the changes they wrought are evident forty years later. And like the musicians who brought them to prominence, L.A.'s young record men would spend a lot of time in Laurel Canyon. Among them were Elliot Roberts, David Geffen, John Hartmann, and Kim Fowley.

It can be argued that Fowley isn't remotely in the league of Roberts, Geffen, and Hartmann, who together and separately controlled the careers of Joni Mitchell, Crosby, Stills & Nash, Neil Young, Jackson Browne, America, Poco, and the Eagles. Fowley never landed a cash-cow artist, never headed a label of commercial consequence, and presided over a career that, while prescient, always seemed just shy of critical mass. Geffen parlayed agenting for Laura Nyro into his own record label, Asylum, before ascending to true Hollywood moguldom in the 1990s by co-founding the DreamWorks movie studio with Steven Spielberg and Jeffrey Katzenberg; Fowley's chief claim to fame was producing and managing the Runaways, an all-girl '70s band notable mostly for launching the careers of Joan Jett and Lita Ford. Nevertheless, Fowley was among a handful of key figures present at the dawn of L.A.'s rock-and-roll renaissance, and he possessed a street hustler's appreciation of heat and hype, and an acute sense of how the rawest talent, if genuine, could be marshaled. "He's an amazing, amazing Hollywood character," says Michael Des Barres.

Unlike Geffen and Roberts, who came to L.A. from Brooklyn and the Bronx, respectively, after apprenticeships in the William Morris mail room, Fowley was uniquely the product of postwar Southern California. In a chaotic upbringing that ranged from Malibu to Hollywood—his mother, Shelby Payne, a Goldwyn Girl and Warner Brothers contract player, abandoned him to a foster home "so she could marry William Friml, son of one of the co-founders of ASCAP," he says—Fowley had survived two bouts of nonparalytic polio by the time he was a teenager and emerged in the late 1950s a gaunt postadolescent standing six feet four inches. His Dickensian upbringing imbued him with a survivor's bravado that made him naturally resentful of interlopers from New York sniffing around the reemergent rock-and-roll scene. "All the guys who lived in California—Kim Fowley, Brian Wilson from Hawthorne—we were natives," Fowley says. "We didn't have to learn this shit; we *lived* it. This was our town, our hometown. We were cool. Those guys weren't as cool."

Fowley was introduced to Laurel Canyon in 1946, when his father, Douglas—a weedy ladies' man recently discharged from the Navy—plucked him from the foster home and installed him in a house in Malibu that he shared with "a bunch of actors and guys from the Navy," Fowley says. "He was a B-movie actor in the '30s and early '40s, playing in a variety of Charlie Chan and Hopalong Cassidy films. [The young Fowley appeared with him in the 1950 RKO picture *Rio Grande Patrol*.] His concept was that by living at the beach no one would think he was broke. The guys would pool their money and throw big parties. They used to do Shakespeare on Warren Baxter's tennis court on Sundays.

"It was the custom in those days to dress your child in a miniature version of whatever the military uniform was that you wore. So I was a six-and-a-half-year-old guy in a Navy outfit, and my dad and all his buddies decided to go to Hollywood and score opium at Robert Benchley's place at the Garden of Allah at the foot of Laurel Canyon. We went from Malibu to Beverly Hills, where he showed me where Bugsy Siegel had been shot—that's a nice fatherly thing to show a child—and then we went to a photographer named William, who took a picture of me in the sailor suit. His studio was next door to the Canyon Store, right there above the dry cleaner's. Afterward everybody cheered, and then we rolled down to Schwab's, where

Doug Fowley put me on the bar and said, 'Gather 'round! Son, welcome to Hollywood! This is a Jewish manager. This is a Mafia enforcer. This is a fag. This is a whore. This is a phony. This is an out-of-work actor. This is your world now, son! Welcome!' And everybody cheered and two chorus girls grabbed my six-year-old cock and balls and stuck a candy cigarette in my mouth. And I stood there being massaged by these two goddesses, and everybody was cheering, and I said: 'Okay! This is better than the foster home!'

"And then Douglas Fowley announced it was time to go get high. 'Let's go down to Benchley's and get some opium. You're the lookout.' He had a little boat he bought me in the drugstore. He said, 'You can sail this boat around the fountain in front—we're going to be smoking pipes and lying down on bamboo mats. If the cops come, you jump in the water and start yelling and screaming like a bored six-year-old having a tantrum and we'll flush the stuff down the toilet.' That was the day I decided Hollywood wasn't what it was cracked up to be. Suddenly I was a lookout for these imperfect humans who had to get high. I had heard you could leave home at eighteen—I was six and a half—and that was the day I plotted my escape. Then they came out with big guilty smiles on their faces and we rode off back to Malibu."

Fowley next came into contact with Laurel Canyon's environs in 1949, at Preston Sturges's Players club on the Sunset Strip, "where divorced guys between marriages would go to get laid," he says. For this engagement, Fowley's irrepressible father drafted his seven-year-old son into service as bait for feral women. "I would go up to a girl and I'd say, 'Could I talk to you, pretty lady?' 'Oh, what a cute little boy.' 'Do you have a little boy, too? Are you married?' I'd find out right away. 'Do you like womens? You like drugs? What do you like?' If she answered with something the father would find seductive, I'd tug

my ear and that would mean, Get over here. He'd say, 'Is he both-
ering you?' 'No, is this your kid? What a delightful little boy. Oh?
You're his dad?' And then I'd take off and he'd move right in. It
was like having a dog or a red Cadillac—you put the right dog
on the beach, you can meet any woman. He failed with Joan
Caulfield, though. I tried to break the ice, but he didn't get anywhere with her."

Before Fowley's second bout with polio—in Ontario and
Saskatchewan, Neil Young and Joan Anderson, later to become
Joni Mitchell, were likewise stricken—he had taken to riding
into Hollywood with Ryan O'Neal on weekends and "fighting
anybody we didn't like the looks of. Anybody who wasn't cool
got it," Fowley says. "You always had the right record on the car
radio so you could fight to 'Great Balls of Fire' or 'Whispering
Bells' by the Del Vikings. Man, nobody could hurt you when
those records came on."

Fowley's father had by then abandoned him. "My dad
looked like Errol Flynn and he didn't need an Ichabod Crane/
Scarecrow of Oz walking down the boulevard with him. So
there was no more cute kid to show off to Joan Caulfield. Suddenly I was out there on the tightwire. I became a petty thief
and a burglar—a crippled burglar—and male prostitute for old
desperate women who saw me as Lord Byron with a limp,
which I worked at, and eased into my senior year in high school,
or hobbled in, as it were. From there it was into the Army National Guard. When I got out, I made peace with my dad, but
then broke his confidence when he went off to direct June
Wilkinson in *Macumba Love* in Brazil. I stole his car, clothes, and
TV set, which I used for bartering, masquerade, and transporta-
tion purposes."

There were men with life stories as outrageous as Fowley's
at that moment taking up stations in New York, San Francisco,
and London who would shape rock in the 1960s. As a group,

they were fearless, cunning, profane, and fiercely protective of the musicians they represented. Bill Graham, founder of the Fillmore ballrooms in San Francisco and New York, soon to become rock's Carnegie Halls, escaped the Nazis as a child by literally walking out of Poland and later studied Method acting with Lee Strasberg in New York; Peter Grant, fearsome manager of the Yardbirds and Led Zeppelin, had been a bouncer, professional wrestler, stuntman, and actor (he appeared in *The Guns of Navarone*). Their outsize personalities and street radar made them unsuitable for conventional careers but were tremendous assets in an enterprise where fast thinking, fast talking, and sheer brazenness could carry the day. "When you're nineteen and you've already done thirteen years of opium runs with Dad and been a kind of marriage/seduction advance man, you know how to talk to people," says Fowley.

Michael Des Barres sees in Fowley's early ambitions an attempt to belatedly take control of his chaotic upbringing. "Here's this hurt, almost destroyed boy," says Des Barres, whose own childhood—his father was a French marquis, his mother a London stripper—was a delirium of boarding schools and abandonment. "What do you revert to, what is the procession, especially being the son of a B-feature actor and experiencing all of that rejection through his father, and then being abandoned by his mother? He reinvents himself as this Svengali guy. Now, what do you choose to be a Svengali about?" Alone among Fowley's career options at the time, the business of rock and roll had no prerequisites beyond sheer ambition. "I mean, he had no musical ability," Des Barres says, "but incredible chutzpah and vision. It's the Oscar Levant of the situation—the witty, brilliant sort of specific point of view like Levant had. And Kim's got that. Hollywood is based on all of that."

Fowley began managing, producing, writing songs for, and

performing with a range of nascent L.A. rock talent, most profitably with Gary Paxton and Skip Battin, who as Skip and Flip scored a Top 20 hit in 1960 with "Cherry Pie." (Battin would later join the Byrds.) With Paxton, Fowley formed the Hollywood Argyles and recorded the No. 1 smash "Alley Oop." Two years later, under the guise of the Rivingtons, they hatched the novelty hit "Papa-Oom-Mow-Mow." Fowley, meanwhile, wrote and produced B. Bumble and the Stingers' "Nut Rocker," a piano-pounding adaptation of Tchaikovsky's "March" from the *Nutcracker Suite* later covered, to the relief of anyone who ever slogged through the entire album, by Emerson, Lake & Palmer on the ponderous *Pictures at an Exhibition*. Fowley also worked early records by Paul Revere and the Raiders.

Fowley's travels in these ventures took him all over Hollywood and to rock-prehistoric Laurel Canyon, then in its moldering postwar doldrums. "As a nineteen-and-a-half-year-old hustler, I realized there was no money up there," Fowley says, "but I could get laid. You could go up there and maneuver those tiny streets and nail thirty-two-year-old women in their ticky-tack houses and dodge the gay men: *Hi, are you an actor? A musician?*" Fowley says the canyon in those days was populated with "people who wanted jazz to come back, who wanted the Co-existence Bagel Shop not to have gone to San Francisco and become City Lights. They wanted Greenwich Village on a cliffside, they wanted bohemia, they wanted literature to be the backdrop to their debauchery, but literature had gone to San Francisco from Venice with the beatniks."

All that was about to change. Fowley had produced yet another will-o'-the-wisp hit, "Popsicles and Icicles," by the Murmaids, which floated all the way to No. 3 in January 1964, the same month Capitol Records finally released the Beatles' "I Want to Hold Your Hand." Fowley was friends with Danny Hutton,

an L.A. singer who would soon found Three Dog Night and
move to the canyon. "Danny Hutton summed it all up by saying: 'The Beatles are going to replace everything, and we all have
to reinvent.' And he was right."

The change between 1964 and 1965 in Los Angeles was as-
tonishing. In a photograph of a Johnny Rivers performance at
the Whisky in 1964, the patrons look like extras from an episode
of *Dobie Gillis*: short brilliantined hair and skinny neckties for
the boys, Doris Day–style bouffants and sack dresses for the
girls. One year later, post-Beatles, the Byrds are onstage—David
Crosby has grown his hair and Yosemite Sam mustache and is
wearing fringed buckskin; the audience appears to have been
made over by some species of hip aliens. "It was like a thousand
years had gone by," Fowley says.

Across Los Angeles there was the sense that a new order had
just been decreed, and that it was finally acceptable to look and
act one's age. "The Beatles brought stupidity and working-class
magic to teenage culture for the first time since Elvis—who, by
the way, appeared only after James Dean died," Fowley says. "It
seems there's a thing in American culture: James Dean dies—
Elvis Presley; John F. Kennedy dies—the Beatles. America's youth
was mourning for those guys, and Elvis and the Beatles stood up
at the plate and delivered the home run and extended the youth
culture." It was the beginning of a seismic shift. "The '60s didn't
start until 'I Want to Hold Your Hand' was number one in
America," says Fowley. "And then suddenly: no underwear and
bras, and drugs and long hair. We all had Hugh Hefner's lifestyle,
and we were all in our twenties. Everybody showed up and celebrated hedonistically. You threw away your suit and you put on
your thrift-shop clothes, the shabbier and dumber the better.
You could live in a dirty room, and you would get the same
pussy as Steve McQueen. Everything was a level playing field."

When John Hartmann reported for work at the William Morris Agency's Beverly Hills office, his hair was so short "it looked like it was painted on," he says. He also affected a pinkie ring, a gold chain-link watch, and a black mohair suit. He was twenty-three. "I was there two days and said, 'I could do this better than any of these guys.'" Elvis Presley was signed to the agency, and Hartmann was duly shipped off to work for Colonel Parker. "I was on his staff for six months, and I saw the music business at the highest possible levels," he says. "I became infected." Back at Morris, Hartmann was reassigned to the television department and booked acts on *Shindig!*, a rock-and-roll variety show on ABC launched six months after the Beatles' *Ed Sullivan* appearances. The experience would be life changing. "*Shindig!* was the MTV of its day," Hartmann says, "and I owned *Shindig!* I signed many artists because I could guarantee *Shindig!*"

One of the acts Hartmann found through the show was a Los Angeles husband-and-wife singing duo who had recently dropped their appalling stage name Caesar and Cleo. Salvatore "Sonny" Bono had been knocking around the L.A. record business as a singer, songwriter ("Needles and Pins," co-written with Jack Nitzsche), record plugger, and flunky for the legendary producer Phil Spector. He met sixteen-year-old Cherilyn Sarkisian LaPierre in a coffee shop, and their singing act became popular at clubs on the Sunset Strip. They were to become, through their television appearances and hits like "I Got You Babe" and "The Beat Goes On," the king and queen of early L.A. hippiedom—Sonny took to appearing in Paleolithic-looking fur vests and grew his hair to incautious lengths for 1965. Hartmann had a moment of clarity watching them perform one night on *Shindig!* "I remember when I knew Sonny and Cher would be a huge success," he says. "The Rolling Stones were onstage live and the kids in the audience were going 'SONNY!' They were more interested in Sonny standing in the wings watching the Stones than they were in the Stones."

Before long, Hartmann was "the rock-and-roll agent of William Morris," he says. "The things I learned with the Colonel I was seeing now in this other musical context and I went, This is for me." But representing scruffy rock-and-roll acts was not a fast track for ambitious young men at the agency, Hartmann's colleague and future partner David Geffen hectored him from the Morris office in New York. "He said, 'Why are you signing all these musical acts—don't you know movies are where it's at?' I said, 'Yeah, I know movies are where it's at, but how are we gettin' in? All these other guys know it, too. The only way you get in is on the back of a star, and the only stars we have access to are in music because they don't care.'"

While Hartmann fattened the Morris roster with Sonny and Cher, Chad and Jeremy—a genteel British pop duo—and L.A.'s psychedelic garage band the Seeds, he experienced two epiphanies. One occurred the night he went to see a rising young band with the vexing name Buffalo Springfield. The band's lineup now seems like a dream: Stephen Stills, Neil Young, and Richie Furay, later of Poco, on guitars and vocals, for starters. They had formed in 1966 after Furay and Stills pulled up next to a 1959 Pontiac hearse with Ontario license plates driven by Young, with future Spingfield bassist Bruce Palmer aboard, on the Sunset Strip. After the Byrds, the Buffalo Springfield were the dominant folk-rock band on the Strip, although their repertoire was far more eclectic, ranging from proto-psychedelia to primitive banjo plucking. They developed a devastating live show built around Stills's impeccable songwriting, his and Young's ferocious guitar interplay (and Young's occasional epileptic seizures), and the band's three-part vocal harmonies. At the Whisky,

Hartmann watched them kick into their first song. "I knew this was a hit," he recalls. "I turned to their manager before the song was over and said, 'I'm in.'" Back at William Morris, Hartmann dispatched a memorandum: TO ALL AGENTS, COAST, NEW YORK AND CHICAGO. REGARDING BUFFALO SPRINGFIELD, PLEASE BE ADVISED THAT THEY ARE THE NEXT THING TO HAPPEN TO THE WORLD BUT DON'T WORRY, THEY'RE IN OUR HERD.

Hartmann's second epiphany occurred after an acquaintance told him: "You think you know what's happening but you don't." "I said, 'What are you talking about?'" Hartmann says. "He said, 'It's happening in San Francisco.' So one night Skip Taylor, who was an associate at William Morris, and I went to San Francisco and at Winterland saw the Jefferson Airplane, the Grateful Dead, and Paul Butterfield Blues Band." Hartmann and Taylor were stunned. "I knew two guys in L.A. with long hair. One was Sonny, [whose hair] came to here and wasn't really long hair, and the Seeds, whose hair was truly long. No one else in L.A. or in the music business had long hair. That night at Winterland *every single guy* had hair down to here. The other thing I saw that totally defied the rules was that unknown acts could fill a hall. That is not humanly possible. Then I go up there and see three acts I had barely heard of fill a five-thousand-seat venue. That shocked and amazed me."

Hartmann and Taylor, having glimpsed the future, made plans. It was common in those days for bands in L.A. and San Francisco to build an audience during an extended run at a single club—the Doors would log untold nights at the London Fog on the Strip in this fashion before hitting it big. "We realized that artists broke out of venues," Hartmann says. "Trini Lopez broke out of P.J.'s, Johnny Rivers broke out of the Whisky, the Airplane broke out of the Fillmore. So we figured all we need is a venue and we'll break the Buffalo Springfield out of it and we'll have the number-one act in the world."

Soon thereafter, Hartmann's sideburns got longer, a mustache creeped over his upper lip, and the mohair suits stayed on their hangers. Hartmann's bosses at William Morris were growing restive with their young "rock and roll" agent, particularly his and Taylor's extra-agency forays into the rock scene. Also, Hartmann's unsolicited advice. "I wanted them to start a San Francisco office," he says. "I said, 'Look, you've got to go up there. There's no professional business, it's all amateurs, and they don't know what to do. If we get a hold of it, we will make it do the right thing. If we don't, it will fall apart,' which is what happened. William Morris said, 'You sit down and stay out of San Francisco.' So we quit and went off to do it for ourselves."

Hartmann and Taylor, with Gary Essert, who'd just graduated from UCLA, opened the Kaleidoscope, their take on the San Francisco psychedelic ballroom experience. The Kaleidoscope was housed in the former Earl Carroll Theater at the corner of Sunset and Vine in Hollywood, home to the Moulin Rouge nightclub in the 1950s. It boasted a lazy Susan stage, which proved handy when presenting the multi-band bills typical of the day; as one band played, the equipment for another could be set up in advance and rotated into place. Hartmann loved the ravishing light shows projected behind the San Francisco bands while they performed and incorporated them into shows at the Kaleidoscope. "We built the first truly huge PA for rock," he says. "We had four of those ten-foot Voice of the Theater speakers, plus six of the regular ones."

But the band that was supposed to burst out of the Kaleidoscope and take over the world was collapsing under internecine rivalries, chiefly between Stills and Young, after barely two years. The band's inventive, eccentric songs weren't a good fit for Top 40 radio, still the arbiter for breaking a rock act. "Their singles came out and missed," says Hartmann, "and you had to get a hit single. They came out with 'Nowadays Clancy Can't Even Sing,' a truly brilliant song. It was the only rock song up to that point to have a time change, and that shocked radio and they didn't play it. 'Mr. Soul' bombed, and by then the band was broken up."

Ironically, Buffalo Springfield's sole hit, which would end up a '60s anthem, wasn't even on their debut album. Hartmann explains: "What happened was there was a string of nightclubs on the Sunset Strip from Crescent Heights to Doheny, maybe twenty-five clubs with live bands every night, and there was a whole movement of people that went there every night and walked up and down Sunset—hundreds and hundreds of people. Pandora's Box was a tiny little joint. It was on an island in the middle of the intersection of Sunset and Crescent Heights surrounded by a white picket fence. You could get maybe fifty people in the club, but two hundred people would be in this little yard. The cops didn't like it and they closed it down and the kids rioted and there were people going to jail."

Stills knew a budding revolution when he saw one, and promptly wrote "For What It's Worth." With its chilling guitar harmonics and peer-to-peer admonishment to hassled longhairs everywhere—"stop, children, what's that sound / everybody look what's going down"—"For What It's Worth" was a rallying cry and proof that rock could create music as vital as it was hummable. "In those days you could get a record on the radio in a minute if you wanted to," says Hartmann. "And so they went on KHJ with it and it was a hit." Atlantic Records belatedly added "For What It's Worth" to the second pressing of Springfield's debut album, but the band's momentum had by then been spent. A second album failed, and the band, though continuing in name through retrospective releases, was over almost as soon as it had started. Hartmann was devastated. "The failure of the Buffalo Springfield I took as a personal failure. My first failure in show business was their failure. I didn't want to be an agent anymore."

Free from William Morris and with the Kaleidoscope at their disposal, Hartmann and Taylor started a management company, their most successful act being Canned Heat, a blues-and-boogie quintet from the San Fernando Valley suburb of Northridge. (The band's house, next door to Mitchell's on Lookout Mountain, later burned to the ground, leaving ghostly charred amplifiers and speaker cabinets used by Henry Diltz and Gary Burden as an apocalyptic mise-en-scène for the cover of Steppenwolf's *At Your Birthday Party*.) The Kaleidoscope, as planned, became the Los Angeles equivalent of San Francisco's LSD-soaked ballrooms. "We were the L.A. hippies, just like the Family Dog"— San Francisco's confederation of hippie dance promoters— Hartmann says. "We had more of an artistic sense than a keen business approach. We had an elephant on opening night. We had fireworks onstage, we did crazy shit you couldn't get away with now. We didn't make a fortune doing it but we had a great time."

The night of the 1968 California Democratic primary, the Kaleidoscope presented a Pat Paulsen for President rally, featuring the comedian dressed as George Washington riding onstage on a white horse. Mama Cass Elliot appeared as Betsy Ross, sewing an enormous American flag. Hartmann estimates there were five thousand people in attendance. "You couldn't move, we had TV sets everywhere," he says. "Then it comes over our own TVs that Robert Kennedy was shot at the Ambassador Hotel, and it just blew the bubble. The whole fun of Pat Paulsen's running for president was over, because we really wanted Kennedy. Chad and Jeremy put RFK's logo on their album; that's how committed artists were to the political process in those days."

Hartmann presented twenty-two major concerts at the

Kaleidoscope but increasingly spent his time managing. While still at William Morris he had taken up residence on Willow Glen Road in the canyon. His neighbor was Gene Clark of the Byrds. "He had a purple Porsche and I had a gold T-bird," Hartmann says. "We used to pass on the road—his music would be blaring, my music would be blaring." The sight and sound of so many people under thirty living cheek by jowl and, it seemed, philosophically united was reinforcing. "There was a definite peace-and-love ethic, and it was solid as a rock," Hartmann says, "whether you tuned it in or not, and the majority were tuned in to it. Trust me, it was real, because the antiwar sentiment was so high. Everybody visibly identified himself on which side of the war he was on by his clothing and hair. The Jefferson Airplane's original promotional button just said: JEFFERSON AIRPLANE LOVES YOU. You know how exotic that statement was at the time? That a band loved you? That was unheard of. There was no vibe like that coming off the Beatles."

There was also FM radio, which would prove indispensable to disseminating the sort of music being made by Hartmann's neighbors and clients. "Suddenly there was a tool that made the business able to deal with a whole lot more acts in a whole lot bigger way," he says. "The record companies got it a little later than we did, or Buffalo Springfield would have made it." The confluence of free-form radio, the fecund creative atmosphere in the canyon and on the Strip, the emerging hippie ethos of psychedelics and generational reinforcement meant that young men like Hartmann, who knew how to work the business side of the record business but could parse the youth culture and discover and nurture new talent, were in the proverbial right place at the right time, not least because the music men who ruled the business throughout the 1950s and early '60s were suddenly at sea.

"Those guys didn't manage rock and roll; they didn't get it and didn't like it. [We] were a new breed. We had a whole different approach. We were closer to the artist than managers had ever been; we were almost like partners, almost in the band." In photographs taken during the era, it is often impossible to differentiate between the managers and their charges. When Hartmann procured dugout seats for himself and his clients Chad and Jeremy at a Beatles concert in Dodger Stadium, he was mortified to discover that he had dressed in almost exactly the same clothes as Jeremy. "The same shirt, the same pants—striped bell-bottoms with a big wide belt. And there was Jeremy in the same outfit. So, yeah, we joined."

Hartmann insists with considerable earnestness that "we worked from our heart, not our pocketbook. We were in it to make music to reach the people, not to make a fortune. Never thought of it. Happened anyway, but it was never the driving force. The goal was not to make money; the goal was to make music." Nevertheless, a lot of money was being made, and Hartmann and the new hippie managers were not at all conflicted about making sure as much of it as possible flowed into their clients' pockets and into theirs. The record companies fiercely defended their largely indefensible standard contracts—which billed the lion's share of the costs associated with recording against the musicians' royalties—but the concert business was another matter.

Rock concerts as we know them today essentially didn't exist until the mid-1960s; before that, bands would travel in package tours put together by impresarios like Dick Clark, who, along with the local promoters, would reap most of the proceeds. The Beatles' second U.S. tour in 1966, which filled baseball stadia across the country, confirmed the enormous potential of rock in a live setting. When it became apparent that American rock

bands with national followings could headline and sell out bas-
ketball arenas without the imprimatur of Dick Clark or an absurd entourage of seven or eight co-stars, the hippie managers
pounced.

"In the beginning the promoters had the power," says Hartmann. "But once the acts realized that they were bringing in the
people, we started to take control." The deals were structured
with a guarantee to the artists that varied by venue, for example,
$25,000 against 60 percent of the box office over $40,000.
"Each venue had to be negotiated specifically based on its size
and the ticket price—all of which we dictated," says Hartmann.
"The managers were very much in charge." Detailed riders were
attached to the basic concert contracts specifying everything
from the size and number of spotlights to dressing room accoutrements.

"We invented the rider," Hartmann says. "I remember the
big thing I wanted was Perrier. I drank Perrier. So I got everybody around me into it, and we ended up putting Perrier on the
riders and no one knew what it was and people were sending to
France to get it. Those kinds of things crept in as the managers
and the artists gained power." As they did, the price of the talent went up, at least as a percentage of what the promoters got
to keep. "That's when managers started going on the road, because they had such huge commissions," Hartmann says. "I
mean, if you're making twenty-five thousand dollars a night in
commission, you're sure as hell going to be there to make sure
the gig goes off."

Hartmann would eventually work for Elliot Roberts before
leaving and taking over some of Roberts's prized acts, including
Crosby, Stills & Nash. By then rock and roll was serious business,
and the hippie managers were sounding and acting more like
P. T. Barnum than Timothy Leary. "The price is always rising,"

says Hartmann. "And it's the manager's job to push it up. And you're really supposed to push beyond what's fair, even. The toughest deal we ever made was a 90-10 split. It was a Neil Young tour right after *Harvest*. Every promoter in the country was rebelling against the deal. And we knew this was the hottest Neil was ever going to be. So we put him out on sixty dates in ninety days and demanded 90-10s and everybody refused to pay. The whole promoter community which is now owned by Clear Channel—the Ron Delseners, the Don Laws—all these guys are holding out on the deal waiting for Bill Graham to beat me up over the money. And the day comes and he goes to Geffen, and Geffen says, 'It ain't my job, talk to Hartmann.' And Bill Graham and I got into an incredibly huge fight: screaming, yelling, insulting. I know that in my office every person in the building was listening to my end. I don't know what was going on in his office, because he was making as much noise as me. I said, 'Okay, Bill, I hear you, but it's 90-10, are you in or are you out?' And he said: 'Mother*fucker*! . . . I'm in.' And then all the other promoters went and that was the deal. Neil made a fortune on the tour, which he deserved because he was coming off a number one single and a number one album, and that's the only time he was going to get those kind of numbers."

The relationships between the hippie managers and their clients would become increasingly fraught as the money being made in some cases went beyond comprehension. Hartmann got a taste of what was to come in the comparatively spartan days of 1968. "The night the Buffalo Springfield broke up there was a wake at [Springfield managers] Charlie Greene and Brian Stone's house, up in the Hollywood Hills overlooking the whole city," he recalls. At the wake, Stills pulled Hartmann aside. "Stills says, 'Can I talk to you?' I said, 'Sure.' And we go outside. We sit down on this little stone bench and we're looking at all of L.A. like a jewel box. And I expect him to say to me: Good job, man. Because I was fuckin' brilliant. I was probably the most brilliant agent there ever was for a specific act. I got them on the Rolling Stones gig at the Hollywood Bowl. I got them on *Hollywood Palace*, where no rock act had ever played. I got them Chad and Jeremy's tour. Everything that had to be done, I did. And he turns to me and says: 'It's all your fault.' Now, I was flabbergasted. Flabbergasted. And he got up and walked away."

Hartmann would extract a measure of revenge, denying a reunited Buffalo Springfield a berth on a benefit concert at the Kaleidoscope until Stills apologized. "We had the Airplane, the Doors, the Dead, and about ten other acts," Hartmann says. "And I wouldn't let them play. I made him apologize to me before they could go on and he did—came to me with a flower and apologized—but he didn't know what he was apologizing for." Hartmann nursed the insult for forty years, including his stint managing CSN in the 1970s, before confronting Stills at a $1,000-a-plate dinner at the Pier in New York honoring Atlantic Records founder Ahmet Ertegun. Spotting Hartmann across the restaurant, Graham Nash invited him to sit at the CSN table.

"Stills was sitting next to me, and it was a wonderful night, and so I decided to clear the decks," says Hartmann. "I said to him, 'Stephen, remember the Buffalo Springfield wake at Charlie's house? Remember you called me outside to talk?' He says, 'I did?' I said, 'Yeah. You remember what you said?' And he said, 'No, what'd I say?' 'You said it was all my fault.' And he turns, like, white. And I said, 'You know that's not true, don't you, Stephen?' He said, 'Yeah, I do, but let's not talk about it.'"

———

Ron Stone was halfway through law school when he moved from New York to Los Angeles and opened the Great Linoleum Clothing Experiment, a resale shop on Santa Monica Boulevard in West Hollywood just down the hill from the Sunset Strip. Stone had planned to call the store the Great Clothing Experiment, but ripping out its floors had proven hideously memorable, and the amended name complemented the taste among hippies for inscrutability in all things. Stone got the idea to sell used clothing from a store in the East Village called Limbo, but he might as well have looked no further than the Village itself, which was bestirring itself for its moment in the great Haight-Ashbury/Sunset Strip/Rush Street hippie gala.

There were pilgrimages like Stone's, physical and metaphysical, all over the country in the mid-'60s. A lot of them were made by restless young men moving from New York to Southern California, if for no other reason than the place where pop culture and its sundry lifestyle ancillaries were created was moving, too. The motion-picture business had forsaken its studios in Queens and New Jersey for Burbank and Culver City in the 1920s; now the television and music industries were shifting their operations from East Coast to West. The folk-music movement and the Beatles legitimized performers who wrote their own material, decimating the Brill Building songwriting assembly line. What demand still existed for pop and rock songwriting for hire increasingly went to L.A.-based writers like Jimmy Webb ("Wichita Lineman"). It was telling that Carole King, who with her husband, Gerry Goffin, wrote sophisticated teen anthems like "Up on the Roof" in the early '60s and embodied the Brill Building's golden era, moved to a house on Lookout Mountain, where she reinvented herself as a hugely successful singer-songwriter.

As it happened, Stone's Great Linoleum Clothing Experiment was located next door to the Troubadour. Stone kept the store open late to poach customers from the long lines that formed outside the club. Along with selling a few extra pairs of exquisitely faded Levi's, he came to know many of the Trouba-dour's regulars, who would wander in and kill a few hours while he waited for the post-performance stampede from the club. "Janis Joplin used to come to the store a lot," Stone says. "She looked like a bag lady, like a little old Jewish woman. Believe me, the character of Janis Joplin onstage had nothing to do with who she was offstage."

Another regular was a young musician who at the moment had plenty of time on his hands. "David Crosby had just gotten thrown out of the Byrds," Stone says, "and he was hanging out at the store. We had a mutual interest in smoking pot, and we played chess. There'd be that quiet time, a couple of hours while the Troubadour had the show on, and David and I would sit in the store, smoke dope, and play chess. We got to be pretty good friends. It was six months after the Byrds chucked him out, and he was trying to figure out what was going on." So was Stone. His wife, who ran the store with him without pay, was getting restive. "We argued about running the store and she was right and I was wrong, which I never admitted." Thanks to his dope-smoking, chess-playing friend, and the many other musicians who frequented the Troubadour, Stone found himself drifting into the music business.

One of Stone's friends from the Bronx, Elliot Roberts, né Rabinowitz, had worked in the Morris mail room alongside David Geffen in New York but abruptly left the agency after seeing Joni Mitchell at the Café au Go-Go. Floored by her per-formance and the buzz building around her songwriting, he of-fered to manage her. "She had a backlog of twenty, twenty-five songs," Roberts recalled. "What most people would dream that they would do in their entire career, she had already done it be-

fore she had recorded. It was stunning." Mitchell had no manager or recording contract but was nothing if not a cool customer.
She told Roberts that she was going on the road for three weeks
and that if he paid his own expenses, he could come along.
Roberts did, and got the job at the end of the tour. "Elliot became wildly excited about Joni, and he introduced me to her
and I became her agent," Geffen recalled. "It was the beginning
of her career; it was the beginning of *our* careers." It was also the
beginning of a fruitful partnership between Roberts and Geffen: whenever Roberts signed an act—and he would go on to
sign many—Geffen would become their agent.

Mitchell subsequently left to play a club in Coconut Grove,
Florida, where she was introduced to Crosby, who was nursing
his fractured career amid a scene he had played years before
when he was on his way up. He and Mitchell began an affair,
and Crosby—besotted as much by her talent as by her cheek-
bones—pledged to produce her first record. The couple returned to New York and, with Roberts, left for Los Angeles to
begin work on what would become *Song to a Seagull.* In the
course of recording the album, Mitchell introduced Roberts to
Neil Young, whom she knew from the Canadian folk circuit.
The Buffalo Springfield, beset with internal strife and management woes, was entering its protracted disintegration. "When
the Buffalo Springfield broke up, [Roberts] ended up managing
Neil," says Stone. "I think in the beginning he was trying to sign
the Buffalo Springfield. As he relays the story to me, Neil said:
'You can either sign them or sign me, because I'm leaving.' And
to Elliot's brilliance, he signed Neil." Forty years later, Roberts
still manages Young, although, as Stone points out, "Neil claims
he actually manages Elliot."

With Young and Mitchell signed, Roberts—who was at
the time sleeping on Stone's couch at his house on Lookout
Mountain—asked his old friend to join the management com-

pany he had decided to form, which he named, with refreshing directness in an era of Great Linoleum Clothing Experiments, Lookout Management. Stone accepted Roberts's offer even though, he says, "I'd never been in the music business and quite honestly neither had he." Lookout Management would become, under various names and with the addition and subtraction of the mercurial Geffen, Hartmann, and other partners, Laurel Canyon's de facto talent repository. Its roster almost single-handedly created the folk-rock-country-whatever L.A. sound essayed by Young, Crosby, Stills & Nash, Jackson Browne, America, J. D. Souther, and the future Eagles Glenn Frey and Don Henley.

In addition to bunking at Stone's house, Roberts crashed at Stephen Stills's and Young's before finally renting a place a few doors up Lookout from Stone. Mitchell was about to move into her cottage down the street. "Elliot lived on Lookout," says Stone. "I lived on Lookout, and Joni lived on Lookout—we were all on the same street." By then, Roberts had added Crosby to his list of clients. Crosby set about promoting Mitchell to the Laurel Canyon cognoscenti as aggressively as any agent. His standard gambit was to get them wrecked on primo dope, then have Mitchell make a dramatic entrance with her guitar. "I took her around to people that I knew already loved music, already loved singer-songwriters," Crosby recalled. "I'd roll them a joint, get them high, and sit down and ask Joni to play. And the word spread, pretty much like wildfire." The upshot was that before her album was completed, Mitchell was the talk of the canyon and, by extension, the record industry. "David set it up so that when the album finally came out, everyone in L.A. was aware of Joni Mitchell," Roberts recalled.

In the middle of all this, Graham Nash began an affair with Mitchell while they were staying at Crosby's house. They had previously met when the Hollies toured Canada; now she and Nash moved into her house on Lookout. "David once told me of this woman that he knew called Joni Mitchell," says Nash, "and that if I ever came across her that he felt that we would get on together. In late '66, maybe early '67, the Hollies are playing in Ottawa, and after the show, the Hollies were being thrown a party at the local Holiday Inn. And there was this beautiful blond sitting in the corner. I kept staring at this girl and my manager, Robin Britten, comes up to me and starts nattering in my ear about something. I say, 'Robin, please, leave me alone, I'm looking at this woman.' And he says, 'Well if you'd fuckin' listen, I'm telling you, she came up to me and her name is Joni Mitchell and she has a friend, David Crosby, and she told me to introduce you.'

"I took her back to her hotel, the Chateau Lorraine, on the top floor with the gargoyles outside the windows. Joni had been there for a month—she was doing a series of gigs and so she had the hotel room set up as her own living room, with beautiful colored drapes, and candles and incense going. Very romantic. Then she picks up her fucking guitar and starts to play me twenty of the greatest songs that I'd ever heard in my life at that point: 'Michael from Mountains,' 'I Had a King,' 'Both Sides Now,' 'Circle Game.' And with every song I'm getting deeper and deeper in love with this woman."

Reunited in Laurel Canyon, Nash and Mitchell rekindled their romance. Crosby, famous for keeping a virtual harem of women in his orbit, took Mitchell's departure in stride, hewing to the canyon's what's-mine-is-yours ethic. "Obviously Crosby had a relationship with Joan because he discovered her and brought her to Los Angeles to record," says Nash. "And they were lovers, of course. But with all due respect, I mean, it was probably part of that Laurel Canyon thing. It was nothing to me and David that I would go live with Joan. It was all right all the way around."

Nash and Mitchell conjoined at what turned out to be the

height of Laurel Canyon's generational cohesiveness. "There was a camaraderie among all the artists," recalled Roberts. "There was always people coming over up and down the canyon, going from one house to another playing new songs for each other." Says Nash: "That was a remarkable situation for me. Because it may have been what they did in Laurel Canyon but it wasn't part of my life. So when I got there and actually immersed myself in that Laurel Canyon culture, it was really amazing to me. It was very much like maybe Vienna was at the turn of the century or Paris in the '30s, where something happens and you don't know what it is and it's catching fire and there's more music coming out and more people making music and more people discovering each other and discovering the fact that love is better than hate and peace is better than war and really trying to emphasize those kinds of things that we all truly believed in." As Mitchell told the L.A. disc jockey Jim Ladd: "Ask anybody in L.A., you know, where the craziest people are, and they'll say Laurel Canyon, and what was the craziest street? Lookout Mountain. So there we were, Elliot, myself . . . and a whole lot of us strung all the way through the canyon. The Eagles came in later, and it was quite a neighborhood."

Mitchell's house was set back from the street against the hillside, with a smaller cottage in front. The exterior was covered with cedar shakes painted pale green; the interior sported tongue-in-groove knotty-pine ceilings and floors. A reporter from *The New York Times* visiting in 1969 described it as "lovingly cluttered with two cats"—soon to be immortalized in Nash's "Our House"—"a stuffed elk's head, stained glass windows, a grandfather clock given to [Mitchell] by Leonard Cohen, a king's head with a jeweled crown sticking out from the brick fireplace, votive candles, blooming azaleas, a turkey made of pinecones, dried flowers, old dolls, Victorian shadow boxes, and an ornamental plate from Saskatoon, Saskatchewan." A reporter

from *Rolling Stone* visiting the same year painted a scene of
countercultural domestic bliss: Nash perched on an English
church chair in the living room while Mitchell busied herself in
the kitchen making a crust for a rhubarb pie. Yet for two intense
personalities on the verge of, literally, fame and fortune, living
in what was, for all the hand-sewn hippie accoutrements, a smallish, gussied-up hunting shack, the atmosphere was increasingly
claustrophobic.

"It was a small house," says Nash, "and it was a thing of,
who got to the piano first? She was in the middle of a record
and was writing daily; and I was in the middle of a record with
David and Stephen and I was writing daily. It just got to be
crazy, y'know. Okay, she's playing, and then: 'Shall we have
some lunch?' And then we'd have lunch. And then maybe I'd get
to the piano."

Nash hadn't consciously set out to immortalize their life in
the canyon; the song that would come to embody the baby
boomers' longing for their own flavor of domestic intimacy
came about, prosaically enough, after an errand to the Valley.
"There's a delicatessen on Ventura Boulevard called Art's Deli,
and often Joan and I would go there to breakfast," says Nash.
"As we were walking back to the car there was this little antiques store, and in the store was this beautiful vase. Joni loved it
and I said, 'Well, great, I'll buy it for you.' And she said, 'No, no,
I can buy it myself, let me see . . .' I mean, with all due respect,
Joan still has her first dollar; she's not one to spend wildly—and
so she bought the vase. It was one of those L.A. mornings that
are gray and not quite rainy; you want to stay in because it's not
sunny. We came back and I said to her, 'Y'know, do me a favor,
why don't you put some flowers in the vase and I'll light a fire
'cause it's getting a little chilly,' and that's what we did. Then I
started to think, Y'know, that's an incredibly domestic . . . Here

we are, Joni Mitchell and Graham Nash and I'm, 'Put the flowers in the vase and light the fire' and stuff. And I thought, I *love* this woman, and this moment is a very grounded moment in our relationship. And I sat down at the piano and an hour later 'Our House' was done. It was kind of amazing."

While Mitchell and Nash explored the joys and terrors of cohabitation, Roberts was puzzling out how to land Crosby, Stills & Nash a recording contract. Each musician was already signed to competing record labels, and the machinations involved in releasing them from their commitments were beyond Roberts's experience. He turned to his friend and increasingly close business associate Geffen, who in short order got Columbia Records to take the former Buffalo Springfield singer Richie Furay and his new band, Poco, in exchange for releasing Nash. Stills was already signed to Atlantic Records, which ultimately signed CSN. Crosby's stock in the industry had sunk to the point that Roberts was able to extricate him from his Columbia contract, left over from the Byrds, with a single phone call to the label's chief, Clive Davis. When the album was finally released in 1969 and became a major hit, Geffen—then at Creative Management Associates, the forerunner to International Creative Management—proposed leaving the agency and teaming with Roberts in Lookout Management. Roberts was intitially skeptical, but Geffen carried the day, insisting, "Don't be stupid, I'll make you more money than you've made alone." Geffen, it turned out, was right, and Lookout Management morphed into the Geffen-Roberts Company.

Roberts had taken office space in the felicitously named Clear Thoughts Building on La Cienega Boulevard in West Hollywood, not far from the Troubadour. Stone stayed on in his apprenticeship. "We had the offices upstairs," he says. "Later on, Jim Morrison's girlfriend opened a clothing store underneath."

Morrison himself kept a room at the Alta Cienega Motel nearby, where he would crash after his monumental benders. The Doors had offices and a studio around the corner. Everywhere you looked, it seemed, was evidence that Los Angeles, thanks in no small measure to the Laurel Canyon/Geffen-Roberts stable, had eclipsed San Francisco as the music capital of America. "The impact of the '60s music scene on L.A. was quite spectacular," Stone says. "When Geffen left the agency business and went into partnership with Elliot, we represented all those artists: Jackson Browne, America, the Eagles. All of them came through our company. That was our raison d'être."

Geffen-Roberts quickly gained a reputation as a fierce advocate for its charges. Generational solidarity was part of the equation, but the company's percentage of its clients' gross compensation was equally compelling. And the partnership was not about to repeat the outrageous fleecing that rock's first generation received at the hands of agents, managers, and record labels. "During this period of time that this hothouse environment in Laurel Canyon is nurturing all these new and young artists, we were kind of reinventing the business to become more artist-friendly," says Stone. "David and Elliot really were committed to the artists."

The Troubadour's owner, Doug Weston, Stone's neighbor during the Great Linoleum Clothing Experiment days, may have presided over one of the most beloved institutions in L.A.'s folk-rock convergence, but he could be a blunt businessman. "He had a very interesting contractual arrangement," Stone says. "He would let you play the club, but he had four options. So if you became a success, he ended up having you back three more times even if you could sell out gigantic places. He had you by the balls." (There was one escape hatch: buying out Weston's options for the additional nights; Elton John, having gone on to superstardom after appearing at the club as a nobody, reportedly paid Weston $25,000 for his.) Enter Geffen-Roberts. Says Stone: "When Joni played the Troubadour and there were these options [Weston] was prepared to exercise, Elliot somehow managed to extricate her from the obligations. I'll leave it at that." Whatever pressure Roberts applied on behalf of his client, the incident, Stone says, was indicative of "the nature of the business and how embryonic it was then, that the Troubadour was that powerful." And that Geffen-Roberts was powerful enough to defy it.

The advantage increasingly shifted to the musicians as the decade drew to a close. In contrast to the early 1960s, when hit singles and their lower margins were the measure of success, the Geffen-Roberts stable was selling millions of *albums*, which produced correspondingly higher revenue that the partners used as a wedge to extract better royalty rates and other perquisites from the labels, such as artistic control over the recording process and album covers. "You gotta remember Crosby, Stills & Nash's [first] album was a gigantic success," says Stone. "I mean, it must have sold eight or ten million copies, some astronomical number." The numbers from CSN and other big albums of the late '60s permanently altered the dynamic between the labels and the artists. "In a lot of ways, David Geffen, Elliot, and the managers of that time changed how the business dealt with artists," Stone says. "We improved the artist situation fairly dramatically— how they were treated by the label and how they got paid."

At the same time they started making real money, Crosby, Stills, and Nash—now joined by Young—remained committed, at least in word, to the antiwar movement. When Young, outraged by the indiscriminate killing of four students at Kent State University by National Guardsmen, banged out the blistering "Ohio" and CSN rush-released the song as a single, Stone was deeply moved. "I thought that was the greatest thing we ever did, and nothing that has happened since even comes close in terms of making me believe that music had the potential to impact politically," he says. "I mean, I bought it. I was there. I was young and naive and this had a profound effect on me."

But increasingly, the musicians making this music, thanks to their talent, ambition, and the wiles of their managers, were no longer kicking around the canyon and singing for beer and joints, but budding and actual millionaires. That this discrepancy was seldom if ever addressed in their music is casual evidence of just how much the musicians—by then cocooned in an environment of constant recording, touring, and doping—and their audience—who seemed not to mind being herded into sweltering arenas while the "artists" arrived and departed by limo—had invested in keeping alive the myth that they all were really one tie-dyed nation. "There was a trust that you won't find today," Hartmann says. "That drug-ethic thing—peace and love—that made everybody trust one another and dig each other automatically. You didn't dislike someone until he fucked up; now you don't like someone until they're cool, and that's a completely different mind-set."

One canyonite willing to broach the subject was Mitchell, who got right to the point on *Ladies of the Canyon*, her breakthrough commercial album and psychosocial profile of Laurel Canyon at the end of the '60s. It's a testament to Mitchell's wit that on the same album that contained "Woodstock," her earnest benediction for the freak-flag generation, she could also paint withering portraits of the hippie-dilettantes flitting around her house on Lookout, such as Trina with her "wampum beads" and secondhand coat "trimmed with antique luxury." Later, when reminded that some sneered at her financial success, Mitchell shot back: "Wait until they make some money, they're going to turn into hypocrites real fast. What are they going to do with it?" In the meantime, on *Ladies of the Canyon*'s "For Free," Mitchell summed up the dissonance that at least one of the Laurel Canyon elite felt when she discovered that at the end of a decade that had seemed to offer nothing but frontiers and promise, success could be colored with ambivalence:

> Now me I play for fortunes
> And those velvet curtain calls
> I've got a black limousine
> And two gentlemen
> Escorting me to the halls.
> And I play if you have the money
> Or if you're a friend to me
> But the one-man band
> By the quick lunch stand
> He was playing real good, for free.

SIX

1969

Charles Manson comes to the canyon, the boys from Lookout Mountain take on Woodstock, the Burritos survive Altamont, the dark side comes to the fore

The "'60s"—the relentless pop-cultural event, not the actual decade—had barely started when the calendar 1960s ended. The '60s that were soon to be ossified by nostalgists begin in 1964 with Beatlemania and end, with several bangs and whimpers, right on schedule. A triptych of events conveniently arrayed in the final months of 1969—the Charles Manson murders in Los Angeles, the Woodstock Music and Arts Fair in upstate New York, and the Rolling Stones' free concert at the Altamont Speedway outside Livermore, California—provided a tidy metaphorical conclusion to the '60s, just as the 1929 stock market crash became the preferred denouement for the Jazz Age.

In both cases, the reality is somewhat less circumscribed. Dorothy Parker and her gang were still raising hell in Paris in the late '30s while Nazi reconnaissance planes droned overhead. The songs of Crosby, Stills, Nash & Young most tenderly associated with the '60s—"Our House," "Almost Cut My Hair," "Teach Your Children," even "Woodstock"—weren't released until 1970. There is among Americans especially a puritanical imperative that wishes for times of great sexual, personal, and artistic liberty to end apocalyptically so as to punish the participants for upsetting, if not God's plan, then the orderly procession of things. Which is how the happenstance and coincidence of three otherwise random events in 1969—Manson could have struck just as easily in 1968, or not at all—were turned into a solemn cultural bookend.

Nevertheless, the last five years of the '60s had been building, inchoately and chaotically, toward a crescendo; a moment that most of those in the thick of things didn't realize they were living was defining itself. The "'60s" didn't end in 1969 any more than the "'20s" did in 1929; instead, 1969 happened to be the year that so much of what the '60s were about reached an apogee. It was also the year that showed everyone just how fragile the peace-and-love underpinnings to the '60s really were, and that the baby boom's great unifying constant—the music pouring out of Laurel Canyon and L.A.—could also be a nexus for the most appalling aspects of humanity.

Charles Milles Manson had been in reformatories and prisons for more than half of his life by the time he drifted into L.A. in 1968. He was born in Cincinnati in 1934, the illegitimate son of a sixteen-year-old mother convicted of armed robbery when he was five. Manson spent most of his adolescence and young adulthood in juvenile detention centers and federal prisons, convicted of armed robberies, car heists, pimping, and check forging. By 1967 he'd married and divorced twice, had fathered two sons, and was about to be paroled from the Terminal Island prison in San Pedro, south of L.A., after serving seven years of a ten-year sentence for cashing a stolen check (his request to remain in the prison was denied).

During his incarceration Manson had become obsessed with the Beatles and taught himself to play the guitar and write songs. After hitting the bricks at Terminal Island, he insinuated himself into the Haight-Ashbury scene in San Francisco, where he looked like just another guitar-toting, songwriting freak. It was there he began collecting the beginnings of his Family— young, attractive girls, often from privileged families, all of them damaged to one degree or another and susceptible to the blandishments of an intense, charismatic "hippie." With a grow-ing entourage of impressionable young women in thrall to his philosophies—a hash of biblical revelations, Scientology, and his own song lyrics—Manson moved to L.A., where he hoped to secure a recording contract. He fit in so seamlessly at the parties and clubs that many were later shocked to realize they'd unwit-tingly shared a joint with him or listened to him deliver one of his ponderous raps.

Sally Stevens, an L.A. record executive who lived on Look-out Mountain at the time, recalls, "I was kind of wandering about this party and there was a door slightly open and I could see people all sitting in a circle. There was a candle in the mid-dle of the floor, and there was this guy sitting in the corner. He was kind of holding forth to everyone, and they were all sitting there like a bunch of sheep. And as I looked in the door, he said, 'Come in, come in.' I just got a bad feeling from him and said, 'No, that's okay.' Later on, when they arrested Manson, I went, God, that's that guy."

Manson hit pay dirt, or so it must have seemed, when Den-nis Wilson, the Beach Boys' drummer and singer, picked up two Family members and had sex with them at the Sunset Boulevard mansion he was renting. When Wilson returned from an errand, he found that Manson and the rest of the Family had simply moved into the house. Wilson was placated by the prospect of unlimited sex and, for a while, Manson's hippie-apocalyptic ravings and songwriting. Wilson paid for the Family's food and drugs—even penicillin shots when the girls came down with the clap. Manson meanwhile made demo tapes of his compositions and got them to Terry Melcher, the son of Doris Day and a popular young record producer who'd recorded the Byrds and Paul Revere and the Raiders. The tapes made the rounds at L.A. record labels but were invariably rejected. (The Beach Boys would nevertheless record one of Manson's songs, "Cease to Exist"—retitled "Never Learn Not to Love"—and release it exactly eight months before the massacre on Cielo Drive.)

"Circulating around Elektra Records or A&M when I was there was some Manson tape that had come in, gotten rejected, come in, gotten rejected again," says Michael James Jackson, an A&R executive soon to become a successful record producer. After Manson's arrest, Jackson says, "people remembered that tape suddenly, and some people were thinking, Gee, glad we didn't sign him; and, Gee, wonder if our rejecting him played a role. There was this vague sense of not so much guilt that anyone contributed, but that they were part of a chain of events that, unknowingly and unwillingly, led to the outburst of whatever all this rage was."

Manson didn't take the rejection well. By 1969 he and the Family had holed up at the Spahn Movie Ranch, a dreary redoubt in the Santa Susana Mountains that had served as a set for Westerns in the 1950s. There Manson inculcated his followers in his fantasy that an epic race war was at hand; he dubbed it "Helter Skelter," an homage to a song on the *White Album* whose lyrics Manson was convinced were a personal message from the Beatles to him confirming his vision of the coming apocalypse. Once Helter Skelter started, Manson preached, the blacks would rise up and kill the whites, but he and his disciples would retreat to Death Valley and later emerge to inherit the earth. When

Helter Skelter failed to materialize, Manson told his followers that they'd have to show the blacks "how to do it." On the night of August 8, 1969, the Family set out from the Spahn ranch.

Manson's instructions were concise. Family members Patricia Krenwinkel, Tex Watson, Susan Atkins, and Linda Kasabian were to drive to 10050 Cielo Drive in Benedict Canyon and massacre everyone there (Kasabian was lookout). The next morning a housekeeper found the bodies of Steven Parent, the actress Sharon Tate—eight months pregnant by her husband, the director Roman Polanksi—the hairdresser Jay Sebring, and coffee heiress Abigail Folger and her boyfriend, Wojciech Frykowski, who lived on Woodstock Road in Laurel Canyon. (Polanski was shooting a movie in Europe the night of the murders.) Tate, Sebring, Folger, and Frykowski had been stabbed 102 times; Parent had been shot. "PIG" was scrawled on the front door of the house in Tate's blood.

Before dawn the next morning, Manson, Watson, Krenwinkel, Kasabian, and Leslie Van Houten drove to 3301 Waverly Drive in the Los Feliz section of Los Angeles. After helping Watson tie up Leno and Rosemary LaBianca and assuring them they were only going to be robbed, Manson left the house while Van Houten, Krenwinkel, and Watson murdered the LaBiancas. Police found Leno's body the next morning with a carving fork protruding from his stomach and "WAR" carved into his skin; Rosemary had been stabbed forty-one times, thirty-six more than was necessary to kill her. Smeared in blood on the walls and refrigerator were the legends "DEATH TO PIGS" and "HEALTER [sic] SKELTER."

Police initially botched the case so badly that they actually arrested Manson and the Family on suspicion of auto theft and released them. Months later, after the Family had been re-arrested and jailed on car-theft charges, Atkins bragged to her cell mate about the Family's responsibility for the Tate-LaBianca murders, and Manson was finally charged in the killings. After a spectacular trial, Manson, Watson, Krenwinkel, and Van Houten were convicted of murder and sentenced to death, later commuted to life in prison after California briefly rescinded the death penalty. Kasabian, who hadn't participated directly in the murders, was granted immunity in exchange for her testimony.

In the months between the murders and Manson's arrest there was terrified speculation in the canyon about the identity of the killer, in no small measure because everyone knew that, before Tate and Polanski, Melcher had lived in the house on Cielo Drive with Candice Bergen. As a record producer and generational peer, he was one of them. "The paranoia started to come down," says Stevens. "It was fairly frightening because no one really knew who was responsible for this. A lot of people left town because they thought they were gonna get it from whoever they imagined it was. Everyone thought at first it was a big dope dealer who was revenging himself on people. There was one guy, a boyfriend of Cass Elliot's, everyone thought it was him, and he'd fled for Algiers or something."

Once Manson was charged with the murders, the paranoia only increased. Plenty of people suddenly remembered interacting with the Family when they had seemed like just another off-kilter hippie retinue—they had frequented the gatherings at Elliot's Woodrow Wilson house and the canyon's other party scenes. It was said that Manson had meant to kill Melcher as revenge for not securing him a record deal but didn't know that Melcher had moved to Malibu and had had the Family butcher the wrong victims. A competing theory was that Manson knew full well Melcher no longer lived on Cielo Drive but wanted to use the murders to send him a message. During the trial there were plenty of Family members not charged in the murders floating around town; some of the women shaved their heads, carved Xs on their foreheads, and hung around the Federal Building downtown giving chilling interviews about their "father" on trial inside.

The effect of the Manson murders on the canyon was profound. "That's when it really started to turn weird," says Nash. "Because up until then everybody's door was open, nobody gave a shit—y'know, come on in, what the fuck—and then all of a sudden it was like: I gotta lock my car. I gotta lock my door. It was the beginning of the end, I think." "Once people found out that hippies were killing people, it was a whole different thing," says Paul Body, a musician and a doorman at the Troubadour. "It was really scary suddenly," says Stevens. "People used to just hitchhike merrily everywhere and that really slowed down."

David Strick, an L.A. native soon to become a prominent entertainment-industry photographer, entered the business shortly after the murders. "A kind of lurking dread developed," he says. "There was a huge number of whacked losers who were part of the hippie scene—I mean, they were absolutely demented—and you might well have grown up with them. One of the Manson girls went to junior high school with my sister. They were just kind of like in the general mix." Body went to high school with Van Houten, who delivered sixteen stab wounds to Rosemary LaBianca. "She was in my French class. Sweet little girl, homecoming princess and all that bullshit. We hung around the same sort of people. Then she got into the drug thing, then LSD, and that just ruined her. Then she hooks up with Manson and becomes totally different than anything I remember."

The murders forced L.A.'s counterculturalists to confront the possibility that not everyone with long hair under thirty was their brother. "The Manson murders changed the idea that hippies were safe, that hippies were harmless, that hippies could inflict no harm on anybody," says Pamela Des Barres. "That the guy with long hair and the beard could turn out to be the devil was really a nightmare." Before the Manson murders, says Strick, "when you had a party, there was no such thing as crashers. It was nonterritorial and completely open. That's why people could see hippies they've never seen before walking in and out of their wealthy houses and wealthy lives and not think they were going to kill them. These were the same people you were passing a joint to."

"If you were surprised by the Manson murders, you weren't connected to what was going on in the canyon," says Gail Zappa. "I don't think that you could have neccesarily predicted it, but those people were dangerous and everyone I know knew it. They did not have the same character or quality of life that you were witnessing elsewhere. I think it's also part of the drug culture; it got to be a very exploitive business and people were owing people lots of money and there was a lot of drugs involved around that whole scene. If you took drugs and dampened your perception, then that's why you didn't notice. But for those of us who were drug free? Oh, we noticed."

What was particularly frightening for the canyon's young stars was that, according to Atkins, there were plans to attack high-profile entertainers, ostensibly to incite Helter Skelter but just as plausibly to avenge his thwarted dreams of stardom. Elizabeth Taylor was to have had "HELTER SKELTER" carved onto her face and her eyes gouged out, Frank Sinatra would be skinned alive while his music played, and so on.

"It was so close," says Nash, "not only physically was it close, but he was a musician. I mean, fuck, he auditioned for Neil [Young] for fuck's sake. And it was brutal and horrible and the entire antithesis of what the peace-and-love movement was about. Slaughtering pregnant women? For what reason? Everybody knew that something had happened that had changed the vibe of the area dramatically forever." It had become fashionable for rock stars in town to record or perform to rent houses in the canyon instead of staying at the Chateau Marmont; post-Manson, they went back to the hotels. Strick photographed a story on the Manson followers during the trial. "They were vicious, weird people. Afterward the editor of the newspaper said: 'Don't ever talk to them again, don't go near them.'" Strick says the writer of the story refused to answer his door for months afterward.

Probably the most unsettling aspect of the murders was the parallels between Manson's Family and the cliques around L.A. centered on charismatic men inside or on the fringes of the music industry. Manson may not have gotten a record deal, but he did have the trappings of rock stardom—the Jesus-like beard and hair, the trunkful of songs, the beautiful, sycophantic young women otherwise known as groupies had they coalesced around, say, Frank Zappa's scene at the log cabin or Vito Paulekas's studio. "I wouldn't say Frank was on a power trip about it, like Manson probably was, and Vito wasn't either," says Pamela Des Barres. "It was more of a gathering of the tribes and bringing the people together."

Still, there was and remains something cultish about rock stardom. Manson was the first of the hippie generation to show how, with a few turns of the wheel, it could become lethal. "There was always a real undercurrent of very nasty stuff," says Strick. "The rules of nature hadn't been changed by a few records." The point was driven home twenty years later by the rock-and-roll aspirant David Koresh, who harangued his flock of Branch Davidians in Waco with electric guitar solos and doomsday scriptures until, with an assist from the Bureau of Alcohol, Tobacco, and Firearms, he created his own private apocalypse, taking seventy-six men, women, and children with him.

"We were in this peaceful mentality about sharing, that it

was a community, that there was no judgment," says Jackson. The
Manson murders served notice that your "brother" could be your
killer as well as your keeper. "I'm not a fan of the word 'evil,'
because 'evil' sounds religious to me," Jackson says. "But it [the
Manson murders] had a cruelty to it that was not just unaccept-
able but literally unthinkable. The fact that Manson was persua-
sive enough that he had created this little following and they
could actually think like that, as if they had some sense of purpose, and were then capable of doing it, was purely frightening."

Allowed to address the court during his trial, Manson famously blustered, "These children that come at you with
knives, they are your children. You taught them. I didn't teach
them. I just tried to help them stand up." Later in the screed he
added, "Is it a conspiracy that the music is telling the youth to
rise up against the establishment . . . ? It is not my conspiracy. It
is not my music. I hear what it relates. It says, 'Rise,' it says, 'Kill.'
Why blame it on me? I didn't write the music." Manson, in
other words, blamed the Beatles and, implicitly, the rock culture
to which he'd been given a tantalizing glimpse only to have the
door slammed in his face. For years, religious fundamentalists
had been decrying rock and roll as the devil's music; now a failed
rock musician who plenty thought *was* the devil was confirming
their worst fears.

"In truth, the devil had always been there," says Michael Des
Barres. "The '60s created the devil, and Manson came out of
that."

Five days after the Manson murders, the Woodstock Music and
Arts Fair opened in a pasture in Sullivan County, in upstate New
York. Whereas Manson would soon be cited as evidence of the
counterculture's internal rot, Woodstock was hailed as proof of

its resilience. Woodstock drew 450,000 (some estimates are much lower), lasted four days—from Richie Havens's stirring and hastily improvised opening set to Jimi Hendrix's "Star Spangled Banner"—and cost in the neighborhood of $2.4 million versus $1.1 million worth of tickets sold. There were 5,162 medical cases and three deaths, two of them drug overdoses, the other a young man run over by a tractor while in his sleeping bag. Laurel Canyon was represented by Canned Heat and Crosby, Stills & Nash, joined by Neil Young.

CSNY rehearsed for this, their second official live performance—the first would take place at Chicago's Auditorium Theater the night before their Woodstock slot—at Shady Oak, a house nestled in the hills on the Valley side of the canyon. Formerly owned by Wally Cox, it was purchased by Peter Tork at the height of his Monkees fame. Tork's tenure there was already legendary for marathon parties and the abundance of young women in states of undress in more or less permanent residence around the swimming pool. When Tork blew through his Monkees money, he rented the house to his old folkie pal Stephen Stills, whereupon the jam sessions in the downstairs music room and the Möbius strip of parties-cum-hangouts continued unabated.

Stills added a special touch by rehearsing Crosby, Stills, Nash & Young, complete with screaming amplifiers and pounding drums, on the patio. "One day Stephen says: 'It's a beautiful afternoon—I want to hear how this sounds in the outdoors. Let's just set up all the instruments outdoors and play for a while,'" says Nash. "And we did." When Crosby questioned the wisdom of openly provoking the neighbors, Stills accused him of betraying his freak-flag allegiance. ("I think David was a little more paranoid about the police than Stephen was, y'know?" says Nash.) It was typical of the band's heated infighting, in which one member would hurl another's lyrics at him as evidence of mendacity or the dreaded "cop-out." Dallas Taylor, the band's drummer, recalled one evening at Shady Oak "sitting there, taking a long hit off of one of Crosby's killer joints, vaguely aware that an argument was going on around me: 'Fuck you!' 'No, fuck *you!*' 'That's a cop-out, man!'" The next thing Taylor knew, Stills had escorted him downstairs to the music room to jam with Jimi Hendrix and Buddy Miles. The refreshments, according to Taylor, included a large mound of cocaine sitting on a mirror on the Hammond organ. (The Rolling Stones, connoisseurs of bad behavior and rock-and-roll pedigree, would later stay at the house.)

Crosby, Stills, Nash & Young went on well past dark the second day of Woodstock after seven bands, including Jefferson Airplane, Joe Cocker, and Ten Years After, in a career-making performance, had wrung the crowd all day and night. Opening with Stills's masterpiece "Suite: Judy Blue Eyes," written about his affair with Judy Collins, whom he met on Ridpath Drive in the canyon, they faced the enormous audience with only their acoustic guitars and harmonies. The sixteen-song set went well, despite Stills's gold-plated ad-lib that the band was "scared shitless." David Geffen later strong-armed Warner Bros. into using CSNY's version of Joni Mitchell's "Woodstock"—written in a New York hotel during the festival—as the closing music for the Woodstock movie by threatening to withhold the band's performances from the film.

CSNY's harmonies and ethereal musings on love and mythology captured the festival's gentle spirit, which itself seemed to confirm the freshly christened Woodstock Nation's possibilities for forging a new sort of social contract. Despite rain, mud, bad acid, and lack of food, sanitation, and crowd control, the festival managed to make it through four days with no major incidents.

This was interpreted by the straight press as nothing short of a miracle—which indeed it was—while the freak contingent tended toward the point of view that it was all somehow inevitable, that hippie values of tolerance, love, and use of mind-expanding substances could deliver on the rhetoric.

Still, there were a hundred, a thousand circumstances that, had they gone the other way, could have turned Woodstock into a hellish countercultural station of the cross (as evidenced thirty years later at the disastrous Woodstock '99). Henry Diltz, the festival's official photographer, arrived from Laurel Canyon two weeks before the concert. At first, he recalled, the site was "an idyllic summer camp—hippie carpenters hammering nails, the field a sea of green alfalfa. Then one day there was a little group of twenty or thirty people sitting out there. And the next day there was a thousand and the next day four thousand." By the time the concert officially opened, it was clear much of the crowd had simply walked in ahead of time. There was actually a discussion on opening day about forcing the entire crowd to walk out and come back in again to pay or show tickets. That became moot when the tens of thousands still outside the perimeter came pouring through a chain-link fence opened up by the festival's own security under the sensible premise that they would face a riot of epic proportions if they attempted to eject everyone who hadn't paid.

So from the standpoint of what could have happened, Woodstock got off easy. And as the images of the festival were beamed around the world, it was inevitable that someone would try to replicate it whether for profit or, in the case of the band second only to the Beatles in the '60s rock pantheon, in a burst of altruism mixed with opportunism. As it happened, the Rolling Stones had already planned to end their 1969 tour in December with a free concert in San Francisco. They'd held a similar gathering in London's Hyde Park earlier in the year to honor founding member Brian Jones, who'd been discovered floating dead in his swimming pool. The Hyde Park concert attracted several hundred thousand and went off peacefully, and it seemed plausible that the San Francisco show would, too. Woodstock's tremendous spectacle inevitably ramped up the expectations for a free concert featuring "the world's greatest rock and roll band," as the Stones had taken to billing themselves, in the counterculture's very epicenter. And so the Stones' relatively straightforward free concert metastasized into the "West Coast Woodstock." At a press conference several weeks before the festival, Jagger said of the concert, "It's creating a sort of microcosmic society which sets an example for the rest of America as to how one can behave in large gatherings."

Henry Diltz, beholding Woodstock's sad, sodden detritus from the stage as Hendrix played the last morning of the festival, had a vision that, in hindsight, would be an omen for what was to come. "There were probably just a few thousand people left. And I remember looking around, and the mud, with the forgotten sleeping bags and flotsam in the field, reminded me of an old Civil War image—after the battle. And when he played that 'Star Spangled Banner,' with the notes crying out, it bounced off the hills because there was no crowd there to absorb it. It was the most eerie thing."

The notion of Altamont as the "anti-Woodstock" was burned into the cultural consciousness practically before the last notes of "Street Fighting Man" decayed in the chilly predawn hours in the countryside east of San Francisco later to be dubbed Silicon Valley. While there had been, as at Woodstock, three deaths by prosaic mishap, there was nothing at Woodstock remotely like Hells Angels beating audience members with pool cues or the fatal stabbing by an Angel of Meredith Hunter, an eighteen-year-old black audience member in the overwhelmingly white crowd of 300,000, who charged the stage with a gun while the Stones played "Under My Thumb."

Rolling Stone weighed in six weeks after the concert with "Let It Bleed," an epic recapitulation of the day's misadventures; it was followed by *Gimme Shelter*, a devastating account of the 1969 tour and its benighted finale at Altamont financed by the Stones and directed by the documentarians David and Albert Maysles and Charlotte Zwerin. The *Rolling Stone* article advanced the theory that the Stones had cynically used the audience at Altamont as "unpaid extras" in the film, with the Hells Angels as their brutal Praetorian Guard hired for the now-legendary "$500 worth of beer." As the critic Michael Sragow pointed out in his history of *Gimme Shelter* on its twenty-fifth anniversary, "The legend of Altamont as apocalypse was largely based on that *Rolling Stone* cover story," which set the tone for future coverage and may have influenced the rough treatment the film was given by critics like *The New Yorker's* Pauline Kael.

Altamont was unquestionably a dark day. Not even the musicians, accustomed to imperial deference from fans to flunkies, were spared. No sooner had Jagger alighted from his helicopter backstage than a bystander coldcocked him in the face. Marty Balin, singer in Jefferson Airplane—Santana, Crosby, Stills, Nash & Young, and the Flying Burrito Brothers also performed—was knocked unconscious while attempting to intervene in a skirmish between the audience and the Angels. Says Chris Hillman, who played with the Burrito Brothers: "I went from playing Monterey"—1967's evanescent Monterey pop festival—"which was one of the greatest musical festivals, to playing Altamont. And that was like going from heaven to hell."

Altamont was no more inherently evil than was Woodstock. It can in fact be argued that it was the "purer" of the two enterprises. For while Woodstock was conceived as a profit-making venture, Altamont was from the start planned as a free concert, albeit with full understanding of the benefits to be derived from the Stones' largesse, not the least of which was bonding with San Francisco's storied hippie culture, whose rapid decline was hard to discern five thousand miles away in London. What prevented disaster from striking Woodstock had more to do with luck and marginally better planning. "As chaotic as Woodstock was, it was relatively well organized," says Nash. "Altamont was a complete mess. We had no way to get our gear in. I think that was the day that Melvin Beli hot-wired a fucking truck to get our equipment in there to get to the stage. Melvin Beli! A famous lawyer hot-wiring a truck and stealing it!"

The presence of the Angels at Altamont—drugged, drunk, and surly—was also unique to the Bay Area rock scene. While the Stones had used the London Angels as an "honor guard" at the Hyde Park free concert, they were nowhere near as violent as the California Angels, who had nevertheless been courted by slumming San Francisco counterculturalists for years. Hunter Thompson, while researching his 1967 book about the gang, had brought the two camps together at Ken Kesey's ranch in La Honda, south of San Francisco. Thompson was certain the Angels would run amok at the party; instead, they sampled LSD and were fawned over by Kesey's Merry Pranksters, and an uneasy alliance was struck. (R. Crumb's iconographic cover artwork for Big Brother and the Holding Company's *Cheap Thrills* album included the legend APPROVED BY HELLS ANGELS FRISCO.) So the San Francisco rock scene and the Angels had some history of peaceful coexistence. Given the lack of trouble at the Hyde Park concert, Sam Cutler, the Stones' road manager, arranged via the Grateful Dead for the Angels to fulfill the honor-guard role at Altamont.

The Angels, as it quickly became apparent, served to greatly exacerbate problems that already existed. The location of the concert had bounced from Golden Gate Park, after San Francisco city officials refused to issue a permit, to the Sears Point Raceway outside Sonoma. The stage and most of the equipment had been readied at the racetrack when Filmways, Inc., which controlled Sears Point, attempted to wring a distribution deal for the movie. The Altamont Speedway was secured just twenty-four hours before the concert. It was too late to pull down the elaborate staging already in place at Sears Point, so a makeshift stage, built so low that those in the front row could rest their elbows on it, was cobbled together. On December 6, 1969, the roads leading to the racetrack were clotted with cars as far as the eye could see. Altamont was on.

Chris Hillman had bad vibes about the concert even before the Burrito Brothers left Los Angeles. "I felt it was wrong when it was offered to us. Gram Parsons was begging the Stones to let the Burritos be on the show. And I kept saying, 'Why are we doing this? Why are we spending money to go up and play this? It doesn't feel right.'" Two days later, the car carrying the band to the concert was involved in a minor accident in the morass of traffic on the fringes of the festival. "We get out," says Hillman, "there's no parking, there's no order. I literally had to inch through the crowd holding my Fender bass over my head. It was like being in New Delhi and trying to walk through a mass of people on pilgrimage. I get to the stage, and there it is: the Hells Angels are beating people up and it was just like a nightmare. I had to argue with two of the Hells Angels to get on the stage to play. They were like ready to beat *me* up. I had to talk to them real slowly, they were so out of their minds."

Nash, too, was less than enthused about the prospect of playing the festival. "We only did it because Jerry Garcia asked

Crosby to get Crosby, Stills, Nash & Young to play Altamont," he says. "We did it as a favor to Jerry. It was certainly one of the weirdest shows I ever played. They were playing this electronic music really loud in between acts. It was really tense." (Reminded that few people even realize CSNY played Altamont, Nash says, "I know. We left that to Mick and the lads: 'Nope, that's a Rolling Stones concert, thank you very much!'")

All day, the stage front was racked by sullen outbursts as the Angels wielded their pool cues. Nash says that although there was a lull in the violence during CSNY's set, "everybody in our band knew we needed to get on with our show and get the fuck out of there. This did *not* feel good. It was clear this was going to be an ugly scene. It was obvious to everybody." After Balin's knockout, Jefferson Airplane's Paul Kantner berated the Angels over the loudspeakers; an Angel on the opposite side of the stage grabbed a mike and menaced Kantner. A tense standoff ensued before the band started playing again. The Manson murders would soon confirm that not all longhairs were hippies; the Angels were now demonstrating that the fey mutual admiration between the gang and the hippies—Allen Ginsberg had gone so far as to write a mealymouthed poem, "To the Angels," pleading that they stop beating people up—was bullshit.

There were also class considerations at work. The Angels were typically blue-collar and delinquent; the hippies just as typically white-collar, college educated, and—illegal drugs and minor civil disobedience aside—law-abiding. Preserved in the Maysleses' unblinking documentary, Altamont literally becomes a stage where social castes from the same, supposedly monolithic generation—each with long hair and a mutual interest in getting high, getting laid, and listening to rock and roll—reveal themselves to be two species. Stan Goldstein, the Maysleses' deputy, pointed out that away from the stage and the Angels' glowering presence, the audience at Altamont looked and behaved much as the audience had at Woodstock. "Tens of thousands of people had no idea of what was going on just a few dozen feet away. They knew only that the music was interrupted frequently."

By the time the Stones finally hit the stage in the cold pre-winter darkness—the Grateful Dead had been scheduled to go on before but bowed out so the concert would not run desperately over schedule—there was nothing left but the inevitable. Twice during the opening number, "Sympathy for the Devil," the band had to halt as melees with the Angels erupted in front of the stage. At one point Jagger pleaded for order while the audience—one eye cocked for the next attack—looked back at him blankly. "Brothers and sisters!" he cried, sounding genuinely perplexed. "Why are we fighting? Who wants to fight?" The audience, having no answer, stared back.

As the band hit the closing notes of the second number, "Under My Thumb," the stage front suddenly cleared. It wasn't apparent to the band or even to those in the front rows, but Meredith Hunter had rushed forward, gun drawn, and been stabbed in the head and back by the Hells Angel Alan Passaro. (A jury later acquitted Passaro of murder, ruling he had acted in self-defense.) Hunter died before he could be transported to the hospital. Jagger and the band knew none of this, only that someone had apparently been wielding a gun and that the Angels kept wading into the crowd and assaulting people. After playing an abbreviated set, the Stones and their entourage hastily crammed into a helicopter and evacuated the West Coast Woodstock as if fleeing an insurrection.

Altamont wasn't the apocalypse of the '60s but rather something much less and much more. The baby boomers' sense of invincibility had been steadily battered as the decade wound down; now the generation's absolute conviction that the rules didn't apply to it, that anything was possible, including fielding immense, lackadaisically planned festivals where no one would be harmed, had been debunked with terrible finality. Altamont's power lay not in its supposed evil but in showing baby boomers the folly of believing their own hype, at such a portentous moment, with cameras rolling. It was a stunning repudiation. Back in Los Angeles and Laurel Canyon, where so much '60s hagiography had been created and perpetuated, there was no question that it was anything else. "Suddenly the dream was over and the dark side came to the fore," says Gary Burden, "and it was never the same."

PART TWO

COCAINE AFTERNOONS

SEVEN

TROUBADOURS

*The canyon's singer-songwriters take on the Troubadour, John Lennon heckles the
Smothers Brothers, the Eagles take flight, Jim Morrison's six-month apology*

On Tuesday, August 25, 1970, an obscure twenty-three-year-
old English singer-songwriter took the stage at the Troubadour
for the first night of a six-night stand. Sally Stevens was at the
club that night with a sad-eyed musician from Detroit who had
recently arrived in L.A. The Troubadour, then as now, is divided
into a bar and a performance room. "You couldn't get into the
playing room without paying," says Stevens, "but the bathrooms
were through the playing room. So what everybody used to do
was, if you heard something from the playing room that
sounded interesting, you'd say to the guy at the door, 'I'm going
to the bathroom,' and then be able to stand in the back for at
least twenty minutes before they'd come and make you go back
to the bar."

That night her friend excused himself and left for the bathroom. When he finally returned, he grabbed Stevens. "He just
went, 'You've gotta see this guy, this guy's amazing!'" Whereupon Stevens and her friend, the pre-Eagles Glenn Frey, took in

Elton John's first American performance. "He was playing to an almost empty room," Stevens recalls. By the end of his sixth night, John's performances at the club had passed into legend. That run at the Troubadour turned Elton John from a promising nobody into a star almost overnight. It also cemented once and for all the Troubadour's status as a kingmaker.

Since moving the club near the corner of Doheny Drive and Santa Monica Boulevard on the edge of Beverly Hills in 1957, the Troubadour's owner, Doug Weston, had adroitly managed to keep it at the forefront of musical trends. In the '60s it had been indispensable in bringing together the first wave of L.A. folkies; in the '70s it became the stage, salon, and saloon for the singing-songwriting young men and women flocking to Laurel Canyon. If the canyon was where everyone in the L.A. music scene lived either in fact or in spirit, the Troubadour was where they played. A fifteen-minute drive or hitchhike from Lookout Mountain and the Kirkwood Bowl, the club provided a stage where canyonites could hone their performances and—thanks to that bar next to the playing room—a rendezvous where contacts could be made, partnerships started and finished, romances kindled and ruined, while the Cuervo and Sauza flowed.

"Everyone would end up at the Troubadour at night," says Henry Diltz. "These would be the same people you might bump into in the daytime, but you'd be sure to bump into them at night at the Troubadour." The Eagles probably wouldn't have existed without the Troubadour. "The Troubadour was the first place I went when I got to L.A.," recalled Don Henley. "The first night I walked in I saw Graham Nash and Neil Young, and Linda Ronstadt was standing there in a little Daisy Mae kind of dress. She was barefoot and scratching her ass. I thought, 'I've made it. I'm here. I'm in heaven.'" At the same time, the club was a competitive sweat lodge where male egos locked antlers amid the boozy camaraderie and long sniffs of coke. "It was a very predatory atmosphere," says Stevens. "Everyone was after something. Everyone was on the hunt. Just a mass of alcohol and testosterone. It wasn't benign. It was very definitely a hunting ground for success, for sex, whatever you could get."

From Elton John's star-making appearances until the mid-'70s, when Weston's hubris and draconian booking policies nearly sank it, the Troubadour was the most important popular-music venue in the world. "It went through this real exciting period when it peaked," says Paul Body, who worked as a door-man at the club from 1973 to 1980. "All the songwriters played there—J. D. Souther, Warren Zevon, Wendy Waldman, Karla Bonoff, that's how a lot of them got their contracts." The rhythms of the club bled into everyone's lives. The Monday night Hoots, a holdover from the folk days, were followed by a six-night stand—later to become a point of contention between the performers and Weston. "Tuesday night was opening night," says Colman Andrews, a journalist and author who worked for several record labels. "You'd go over to the Troubadour at eight. The format was always two bands. In those days, God, I remember a double bill of Donny Hathaway and Roberta Flack, the Incredible String Band opening for Tim Buckley."

Unlike the Whisky and other clubs on the Sunset Strip, the Troubadour was more likely to attract young Hollywood: Dennis Hopper, Peter Fonda, Harry Dean Stanton, Ed Begley, Jr., Jack Nicholson. "Jack's an interesting story," says Stevens. "I never saw Jack hang out at the Troubadour. What he tended to do was come in and invite certain people over to the house"—Nicholson's smallish, art-filled compound on Mulholland near Coldwater Canyon. "Then you'd end up at Jack's, and Jack wouldn't be there. He'd be there but he'd be upstairs; only a very few people would actually get up to see Jack. I must have been there four or five times, and there'd be a lot of people sitting around, all very mellow, and you'd go, 'Is Jack here?' 'Yeah, he's upstairs.' You knew not to go." Not-so-young Hollywood was also drawn to the Troubadour—Clint Eastwood, Robert Mitchum, Peter Lawford. "Nicholas Ray, the guy who directed *Rebel Without a Cause*, would come in every Monday on Hoot night at about nine o'clock, and by eleven-thirty he'd be shit-faced, hitting people with his cane," says Body.

The Troubadour's front door opened directly onto Santa Monica Boulevard, and the overflow from the bar would inevitably spill onto the sidewalk. As the evening wore on, a steady stream of patrons coursed between the club and Dan Tana's, an Italian bar and restaurant two doors down and a hangout in its own right. "I remember Harrison Ford used to drink at the bar at Tana's," says Andrews. "Joni Mitchell, David Blue, Jackson Browne, Warren Zevon. You'd walk back and forth and drink all night, do a little coke, maybe smoke a little."

The shows in the Troubadour's performance room could seem like an afterthought compared with the scene raging nightly in the bar. "What really made the Troubadour work was, you had the bar, which was free, you could walk in, and as long as you could buy a beer, you could stay," says Stevens. "You were able to go in there for free and meet people and hang out. At all the other clubs, you were stuck in the playing room, so it was too loud and you couldn't talk and you had to pay. Doug Weston was very smart—he figured: the bar will be the bar and whatever will happen will happen. Then you had Tana's next door, which in those days didn't cost one hundred or two hundred dollars to eat, and you could drink at the bar there for free, too."

Not that there wasn't plenty of drama in the Troubadour's performance room. Body's first night at the club was instructive. "Dr. John was playing and the place was packed. I was working the back door and I hear a knock. And it's Cher. Have to let Cher in. Then a little later it's John Lennon and Elton John. And some of the guys in the Band. Then the next thing I know there's Lennon and Elton onstage, jamming with Dr. John. And this is, like, my first *night*." On another occasion the knock on the door was Miles Davis, reporting for work. "He came in with his band, who looked like a gang. He sits down and motions me over. And he says—he has that voice, right?—'I want a . . .' And I thought he said rum and Coke. I said, 'Oh, Mr. Davis, you want a rum and Coke?' And he looks at me with those eyes, and he said, 'No, motherfucker, a Rémy Martin.'"

The Troubadour's eclectic bookings, from jazz godheads like Davis to Carly Simon, yet another singer-songwriter who launched her career at the club (and met James Taylor back-stage), drew a hip, knowing crowd. "The Troubadour wasn't the rock-and-roll guys with a cucumber in their pants; it was more upscale," says Body. "You know who drew the most beautiful women? Leonard Cohen. All of them dressed in black, all of them beautiful." Compared with the clubs on the Strip, which skewed to a younger audience, the Troubadour was practically sedate. Recalls Morgana Welch, a well-connected L.A. groupie during the '70s: "It was another scene. I just didn't care for the music or the people. There were different cliques of people who went to different bars. I was in the Rainbow-Whisky clique. Those were my people and the Strip was my turf."

Troubadour waitresses were legendary for brooking no bull-shit from the clientele, as Lennon discovered on his fabled "lost weekend" in L.A. during his separation from Yoko Ono. "Ann Peebles was playing and she had that hit, 'I Can't Stand the Rain,'" says Body. Lennon, sitting in the club's VIP section, called the Arena, "was way past drunk. And he was yelling, 'An-nie! I wanna suck you!' Then he goes to the bathroom and

comes back with a Kotex on his head and that was that."
Lennon, Kotex still stuck to his forehead, asked a waitress, "Do
you know who I am?" "And Naomi, the waitress, says, 'Yeah,
you're an asshole with a Kotex on your head,'" says Body.
Welch considered Lennon enough of a hero to break her Troubadour embargo to go see him on the hoof. "I went there a
couple of times specifically to check him out—it was just something I had to do. He was sitting at the bar getting very drunk
and being rather rude, kind of in his own little world. It was
sad; it wasn't what I expected. I met him briefly and that was
a great moment for me, although at the time I thought, Oh,
what a has-been. The opinion of him was pretty low on the
streets at that time, because he was just pretty much a drunk and
a loudmouth."

Three months later Lennon was at it again during a performance by the Smothers Brothers. This time he was accompanied by Harry Nilsson, his Los Angeles drinking partner and
all-around bad influence. "The Smothers Brothers are playing,"
Body says. "Lennon and Harry Nilsson are heckling them"—
Lennon supposedly shouted, "Hey, Smothers Brothers! Go fuck
a cow!"—"and Peter Lawford jumps into the fray. And all hell
breaks loose. Lennon and Nilsson are thrown out. I had to sweep
up all the broken glass and bullshit the next day. What people
don't know is that Lennon and Harry Nilsson felt so bad that
they sent a bunch of candy and roses to the Smothers Brothers'
dressing room." (Lennon later remarked: "It was my first night
on Brandy Alexanders and my last.") For months afterward,
Lennon's trademark granny glasses—knocked off during the
melee—reposed in the Troubadour kitchen as a memento to the
man who wrote "Whatever Gets You Through the Night."
"They were probably the ones he got shot in," says Body.

When not under siege from celebrities run amok—Keith

Moon had to be turned away when he arrived in a Nazi uniform—the Troubadour was cementing a reputation as a clearinghouse for talent. Don Henley arrived in L.A. from Linden, Texas, with a band called Shiloh—mentored by fellow Texan Kenny Rogers—which was failing in the usual fashion. "I really didn't know anybody," Henley recalled, "I just hung around the Troubadour by myself. It was kind of pathetic, really." One night Glenn Frey invited Henley over to his table. Frey had recently departed his own failed band, Longbranch Pennywhistle, founded with J. D. Souther, through which he met Jackson Browne, yet another young songwriter with a backlog of compositions that would soon make him a millionaire several times over. Frey, Browne, and Souther shared grotty apartments in Echo Park, a decaying downtown neighborhood where Aimee Semple McPherson broadcast her sermons in the '20s.

At the Troubadour, Frey got down to business. As Henley recalled, "I said my group's not doing anything. Glenn said, 'Me and my partner are breaking up, too. And there's this guy named David Geffen'—then launching his Asylum label—'and there may be a deal in the works if a band could be put together. In the meantime, do you want to go on the road with Linda Ronstadt and make 200 bucks a week?'" After backing Ronstadt at Disneyland, Henley, Frey, Bernie Leadon, and Randy Meisner regrouped as the Eagles. On May 1, 1972, they released "Take It Easy," and the cocaine cowboys were on their way. It's conceivable that Frey and Henley would have found each other through other channels—the L.A. music scene was still intimate enough for that—but with the Troubadour as midwife the process was sped up exponentially.

The Troubadour was also a useful rendezvous when rounding up the usual suspects; if you were looking for someone, chances were you could find them there. One night Kris

Kristofferson came rushing into the bar and hid behind Stevens and her friend Carol Samuels. "He said, 'She's looking for me! She's looking for me!'" Stevens asked, "She who?" Kristofferson sputtered, "Barbra Streisand's looking for me!" The women mutually decided Kristofferson had lost it. "No, I swear she's looking for me," he hissed. "She wants me to be in this movie"— *A Star Is Born*—"and I've told her I don't want to be in the movie and she won't leave me alone and she's hunting me down. And she's coming in here!" Says Stevens, "Sure enough, about a half an hour later, who walks in?"

The club's networking potential was such that jobs could materialize entirely by happenstance. Stevens briefly worked as a waitress at Thee Experience, a self-consciously psychedelic club far off the Strip at Sunset and Gardner. One evening she was trolling the dreary back room when she noticed, at a table of particularly obnoxious drunks, "this guy giving me dirty looks. I couldn't see who he was, just some big guy with a beard. And as I went by he grabbed me by the hair, hauled me down across his lap, nearly broke my back, and yelled in my face: Get me a beer, bitch!"

Stevens, all of five feet two, was nothing if not self-possessed. "I put my foot on the edge of his chair and kicked him flying. He went over, the table went over, there was complete chaos. I had this tray and I just came down over his face with it and stopped. All I could see were these terrified eyes, like a rat peeking out, and I yelled, 'Don't you ever do that to a woman again! Are you listening?' And then I got up, left him lying there, walked to the front, slammed my tray down on the counter, and said, 'I'm going home.'" The next morning Stevens called the club to get her schedule for the week and was told she was fired. "For what?" she asked, incredulous. "They said, 'Don't you know who that was? It was Jim Morrison.'" Not only had Morrison demanded she be fired, Stevens says, but the incident black-balled her around town. "I was trying to find work, and people wouldn't return calls."

Stevens was at the Troubadour one Monday night when Paul Rothchild, the Doors' producer, stopped to say hello. "He said, 'Oh, how are you doing?' 'Just great, Paul. Now, about your friend . . .'" Stevens told him about her run-in with Morrison. "Paul said, 'Look, do me a favor. Tomorrow morning call Elektra Records'—the Doors' label—'ask for Suzanne Helms. We need a receptionist and you're it.' So I went to work for Elektra the next day."

Six months later, Stevens answered one of the nine incoming lines at the label. "Is Sally Stevens there?" the caller asked. Stevens asked who was calling. "This is Jim Morrison." He was, he said, calling to apologize for getting her fired. "I've been looking for you for six months. Anything you want to say, I'll take it." Stevens was unmoved. "I said, 'Frankly, you strike me as being much too intelligent for what you're doing. Because you're providing amusement for a bunch of idiots who would be only too pleased to see you die for their evening's entertainment. Have you ever thought of that? What is the matter with you?' This conversation went on for more than an hour. I had to keep putting him on hold." Morrison told her he hated being in the Doors. Stevens asked him what the last thing was that had made him happy. "He said, 'I loved being in film school. I have a couple of friends I really want to try to find because we were working on a movie when I left and got in this stupid band thing.'"

Morrison and Stevens became friends. She was still working at Elektra when a "regret to inform you" telex arrived from Bill Siddons, the Doors' manager, saying that Morrison had died in Paris. "Everybody likes to think of Morrison as being this big, bad guy, which he was," Stevens says, "but he also did spend six months trying to find me. The only reason I stopped before smashing that tray down in his face was because I saw the terror in his eyes. I think he'd been waiting for me. Here was finally someone who wouldn't tolerate him. I don't think anyone had done that. I was at a point in my life where I was more angry than Jim Morrison. So he finally met someone who was angrier than he was, and it was a woman."

By 1973 the Troubadour seemed unstoppable, but Doug Weston was about to fatally overreach. More than six feet tall, with flowing blond hair, Weston cut quite a figure among his fellow music entrepreneurs, who tended to be short, balding, and pugnacious. "He was a strange guy," says Andrews, "tall, gawky. Somebody said he looked like Uriah Heep." Which is to say Weston looked like a rock star; now he started acting like one. He kept a private office above the stage, next to the lighting booth, where favored guests could join him during the shows and afterward for marathon coke-and-booze sessions. His behavior became erratic. "One night he pulled a knife on Richie Havens," says Body. "Richie Havens knew it was in fun, but everybody else took it seriously." Weston had built his club on the premise of creating a room where musicians would want not only to play but to hang out, and it had succeeded spectacularly. Now he was growing restive as the talent he'd nurtured went on to reap fortunes but he didn't. "The Troubadour has been a gold mine that's been mined by everybody else," he groused.

The Troubadour's notorious contract—which stipulated that unknowns had to return to play regardless of whether they could fill Dodger Stadium—was meant to give Weston a taste of the bonanza. But it infuriated artists and especially their managers and put the club in a far more vulnerable position than

Weston realized. It's hard to imagine a nightclub wielding such power today, but in the early 1970s a hot run at the Troubadour could still deliver a career, so the musicians and labels tithed through gritted teeth.

What Weston hadn't banked on was competition, and in 1973 he got it. A consortium of industry heavyweights that included Lou Adler, president of Ode Records, David Geffen, and Elliot Roberts—who years earlier had extricated Joni Mitchell from Weston's return-engagement clause—took over the Largo, a former strip joint next door to the Rainbow Bar and Grill on Sunset Boulevard and turned it into the Roxy, a sleek and, more important, larger club that targeted the acts and audience that had been the Troubadour's bread and butter.

The Roxy immediately began siphoning off the Troubadour's business. More devastating, it became the preferred showcase for record labels to break their thoroughbred acts. While Elton John had launched his career at the Troubadour, Bruce Springsteen exploded onto the national scene in a landmark four-night engagement at the Roxy in 1975. "Once the Roxy opened, that was a whole other venue," says Body. "It was bigger; it could pay more money. Originally Bob Marley was supposed to play the Troubadour in '75, and he ended up playing the Roxy. Springsteen, the same thing. And that's when it started drying up."

As the Troubadour's fortunes declined and its prestige faded, the musicians who gave the club its specialness drifted away. "I stopped going to the Troubadour in 1974–75," says Stevens. "That was the last time you sensed that it was a place you'd still run into the old crowd. By then they were all kind of rich and famous. People were on the road, everyone was always out of town, so you didn't see anybody." The days were over when Stevens could pass an afternoon with Janis Joplin at the Troubadour bar, "just the two of us getting mildly bombed and hitting on this surfer guy who got frightened off because we were getting a bit much for him, so we went outside and some people had left a couple bicycles and we started riding around in circles, screaming and falling off. It seemed like every time you went down there something like that was going on, some little drama."

But she also remembered the jockeying of young musicians at the bar, looking for an opening, anything to get ahead. "It wasn't, 'Oh, let's go down and we'll hang out and have a merry old time at the Troubadour.' There was *absolutely* an agenda going on. Glenn Frey . . . I've never seen a guy work a room like that guy could—whatever he could get, to get himself going for his career. He was very, very career-oriented—they *all* were. Anyone who pretends they weren't doing that is fooling themselves. And I think Laurel Canyon probably was a bit that way. All this sort of hippie tripping up and down. It was very ambitious, no doubt about it."

The Troubadour limped through the rest of the '70s until Weston—who'd come close to losing the club—partnered with Ed Karayan and stabilized the operation, but not before irreversible damage had been done to its reputation. It took more than a decade for the Troubadour to regain its footing, playing host to acts like Liz Phair and Fiona Apple in the '90s much as it had showcased Bonnie Raitt and Carly Simon in the early '70s. It must have been gratifying for Weston to see the Troubadour's resurrection. He died, at age seventy-two, in 1999. In Weston's obituary, the *Los Angeles Times* pop-music critic Robert Hilburn wrote, "Weston's contribution to the health of the Los Angeles pop scene in the early days was immeasurable. And it was his love of singer-songwriters that contributed greatly to the development of that tradition in Southern California. He was perfect for the times, and for a time he used his power well."

"My whole life came alive that night, musically, emotionally . . . everything," Elton John recalled of his 1970 stand at the Troubadour, which had been so critical in launching his career and the club's legend. "It was like everything I had been waiting for suddenly happened. I was the fan who had become accepted as a musician."

EIGHT

SHE DON'T LIE

Snow in the canyon, lines on the mirror, platinum records, gold spoons, living large in the gilded palace of sin

No one knows exactly when cocaine supplanted marijuana and LSD as the preferred refreshment among the cognoscenti and hangers-on in the L.A. scene. Most date its arrival circa 1970, but it was certainly around before. In *A Hard Day's Night*, the movie that inspired David Crosby to grow his hair and buy an electric guitar, John Lennon can be glimpsed bringing a Pepsi bottle to his nose and pretending to snort. Paul McCartney later confirmed he snorted cocaine during the year the Beatles recorded their LSD-drenched 1967 masterpiece *Sgt. Pepper's Lonely Hearts Club Band*. *Easy Rider*, released in 1969, commences with Dennis Hopper and Peter Fonda making a cocaine sale to a dealer played by the L.A. record producer Phil Spector. (Spector would send a greeting card that depicted him snorting a line, with the legend "A little snow at Christmas time never hurt anybody.")

That Hopper and Fonda, aside from testing the merchandise, spend the movie indulging in pot and acid but not coke was in line with the piety of the film's intended demographic. Cocaine was at the time still somewhat beyond the pale, a "hard" drug dealt by non-countercultural criminals and thus unsuited for the gentler cravings of the hippies, who conveniently ignored the fact that marijuana was imported by the same criminals who trafficked in heroin and cocaine. On the other hand, before Crosby, Stephen Stills, and Graham Nash became Crosby, Stills & Nash in 1969, Stills and Crosby made an acetate of the future CSN songs "49 Bye-Byes" and "Long Time Gone" under the name Frozen Noses.

Whenever cocaine actually arrived, there is universal agreement that it leeched whatever charm and innocence, real or imagined, the canyon scene still possessed. Whereas pot and acid were seen as tools of enlightenment, encouraging collaboration and damping, as much as was possible, the egos raging beneath the tie-dye and buckskin, coke magnified and amplified the worst qualities of nearly everyone who became heavily involved with it.

"Cocaine ruined everything," says Pamela Des Barres, "because it made people who previously did not have big, egoical ideas about themselves become too self-involved. Of all the drugs, it makes you think you're undefeatable and more important than the next person—believe me, I did enough of it—and it's really false. The infiltration of that particular drug into the rock world, the peace-and-love world, really fucked with it." Says the Turtles' Mark Volman, "It was tearing down a friendship we'd had since high school." Pot and hallucinogenics had actually enhanced the band's interaction and creativity, he says. "But by the time cocaine came along, it really changed everything. It's venomous, poisonous. And what it did to the system of the music industry from the inside out—it really put musicians at the will of the drug. That was a bad period of time, and that whole Laurel Canyon feeling I don't think ever came back from it."

Henry Diltz, canyon photographer and countercultural true believer, says he escaped becoming a coke user except at parties, "when someone would walk up and hold a little spoon under your nose." A first-rate musician himself, Diltz was dismayed at the decline he witnessed among some of his subjects. "I remember one time showing a proof sheet to some singer–songwriter types, and in the meantime they snorted a lot of coke," he recalls. "They took my proof sheet and were sitting around with a blue pen trying to mark which ones they liked. And every frame in the proof sheet had so many marks you couldn't even see the pictures. They were like, '*This-is-good-no-this-is-good-well-not-that-one-well-then-this-one . . .*' I mean, the whole thing was covered with blue marker."

Cocaine made itself known at precisely the moment when the hazy existentialism that had guided the canyon scene was replaced by careerism underscored by the reality that the music being made was suddenly earning unprecedented sums. "Psychedelics disappeared in a way," says John Hartmann. "It took too much. If you took an acid trip, your day was gone. Acts couldn't do that anymore; well, maybe the Dead could." Cocaine's stimulating effect made it the perfect lash both in the recording studio, where marathon sessions were now the norm, and on the grueling months-long tours that bands were expected to endure.

Drug use was also the bona fide that the counterculture held most dear; your parents could conceivably grow their hair and dress like Bill Hickok or Calamity Jane, but never in a million years could you picture them dropping acid—or snorting a line of cocaine. Plus, as drugs went, coke was considered exotic and a touch glamorous. None of the grime associated with heroin or speed, which were at the time being tarred by establishment and hippie alike, clung to cocaine. Not to mention it was a *drug*, and everybody did drugs. "Cocaine came in on the same white horse that all the other drugs came in on," says Hartmann. "It was your *job* to do drugs if you were under thirty and against the war. When a new drug came along, you were supposed to check it out. So there was no stigma whatsoever attached."

And so L.A.'s peace-and-love generation found itself descending a slippery slope into a great fluffy pile of what is now recognized as one of the most viciously reinforcing psychotropics. "That's when the shit hit the fan," says Michael Des Barres. "That's when the peace and love goes right out the fucking window. Peace and love? You'd sell your mother."

Cocaine is an alkaloid found in the leaves of the *Erythroxylon coca* plant of South America. The Incas and other pre-Columbian societies knew about coca's psycho-stimulating effects and used it for medical, spiritual, and nutritional purposes. Chewing coca leaves killed hunger, increased stamina and concentration, and produced mild, enduring euphoria. Spanish conquistadores and the Catholic Church initially banned the natives from chewing coca but relented when they found it increased productivity in the gold and silver mines.

The Spanish brought coca back with them to Europe, where it was alternately vilified as a tool of the devil and celebrated extravagantly. Cocaine alkaloid was first extracted from coca leaves in 1859 by Albert Niemann, a Ph.D. student at the University of Göttingen in Germany. Thanks to Niemann's breakthrough, the psychoactive component of coca could now be consumed in a form vastly more concentrated, amplifying its euphoric and stimulant effects. By the late nineteenth century, cocaine was hailed as a cure-all and endorsed by everyone from Sigmund Freud, whose monograph *On Coca* extolled its palliative effects on concentration and libido, to Ulysses S. Grant and

Pope Leo XIII, partisans of a cocaine-laced wine called Vin Mariani.

Drug companies on both sides of the Atlantic wasted no time exploiting cocaine. Burroughs Wellcome sold cocaine tablets under the chilling brand Forced March, with straightforward instructions: "to be dissolved in the mouth every hour when undergoing continued mental strain or physical exertion." (The British explorer Ernest Shackleton's relentless drive across Antarctica was fueled by Forced March.) In the United States cocaine found its way into powders, elixirs, cough drops, even cigarettes. In the South, where free-floating malaise gripped the population during Reconstruction, "nerve" tonics containing cocaine flourished; especially popular was an extract of kola nut and coca leaf cooked up by an Atlanta chemist named John Pemberton, called Coca-Cola. At the extreme end of the spectrum, Parke-Davis marketed a combo pack containing cocaine and a fearsome-looking syringe. The company claimed cocaine could "supply the place of food, make the coward brave, the silent eloquent, and render the sufferer insensitive to pain." As subsequent events would prove, even this turned out to be an understatement.

Cocaine produces its characteristic high by blocking the brain's reabsorption of dopamine, a chemical messenger that regulates many bodily functions but is best known for its role in modulating sensations of desire and pleasure, from sex to the satiation that follows a good meal. Ingesting cocaine causes dopamine to swamp the pleasure centers of the brain, producing intense, all-consuming euphoria and exhilaration while leaving the user seemingly clear-minded and extremely voluble. The most banal topics—and people—become fascinating on a cocaine jag (inspiring Robin Williams's footnote to coke lore: "Yeah! Teflon!"). The cocaine high is short-lived—twenty to thirty minutes when snorted, even less when injected or smoked—but so fiendishly pleasurable that users are racked with desire to take more. "My senses were lit up like candles," recalled a young woman after snorting her first line. "The effects from the three beers I had drunk were gone completely. I LOVED IT." Recalled another, "In less than five minutes I was jumping all over the place it felt so good. When my high wore off, I begged and begged for some more. Cocaine changed my life forever."

Once cocaine's addictive qualities became evident in the early twentieth century, it fell from favor in mainstream America, then in thrall to the temperance movement. In the South, hideous racial fantasies of the "cocaine-crazed Negro" held that the drug fueled lustful black men to rape white women. Still, it was impossible to suppress a drug so reinforcing and widely available. Even after it had been officially classified an illegal narcotic, Jazz Age revelers would set the tables at fashionable dinner parties with cocaine-filled saltcellars. Cole Porter famously wrote that "some get a kick from cocaine" in an early version of "I Get a Kick Out of You," the opening number in the 1934 Broadway musical *Anything Goes.* (Porter supplied alternate lyrics, including "some like a whiff of Guerlain," when it was pointed out the song couldn't be played on the radio with the cocaine reference intact.)

That a putative highbrow like Porter would devote a quatrain to cocaine, as he might have rhymed it, seems mildly shocking in retrospect, but musicians, dope, and society, high and low, have a long history of co-dependence. The silent-film star Mabel Normand, a notorious cocaine addict, filmed her scenes while a jazz band wailed just out of camera range. Traveling "medicine" shows plied the United States from the turn of the century until the 1940s, presenting sketches, passion plays, and musical interludes. Before the Harrison Narcotics Act of 1914 criminalized their sale, cocaine, heroin, and morphine were primary ingredients in the nostrums hawked at the shows. (The medicine-show format was nominally the template for Lawrence Welk's television variety show, sponsored by—and liberally peppered with pitches for—the tonic Geritol "for iron-poor blood.") "The shows enabled those struggling to earn a living as musicians to find regular work and gave them a chance to travel," according to Harry Shapiro in *Waiting for the Man: The Story of Drugs and Popular Music*. And the musicians were as often as not acquainted with the primary ingredients in the nostrums hawked at the shows. Once they were made illegal, Shapiro noted, "drugs developed their own mystique which was embraced by the outlaw myth of the itinerant musician."

References to cocaine, marijuana, and other drugs were common in blues and jazz compositions before and after Porter's censored lyric. Victoria Spivey's "Dope Head Blues," recorded in 1927, enthused, "Just give me one more sniffle / Another sniffle of that dope / I'll catch a cow like a cowboy / Throw a bull without a rope." Chick Webb and His Orchestra, with Ella Fitzgerald, essayed "Wacky Dust": "So I don't know why it get you so high / Puttin' a buzz in your heart." Some of the cocaine songs sounded a cautionary note. Leadbelly's "Take a Whiff on Me," later covered by the Byrds, admonished, "Cocaine's for horses, not women or men / The doctor said it'd kill you, but he didn't say when." The prodigious subgenre of jazz songs with marijuana themes includes the forthrightly titled "Reefer Song" by Fats Waller and "Reefer Man" by Cab Calloway, who dabbled with opium in "Minnie the Moocher." By the late '40s, jazz musicians were increasingly turning to heroin, prompting Calloway to lament: "Some of my dearest friends have been trapped by this insidious habit, which has fastened upon them like a plague. Drugs have caused a disturbing number of good musicians to deteriorate into hopeless has-beens."

During the 1950s, cocaine and heroin were more associated with the underworld of jazz and black street culture, while marijuana and amphetamines found favor with country, folk, and the early rock-and-roll performers. When Henry Diltz first hit L.A. in 1962 as a banjo player and folksinger, he was swiftly enveloped in a cloud of marijuana smoke. Before moving to Laurel Canyon, Diltz lived at the Tropicana Motor Hotel on Santa Monica Boulevard, owned by the Dodger pitcher Sandy Koufax, a sort of home for wayward musicians where everyone from Warren Zevon to Blue Cheer booked extended stays. At Christmas, the musicians decorated trees in their rooms. As early as 1962, says Diltz, "*everyone* smoked grass. Literally, everyone. It hadn't made the cover of *Time* magazine yet. It was a secret thing. We'd go on the road and have a little toke, which was just a way of life."

At the moment that Diltz and his compatriots were defining the pharmacopoeia for L.A.'s folk-rock explosion, half a world away in Hamburg's Reeperbahn red-light district the Beatles were powering through eight-hour club dates with a little help from Preludin, or "Prellies," a German amphetamine. Amphetamines were first marketed in the '30s to relieve the symptoms of asthma, but once their stimulant properties were manifest, they were administered to treat everything from narcolepsy to morphine addiction. Like cocaine, amphetamines supercharge the body's parasympathetic nervous system and produce feelings of unlimited energy and omnipotence; unlike cocaine, a single dose can last for hours. When taken indiscriminately over extended periods, the result is rage, paranoia, and delusions of grandeur. (Adolf Hitler's increasingly erratic behavior toward the end of World War II was later attributed to daily injections of methamphetamine.) During World War II and the Korean conflict American soldiers were sent into battle with stocks of amphetamine to combat fatigue. The anti-narcolepsy drug Provigil is widely believed to have been dispensed to coalition forces in the most recent Iraq war, while the American pilots who bombed and mistakenly killed Canadian troops in Afghanistan in 2002 were taking Dexedrine "go" pills, which the Air Force still supplies to pilots.

Shapiro traces amphetamine's path to country music, and later to the rock demimonde in London and New York, to soldiers returning from Korea who took up long-distance truck-driving jobs on the new interstate highway system cranked on Benzedrine. When they could tear themselves from the wheel, they frequented honky-tonks and roadhouses, where they cross-pollinated the country and early rock-and-roll musicians with Benzedrine party favors. (German nightclub audiences would pitch Prellies at the bandstand while exhorting the young Beatles to *mach shau*—make a show; the Beatles were happy to oblige.)

More than Vespa scooters and Italian three-button suits, amphetamines defined the Mod movement in Swinging London of the mid-'60s. The house band for the Mods was the Who, whose "My Generation," with its sputtering rage and stuttering cadences, was a naked homage to the Mods' amphetamine-fueled posturing. "These little stuttering pilled-up Mods would come up to me," the Who's guitarist, Pete Townshend, later recalled, "and say: 'You-you-you gotta d-d-do *more*, Pete, b-b-because it's *right*, man.'" (The parallels between the Mod scene of the '60s and the rave scene of the '90s, which was fueled by MDMA, or Ecstasy, a form of amphetamine, are inescapable.) Meanwhile, in New York, amphetamine was coursing through the Andy Warhol–Velvet Underground cult of the hip, thanks

in large part to Dr. Robert Freymann, who from his Fifty-
seventh Street offices injected mixtures of vitamin B_{12} and
methedrine into virtually all comers with the right social cachet.
And on the West Coast, San Francisco's once hippie-resplendent
Haight-Ashbury was turning gray and desperate under its newly
popular street drugs, speed and heroin.

As the decade closed, things had got so out of hand that
an awareness campaign from within the counterculture was
launched. Influential L.A. artists such as Canned Heat, Buffalo
Springfield, and the Byrds contributed antidrug songs for an album; "Speed Kills" public service announcements, featuring
spokesmen like Frank Zappa, were aired on the hip West Coast
FM stations. The "Speed Kills" campaign was a stirring example of the counterculture taking care of its own, and it would be
among the last. If the campaign made a dent in hard-drug taking, it was brief. A blizzard of coke was about to fall on L.A.

Sally Stevens recalls a chilling moment in the early days of cocaine's conquest of Laurel Canyon. "I remember when we first
encountered coke coming in, when it started to be very popular," she says. "And somebody said—he was holding a gram—
'Whoever holds this stuff has got the power. *This* is power. It's
not money anymore—it's this.'" Stevens, revulsed by the memory, adds, "But he was right."

Why did cocaine dominate, especially to a degree that
eclipsed whatever considerable pleasures could be derived from
its consumption, when other hard drugs such as speed were
cheaper, more plentiful, and easier to transport and consume?
More to the point, why did LSD and pot, while not entirely dis-
appearing, become the second or third choice on the drug
menu? One answer was that as the canyon's musicians became

more successful, they wanted accoutrements to match their success that didn't overtly compromise their countercultural values. Cocaine was a perfect fit—expensive, illegal, and unencumbered by heroin's and speed's blackened image. "It was very much a social thing, a cachet, if you like, to have coke," says Stevens.

Here was a delicate balancing act. You could still fly your freak flag high but drive, as David Crosby did, a Mercedes-Benz 300SEL 6.3, one of the era's most exclusive sedans, whereas owning a Cadillac, icon of Establishment bloat and materialism, would have invited charges of selling out at a time when those were still fighting words. Credibility with the hip faction of the baby-boomer audience was not taken lightly. When Sonny and Cher turned up on one too many TV variety shows, they effectively cashiered their equity with the counterculture and perished as commercially viable recording artists. The Monkees' Peter Tork and Michael Nesmith, talented musicians and refugees of the Troubadour scene before becoming teenybop idols, desperately craved, to no avail, the respect accorded to the failed Monkee auditioner Stephen Stills. So newly rich rock stars treaded cautiously. They didn't buy mansions in the flats of Beverly Hills, home to Hollywood's gaudy, toupeed money from the '40s and '50s; they bought in Bel-Air, a woodsy retreat west of Beverly Hills with winding roads and dense stands of eucalyptus and California oak that was sort of an upscale Laurel Canyon and the destination for more and more of the canyonites as their records came in.

Cocaine in L.A. in the early '70s cost roughly $100 a gram, though the price dropped when purchased in volume, typically by the eighth of an ounce, or "eight-ball." Adjusted for inflation, a 1973-vintage gram of coke—which could keep a party of four moderate users more or less happily occupied for an evening—would cost about $500 today. For L.A.'s budding rock royalty, coke was conspicuous consumption as an exercise in meticulous countercultural circumspection, a choice safely within bounds but still a status marker among one's fellow millionaire singer-songwriters. For musicians who liked to project a fastidiously anti-status image, coke was a way of quietly announcing—and only to those in one's circle, since the cost of sharing with strangers, especially those of a lesser station, was so prohibitive as to be pointless—that one had arrived, not in the *Organization Man* sense of the word, but in the hippie-hophead worldview of Gram Parsons's gilded palace of sin.

As cocaine insinuated itself into L.A.'s early-'70s music scene, it radically changed the social contract in the canyon. "Laurel Canyon revolved around social relationships," says Volman. "Once the drug scene got stronger and more dangerous and people got more and more involved with that, the drugs were not social anymore. With marijuana, LSD, peyote, and mescaline, all of those things that were the center of the '60s, those were all drugs that were kind of shareable. The experience of the drugs was in the sharing. It's really different with cocaine. There was more risk involved, it was much more expensive, and it was not something that you shared. With coke, you bought it, cut it so you had twice as much, and then you shared the stuff that was cut, not the good stuff. What it did was make you a liar."

Even for those who didn't partake, coke could be cruelly divisive. Michael James Jackson was visiting a record producer at his Lookout Mountain A-frame when three of the canyon's signature music stars happened by. "They go over on the other side of the room and they're doing something, I'm not sure what," Jackson says, "and [the producer] comes across the room with this piece of paper and he unfolds the paper and inside is this mound of white powder. He says, 'Hey, you want some? It's coke.' I said, 'I don't know. I don't think it's my cup of tea.' He said, 'Just wet your finger and put it on your gums.' So I wet my finger and I put some stuff on it and I put it in my mouth and my whole mouth went numb. And I looked at him with this totally numb mouth and said: 'You want me to put this up my *nose*?' And suddenly I felt out of place, not cool enough, not hip enough, and I left. That was my first exposure to cocaine."

It wasn't much of a stretch to connect the influence of the new cocaine ethic to the demise of hippie-idyllic traditions like the Love Ins in Griffith Park, a sprawling wilderness in northeastern Los Angeles and home to the observatory made iconic to baby boomers the world over in *Rebel Without a Cause*. The Love Ins were semi-spontaneous gatherings of the countercultural tribes of Southern California in the vein of those in San Francisco's Golden Gate Park. "A Love In was just a Sunday afternoon when the word of mouth was, Everyone's going to meet there around noon," says Diltz. "Easter Sunday was always a Love In. Some musicians would bring instruments, sometimes there'd be organized music, but otherwise it was just hundreds of people meeting in the afternoon much as they would in the evening in a club. And they'd dress up really nice, wear tie-dye or beads, colorful clothes."

The quiescent atmosphere at the affairs was, according to Diltz, a direct reflection of the refreshments favored by the participants. "I think most of the people were on psychedelics. You'd just go there and smile at everybody and love everybody. I would go around and take pictures, and nobody ever said, 'Hey, what are you doing?' It was all totally lovely. Never an ugly moment." Says Hartmann: "The Love Ins were phenomenal, and they couldn't be done today. You want to know why? Because of LSD. LSD put everyone under thirty in a mellow mode. You couldn't put all those people together in peace and love today. There ain't enough people feeling that emotion."

Not everyone was blithely accepting of cocaine. Stevens recalls being pulled aside by Chris Jagger, Mick's younger brother, and being given "a big talking-to about cocaine," she says. "He said people were kidding themselves that this is a benign sort of drug and it's good for you and all that. He said it isn't, this is one of the worst things that's ever happened, and that Mick was concerned that Chris was getting into it and gave him a big lecture about it. But it really did take over; it was amazingly scary. People were staying up too long for no reason; they were getting themselves into situations that they would not get themselves into socially because there was coke attached to it. I would run into people that used to be friendly with me and I'd know they were high and they were acting bizarre, paranoid, and unfriendly. It just became a very nasty scene." Cocaine also fundamentally altered the canyon's sexual dynamic, already vastly skewed in favor of the men. "It was unusual to find a woman who was carrying coke," Stevens says. "The men always had the coke, and the women were following them around."

Among its many contradictions, cocaine caused people to talk like mad but made them preternaturally suspicious, validated one's success but encouraged acute parsimoniousness. Volman recognized a link between the rising fortunes of the canyonites and their increasing remoteness. "The more money made, the need for privacy in your mind becomes higher. If you're also using drugs, the need becomes even higher. You don't want anybody coming around, and if you're having drug problems, which a lot of people were, you didn't leave. So then the only people that came in were the people who sold you drugs, and then they left, and you just sort of stayed in your place. It just became that you wanted to have bigger fences up around you."

Canyonites pulling up the drawbridge but still wanting to score didn't have to look far to find well-stocked, and often armed, purveyors. "Laurel Canyon is where drug dealers had valet parking," says Michael Des Barres, who lived with Pamela on Lookout Mountain. "*Every* drug dealer was in Laurel Canyon." Now, in addition to the fragrant eucalyptus, "Laurel Canyon always sort of smelled like what they cut coke with," he says, "which smelled great." There were guns, satchels of cash, and persistent rumors, never realized, that an army of federal agents was about to storm the canyon and round up all the dealers en masse.

One canyonite recalled a visit to one of the manifold neighborhood coke dealers. "He had all the paraphernalia in this room about the size of a walk-in closet," he says. "He was very tidy about it: the three-beam scale, the filters, the big supersize Deering grinders. There's a little four-pane window, and the sun would set straight through it. We were packaging it—I'm talking about a pound and a half, two pounds. We'd do a line once in a while, not like we were big nose-monsters. Anyway, the sun comes down through the window and we look at the room and it's *filled* with, like, Tinker Bell fairy dust, crystals floating in the air, uniform, all the way through the room. It was amazing. And we're like, No wonder we haven't been doing any—we were just inhaling it as we put it in these bags."

Jimmy Wachtel, then a struggling designer of album covers, was sharing a Tudor castle off Hollywood Boulevard in the canyon when the coke blizzard struck. Dealers who had taken to dipping into their product—always a fatal development for their business prospects—started hanging out at the castle at all hours, eager for conversation and generous with their wares, which had positive consequences for Wachtel's work ethic. "I didn't buy it for a long time, because there was so many people dealing they'd just give me coke," he says. "I'd be airbrushing some album cover and these guys would be standing around, just handing it to me." Still, the parade of jaw-grinding cocaine entrepreneurs and their retinues could be wearing. One night the bass player of a prospering L.A. band, known to have a serious habit, was up in the castle's turret when he happened to blow his coke-ravaged nose. The resulting reverberations shook the house like a foghorn. "I swear it did not sound like it came from a human being," marvels Wachtel. "It was unbelievable."

By the mid-'70s, cocaine was integrated into the music business in L.A. at every level. Money for drug purchases was factored into recording budgets and tour logistics; an underperforming single could be magically resurrected by a bindle slipped to a DJ. As the money rolled in and the good times seemed unstoppable, any pretense of discretion went out the window. "Cocaine made a major impact on everything," says Stephanie Spring, who worked all over the record business in the '70s. "First of all, the money that was being made made everybody buy more cocaine. We wore spoons around our necks, had bumper stickers that said MY OTHER CAR IS UP MY NOSE." While working for one of L.A.'s most respected major labels, she says, "the guy who was the photographer for backstage was also a dealer, and in the morning I would call him and say, 'I need all the pictures from last night and an ounce.' And that was on a charge account on the photo session from the night before. My job in the morning was to set it up as grams and distribute it however it was needed. I remember one executive who bought money boxes for one of our larger artists, and in the money boxes was cocaine. It was all on account. We called it 'outboard equipment' when I managed recording sessions."

Roy's, a restaurant on the Sunset Strip popular with the mu-

The Byrds, circa 1966. Left to right: Chris Hillman (with guitar), Roger McGuinn, Gene Clark, David Crosby, and Michael Clarke. Princes of L.A.'s folk-rock movement, the Byrds were the first band with Laurel Canyon roots to hit it big. (michaelochsarchives.com)

The Buffalo Springfield, Redondo Beach, California, 1966. Left to right: Richie Furay, Dewey Martin, Bruce Palmer, Stephen Stills, and Neil Young. Henry Diltz, a folk musician soon to become one of rock's leading photographers, shot this picture after wandering into a Springfield rehearsal in Laurel Canyon. "My career [started] that day, and it was just because I walked down the hill and happened to bump into Stephen Stills." Such serendipitous encounters in the canyon during the '60s created large swaths of indelible popular culture. (Henry Diltz)

LEFT: Frank Zappa, 1971. BELOW: The Laurel Tavern, circa 1916. Home to silent-movie star Tom Mix and later to Zappa and his extended family, for four frenzied months in 1968 the "Log Cabin" was the musical epicenter of the canyon. (Henry Diltz and hollywoodphotographs.com)

The Turtles, 1969, amid canyon eucalyptus. Founding member Mark Volman's (second from left) neighbors included Joni Mitchell, Monkee Mickey Dolenz, composer Paul Williams, and Frank Zappa. Inveterate satirists and iconoclasts, Volman and Howard Kaylan (far right) would join Zappa's band the Mothers when the Turtles broke up. (Henry Diltz)

Joni Mitchell at her Laurel Canyon bungalow, 1970. After moving in with Mitchell, Graham Nash wrote "Our House," the ultimate hippie pastoral, about their life there "with two cats in the yard." (Henry Diltz)

Carl Franzoni (*left*) and Vito Paulekas with son Godot (*below*), 1966. Franzoni, a former salesman of breast pumps, and Paulekas, a sculptor, led a troupe of free-form dancers whose wild dress and coiffure defined the style template for L.A.'s emerging hippie-freak movement. (Henry Diltz)

Kim Fowley, 1966. One of L.A.'s early rock-and-roll entrepreneurs, Fowley managed the Runaways, launching pad for future stars Joan Jett and Lita Ford. "Laurel Canyon was kind of a refuge for people who were incapable of eyeball-to-eyeball hustling on Sunset Boulevard . . . If you took away their tumbleweeds and eucalyptus, they were fucking boring." (Henry Diltz)

Gary Burden, Cass Elliot, and Henry Diltz at Elliot's Laurel Canyon house, 1970. Doyenne of the canyon, Elliot social-engineered the first meeting of David Crosby, Stephen Stills, and Graham Nash. "She had that capacity to know what would be good for you even if you didn't," says Burden, an architect who designed album covers for Crosby, Stills & Nash, the Eagles, and other canyon stars after Elliot encouraged him to switch careers. (Henry Diltz)

Joni Mitchell, David Crosby, and Eric Clapton in Cass Elliot's backyard, 1968. "Whenever things weren't going right, we'd go over to Cass's house—she knew how crazy and fragile artists were," says Graham Nash. Said Elliot: "Music happens in my house, and that pleases me." (Henry Diltz)

Crosby, Stills, Nash & Young rehearse at Shady Oak, Laurel Canyon, for their historic Woodstock appearance, 1969. Left to right: Stephen Stills, Neil Young, Greg Reeves, Dallas Taylor, and Graham Nash. Stills took over the house from his friend Peter Tork, whom Stills recommended after his own failed audition to join the Monkees. (Henry Diltz)

Elliot Roberts, Neil Young, and Stephen Stills, 1970. In partnership with David Geffen, Roberts managed the cream of Laurel Canyon's singer-songwriters, including Crosby, Stills, Nash & Young and Joni Mitchell. Sharing the long hair and lifestyle proclivities of his charges, Roberts radically altered the balance of power between musicians and record labels. (Henry Diltz)

Troubadour owner Doug Weston in front of the club, 1972. A second home to the canyon singer-songwriters, the Troubadour launched the careers of everyone from Linda Ronstadt to Elton John and by the early '70s was the most important popular music venue in the world. (Henry Diltz)

J. D. Souther, John Hartmann, and Jackson Browne in period dress for the cover shoot of the Eagles' *Desperado*, 1972. Souther and Browne, former room-mates, personified the early-'70s canyon singer-songwriter aesthetic. The house "rock-and-roll" agent at William Morris in the mid-'60s, Hartmann co-founded L.A.'s Kaleidoscope, modeled on San Francisco's hippie ballrooms, and later managed Crosby, Stills & Nash. (Henry Diltz)

Crystal Brelsford, with Bart and Cindy Astor, 1971. Brelsford raised the orphaned children after their mother killed herself. Despite the canyon's hippie ethos, she says, "there was an underlying competitiveness that nobody talked about because it was peace and love and everyone was brothers and sisters." Brelsford married Warren Zevon in 1974. (Crystal Zevon Collection)

Marlowe Brien West, circa 1969. West was among the countless young Americans who drifted to L.A. in the '60s. He spent one of his first nights in L.A. in a cave across from the Zappa cabin and later served as one of the family's aides-de-camp. "I swear I saw fairies flying around Laurel Canyon, because everybody had wings." (Trullee)

Morgana Welch, 1972. Morgana was typical of the very young groupies who cruised the Sunset Strip in the early '70s and made the Rainbow Bar and Grill and the Continental Hyatt House (a.k.a. the "Riot House") their second homes. Though only sixteen, she was soon cavorting with Led Zeppelin. "There was a power in being able to provide fulfillment of fantasies of these men [who] were older than me." (Morgana Welch Collection)

Led Zeppelin and friends at Rodney Bingenheimer's English Disco, 1972. Along with the Rainbow Bar and Grill, Rodney's was the preferred boîte of British rock musicians visiting Los Angeles. Note Morgana Welch, center. (michaelochsarchives.com)

Rodney Bingenheimer, Led Zeppelin's Jimmy Page, and groupie legend Miss Pamela, Los Angeles, 1972. Bingenheimer, a genial scenester, was the conduit to the L.A. music scene for British musicians from David Bowie to Zeppelin. Miss Pamela was part of the extended family at Frank Zappa's Laurel Canyon cabin in the '60s, where her groupie clique the GTOs was founded. She later married one of her conquests, British glam musician Michael Des Barres. (michaelochsarchives.com)

Picture Day at the Canyon Country Store, 2003. Once a year, Laurel Canyon residents gather at the store for a ritualistic portrait to reaffirm their neighborhood vows. Throughout the '60s and '70s, the store was the scene of epic countercultural loitering and countless drug deals in the parking lot, "the lobby of the Laurel Canyon hotel," as Michael Des Barres describes it. (© 2006 Michael Jacobs / MJP)

sic industry, featured private rooms where one's cocaine stash could be consumed for dessert, provided anyone bothered with a first course. (Not that coke wasn't simply chopped up right on the table at certain restaurants. As Miles Davis told the waiters at the Black Rabbit Inn on Melrose: "Hey, man, if you find any coke on the table, leave it alone. It's mine.") "I bought my cocaine at Roy's," says Spring. "The food was great, not that we ever ate any of it. The liquor was great, Stolichnaya on the rocks, every flavor. If I got too loaded, I'd get in a limo to the Chateau Marmont, where I'd put it on my expense account."

Michael James Jackson, who didn't use, was in the middle of a job interview at A&M Records when he was offered a line. He politely declined. "One of the things I did at Elektra when I was working there was little promotional items," says Stevens. "And for Carly Simon's 'You're So Vain' I did little coke mirrors. Everybody gave mirrors. It was very socially acceptable." At Elektra's recording studio on Santa Monica Boulevard it was considered great sport to take one of the framed gold records hanging from the walls, lay it on the grand piano, spread a gram or so on the glass, and spin it until the coke arrayed itself in a giant spiral. Straws would be distributed and six or so hangers-on would snort until the spiral was gone. Scenes of gratuitous decadence like this were becoming depressingly common.

"It was *heavily* run on drugs," says Hartmann. "Everybody had a jones, and every manager had to keep track of that act's jones and work it so you didn't have dope dealers all over your dressing room. So somebody, usually on the crew, would be responsible and they would carry the drugs. Or the road manager might sell drugs to everybody. Or the truck driver. It was available and everyone knew it." Drug use was so prevalent that abstinence, or calls for it, seemed perverse. On a tour in 1973, Alice Cooper, by then a serious boozer but not a drug user, stunned his entourage when he called the tour manager over in the middle of a charter flight and demanded that he stop the road crew from using coke and pot.

Musicians who did use were beginning to show the strain. Says Spring: "I went on tour with someone in the South, and when we landed the artist had to be rolled out for the sound check on an Anvil case he was so wasted. We were told to get single rooms. When I checked out the next day I had a three-thousand-dollar hotel bill. They had charged an ounce of cocaine to my room." Likewise, the cocaine-fueled recording sessions were getting out of hand. At A&M, Jackson was forced to shut down an album by a prominent young producer and band because they had essentially stopped recording and were using the hundred-dollar-an-hour studio time doing blow. Inevitably, the music being made under cocaine conditions began to suffer. "Sometimes if you listen to the audio mixes back then, they have a screamy sound to them," says Stevens. "Some of the guys say they'll listen to the work they did in those days and they can't take it." The Troubadour's Paul Body noticed cocaine's influence in the demeanor of the musicians playing the club. "They were a little different, a little colder," he says, "and not likable."

High-profile deaths associated with cocaine were still a decade away, when combining coke with heroin in a single syringe—a "speedball"—became chic among the rock and young Hollywood cliques before claiming John Belushi in a bungalow at the Chateau Marmont (and River Phoenix years later at the Viper Room). But there were warning signs from the beginning that coke had consequences more severe than clogged sinuses. Paul McCartney's dalliance with cocaine in the mid-1960s lasted about a year. "At first it seemed OK, like anything that's new and stimulating," he recalled. "When you start working your way through it, you start thinking, 'Mmm, this is not so cool an idea,' especially when you start getting those terrible comedowns."

In the canyon, the lifestyle havoc abetted by cocaine was decimating personal relationships—Volman's marriage collapsed—but the singer-songwriter juggernaut plowed on with songs about peaceful, easy feelings and romantic succor, even as the songwriters stayed up till dawn with fifty-dollar bills shoved up their nostrils making desperate conversation. "Without mentioning names, I know artists who wrote the most beautiful love songs—songs that are still played at weddings—who couldn't tell you the first thing about love, who couldn't keep a relationship together if their life depended on it," says Spring. Jackson Browne performed a version of the bluesman Reverend Gary Davis's "Cocaine Blues," with lyrics amended with Glenn Frey that even in the snowy mid-'70s sounded a cautionary note: "I was talking to my doctor down at the hospital / He says, 'Son, it says here you're twenty-seven, But that's impossible / Cocaine, you look like you could be forty-five.'"

While managing Crosby, Stills & Nash, Hartmann saw first-hand how ugly things could get. "We were on a charter plane somewhere on tour and Stills had built up some kind of mucus mass because of all the cocaine he was ingesting. We were in a poker game and Stills keeps bumping me. And I'm going, 'Stephen, what?' I'm trying to hold my hand and I look over and he's gone—flipping and freaking and swallowing his tongue and his eyes roll back. I grab him because he's flopping around. I had my hand in his mouth, he's swallowing his tongue, and it was fucking insane. Everybody was totally freakin' and I'm riding this guy who's flipping like a fish out of water. And someone says: 'He's turning blue.' I didn't know what to do," Hartmann says. "Instinctively, I stood up and hit him as hard as I could in the chest. Mucus sprayed out of his mouth and nose, and as he inhaled, I realized I'd done the right thing, so I hit him again—Crosby says later, 'You loved that, didn't you?'—and he's breathing and he settles down. Now he's like sleeping in my arms, like a chick, and I look down at him and his eyes open and he looks at me and goes: 'Hey, man . . . what's happening?' I said, 'Stephen, you had some kind of attack, you weren't breathing, I hit you a couple of times, you're breathing, everything's cool.' 'Oh, okay, man.' And he just lay there in my arms for a while, and there are ten guys standing there looking at us like, *Ho-lee fucking shit*, what was that? And then he finally gets up, kind of brushes himself off, walks to the back of the plane, and disappears. I went into Crosby's little anteroom, and I said, 'What the *hell* was that?' And he told me that Stills had had that kind of attack before and almost died, almost bit his tongue off or something, which would have ruined his singing career."

Even allowing for the economies of scale of buying large lots, cocaine purchases were a relentless drain on even the flushest rocker's finances. Considering Crosby, Stills, Nash, and Young, Hartmann says, "If you look at those guys, the ones who are wealthy are Nash and Neil—and the ones who didn't do coke are Nash and Neil. [CSN] are never broke 'cause they can always go on the road, and there's always ongoing royalties. But Neil and Graham are *wealthy*, in my opinion, and Crosby and Stills still struggle to maintain their lifestyles, because they blew it. I'm not saying that everybody didn't do blow, but some guys did it as a vocation and some guys did it to play. Crosby and Stills took it to a serious life commitment, and then took it beyond health and reason."

At its peak of penetration in the rock industry, cocaine became a pseudo-currency, like cigarettes in prisons. Demand was high and a steady supply needed, and so the entrepreneurial instincts that had served the canyon's managers in making and marketing music were pressed into moving cocaine. "[They'd] buy and sell it, and then the people who were smart made a secondary living off it," says Volman. "And that secondary living wasn't just the money you made off the drug—it was the fact you were able to do the drug for free. The people I noticed who had it first were the people who had made more money than I did, namely some of the producers of records and managers of artists. It kind of seemed that they were the ones who felt, Well, if my artist is going to use it anyway, I might as well get it for them. It gets my needs covered, but at least I know where it's coming from; I'm getting them good stuff. It was sort of looked at as a way of protecting the artist: I'll buy it and I'll sell to them. I actually knew a manager who was transporting massive quantities of it who'd got into some financial trouble and was having people show up at his house wielding guns and threats."

Then there were the icy professionals who cared not at all about snorting cocaine themselves but saw instead a market with the potential to make them richer than the hapless denim-clad singer-songwriters hunched over mirrors in the canyon. "Once you get a drug like cocaine going, you've got the criminal element coming in and the big-money criminal element, too," says Stevens. One night she went to dinner with a cocaine dealer and his wife at a rooftop restaurant on Hollywood Boulevard. "Neither one of them was using cocaine," Stevens says. "They had a business plan: they would bring the raw material out [of South America]; he would then take it to supervise production of the cocaine. This was a one-man, one-woman operation." By the time Stevens joined them for dinner, the enterprise had been going for about year, and they had purchased a private island with the proceeds.

At the restaurant, the waiter approached the table. "The man was sitting there, and he said, 'Bring me the most expensive bottle of wine you have in this place,'" says Stevens. "And the waiter said, 'Well, sir, can you afford it?' He just opened his wallet and said, 'Do I look like I can afford it? Just bring me what you've got.'" The waiter, duly chastened, returned with a bottle of 1899 Château Lafite Rothschild. "It was a fifteen-hundred-dollar bottle of wine and we drank this—it was wonderful, trust me—and then he soaked the label off. They were making this coffee table for their island retreat which was all wine labels and all the bottles of wine were over a thousand bucks. It was all going to be inlaid in Perspex on this coffee table." As the Lafite was emptied, the dealer imparted to the table his secret to success. "He was telling us, 'You know what all these fools do, these cocaine guys? They get involved in their own product, and that's a sure way to lose money. You start using it, you're done for. I don't like the stuff and don't touch it, but I'll sure in heck take the money.'" Stevens was agog. "They retired, I heard," she says. "They did two years of this and did exactly what they said they were going to do. They quit. They were very smart."

Thirty years after the blizzard, Jackson Browne, ageless as ever with his Prince Valiant bangs, addressed the audience at a show on a national concert tour. Over the years, Browne's cover of Reverend Gary Davis's "Cocaine Blues"—like Eric Clapton's version of J. J. Cale's "Cocaine"—had been construed as a winking endorsement of the drug, even though the lyrics of both songs were far closer to indictments. (Browne didn't help matters by ending his version with loud snuffles and the sniggering ramble, "Gotta take either more of it or less of it, I can't figure out which one.") Now, as he introduced the song, Browne made it clear he'd had a change of heart. "You know, I didn't write this song, but I did make up some verses of the things that were said while we were writing it. So tonight I'd like to play an updated version." The audience recognized the song instantly, much the way Clapton, a recovered heroin addict and alcoholic, was greeted with football cheers when he hit the opening lick of Cale's "Cocaine." Then Browne started to sing, literally, a different tune: "Look at me now, sharp as a tack, except for a few billion brain cells I wouldn't mind having back." And, finally, "There was damage to the body, damage to the soul, damage to the quality of the rock and roll. Cocaine."

NINE

THE L.A. QUEENS

Rock and roll's ladies in waiting meet the young princes, orgies at the Riot House, catfights at the Rainbow, what it's like to be sixteen and savaged

When Morgana Welch's mother entertained at their house in the flats of Beverly Hills in the early 1970s, she would serve her daughter a cocktail before the guests arrived. "She used to encourage me to have a drink when I was like sixteen, seventeen," Morgana says. "My mother always thought I was better if I had a drink; otherwise, I'd just sit there pissed off." Morgana's mother and father no longer lived together, a circumstance hardly unique among her classmates at Beverly Hills High. Nor were her poker-straight honey blond hair and doe-eyed beauty, the genetic munificence bestowed by her fashion-model parents who pressed their daughter into the business as a preschooler. She posed for magazines, worked the runway at fashion shows, and shot a Toyota commercial before her agency dropped her when adolescence nudged her out of the adorable-child category.

There were hundreds of teenage girls like Morgana fidgeting around L.A. and Beverly Hills in the early '70s: white, stunningly attractive, overprivileged, and undersupervised, they

shrewdly exploited the social chaos kicked up by the sexual revolution and budding drug and rock-and-roll cultures while their
parents were otherwise preoccupied, as often as not with their
own lifestyle fandangos. They lost their virginity between Bill Blass
sheets on weekday afternoons in silent, over-air-conditioned faux-
Mediterranean manses, smoked Hawaiian primo from gurgling
four-foot-long bamboo bongs, chugged tanniny Châteauneuf-
du-Pape liberated from their parents' wine cellars, and generally
comported themselves in the fashion of rich kids since time
immemorial—the crucial difference being that they considered themselves confederates in the drug, rock-and-roll, and
antiwar countercultures, which colored their teenage alienation
with class consciousness. "My mother was into the whole Beverly Hills scene," says Morgana, "and I was very anti–Beverly
Hills."

In short, the "L.A. queens," as Robert Plant would soon
immortalize them after Led Zeppelin's first voyages to Los Angeles, were Southern California's answer to the debutante Mick
Jagger eviscerated in "19th Nervous Breakdown"—"your
mother who neglected you owes a million dollars tax"—blithely
decadent but still too young to drive the family Benz. "I didn't
really have a strict upbringing," says Morgana. "My mother was
single. She was dating very rich men. She was in the quote-
unquote jet set and flying off here and there, so I was pretty
much left alone."

Morgana's generation had been born five or so years too late
to participate in the first wave of rock-and-roll madness that
swept Hollywood and the Sunset Strip in the mid-1960s. Having watched from the sidelines as their older brothers and
sisters—and frequently enough, their parents—grew their hair,
burned their bras, and slept with whomever they pleased, they
longed for their own salad days to arrive and so decided, in ef-

fect, not to wait. In this endeavor they were, ironically, abetted
by their befuddled elders. Beverly Hills High engaged, at market
rates, Traffic, Three Dog Night, and other top-billing bands of
the day to play for the student population in the school gymna-
sium, sort of million-dollar sock hops. Then there was the
Teenage Fair, an annual battle of the bands held in the Hollywood Palladium's parking lot, where ninety or more groups
would play over the course of a week. An important staging
ground for L.A. rock in the '60s, the Teenage Fair had by 1969
gentrified with contempo flourish into the Pop Expo and
showcased the likes of Jimi Hendrix. And it was there that Morgana, like so many other bored, beautiful teenage girls from
Beverly Hills and beyond, got her first whiff of the rock-and-
roll pheromone.

"That was the place our appetites got whetted," Morgana
says. "I think Three Dog Night was one of the first bands we
ever came in contact with at the Teenage Fair, and one of them
went off with my girlfriend. So it was a place where young girls
could get their look at rock stars and rock stars could get their
look at young girls. That was my initiation into the potential for
being a groupie, that it was a viable path."

Before long—in fact, before she was seventeen—Morgana
and a shifting band of feral young women had abandoned their
sullen teenage lives in Beverly Hills and Brentwood and become
ladies in waiting to the rock-and-roll scene on the Strip and in
the canyon. Their timing at first seemed inauspicious. By 1971,
L.A.'s rock-and-roll arcadia was in decline. The Byrds were sputtering and Buffalo Springfield was gone, as were the Strip's
homegrown heroes, the Doors, silenced after Jim Morrison, fat,
alcoholic, and given to Mansonesque beards, expired in a Paris
bathtub while his long-suffering girlfriend, Pamela Courson,
slumbered in the adjoining chamber. Gone too were honorary

L.A. citizens Janis Joplin and Jimi Hendrix, Joplin from a hot
dose of heroin injected at Hollywood's Landmark Hotel hours
after she recorded the final vocal for "Buried Alive in the Blues,"
Hendrix in a ghastly, banal demise three months earlier, chok-
ing to death on his vomit after ingesting one too many sleeping
pills following several hard weeks in London.

"I caught the tail end of the Strip, where it was a carnival,
the streets were packed, and there were all kinds of things going
on," Morgana says. "It totally immersed me in another world. It
was only blocks away, and it was so vastly different. Then [the
police] kicked everybody off, and it moved down to Hollywood
Boulevard for a while and that didn't last. That's when the Hyatt
House started and Rainbow came along."

The Continental Hyatt House and the Rainbow Bar and
Grill, within blocks of each other on the north side of the Sunset Strip, constituted two stations of the cross of the Strip's resurrection in the early 1970s. As Sunset was overrun in the '60s
by longhairs flocking to the Whisky, Gazzari's, the Trip, the
London Fog, and the other rock-and-roll clubs, the owners of
the Strip's traditional nightclubs and restaurants—many of them
hoary leftovers from the '50s like Dean Martin's Dino's Lodge—
in concert with the Los Angeles County Sheriffs' Department,
launched an uninhibited campaign of harassment on the hippie
element suddenly clotting the sidewalks. "People were locking
their cars long before there was the dimmest awareness of the
Manson element because of the police," says Gail Zappa. "I
think our phones were tapped; the police followed us everywhere." One of the reasons freaks danced in large groups like
Vito's troupe, she says, "was that there was safety in numbers.
You think gay bashing was bad, you should have seen freak
bashing."

Most restaurants on the Strip refused to serve longhairs, and the few that did—notably Ben Frank's, a coffee shop mobbed nightly after the clubs closed at two—were under permanent surveillance by the sheriffs. "The waitresses were known to call the police in to clear out a table of customers, even if they were only suspected of something as innocuous as being the kind of people who might not leave a proper tip," recalled Michael Stuart-Ware, drummer in the seminal L.A. band Love, who was summarily escorted out one night. When a bandmate politely asked the police why, he was smacked on the keister and advised, "Keep walking hippie, they don't want you here." The unrelenting harassment led many to flee the Strip entirely for Canter's, a magnificently tacky Jewish deli a mile south on Fairfax Avenue, where a thriving after-hours scene continues to this day.

In the midst of this, Elmer Valentine and Mario Maglieri, former Chicago cops turned nightclub impresarios who ran the Whisky, were tapped to open a club where musicians and the emerging rock industry's freshly minted "executives" could drink and dine in peace. There would be no live music, just a menu of Italian delights, plus a cover charge convertible to two drinks. And so with backers that included the rock press agent Bob Gibson and Lou Adler, the Rainbow Bar and Grill was launched at 9015 Sunset Boulevard on April 16, 1972, and instantly became the Round Table of L.A.'s rock elite, packed nightly with locals and whatever touring bands, especially British, happened to be passing through town. Behind the Rainbow's ye-olde mock-Tudor facade was a dining room shaped like a horseshoe with a fireplace at one end and banquettes upholstered bordello red, supplemented by two bars and a snug upstairs dance floor. The dark, chockablock layout and mysterious twisting staircases gave the place the feel of a pirate's ship run aground in the middle of the Strip, and rock and rollers took to the atmosphere instinctively.

Meanwhile, several blocks to the east, where Sunset Boulevard bends against the back wall of Laurel Canyon, the Continental Hyatt House was undergoing a shift in clientele that
would make it the most famous hotel in a chain better known
for catering to weary Willy Lomans. As the post-Beatles rock-
and-roll bands from the Strip began touring regularly, they
found that hotels that would tolerate their long hair, aggressively
slovenly dress, and pitiful per diems were hard to come by, even
in cities as large as Los Angeles. Thus was born the rock-and-roll
hotel—the Gramercy Park in New York, the Ambassador East
in Chicago, and, in L.A., the Chateau Marmont, a moldering
Norman pile from the 1920s with a long history of unapologetic behavior.

But by the early '70s, the comparatively spry Hyatt House,
located just around the bend on Sunset, had eclipsed the Chateau as L.A.'s premier rock-and-roll hotel. Opened in 1956 as
Gene Autry's Continental, it was a dreary twelve-story box with
pressed-concrete balconies and a rooftop swimming pool, the
first high-rise on the Strip. By the time the Rainbow opened,
the Hyatt was overrun with touring bands whose excesses—
especially those of the irrepressible Led Zeppelin—had earned
it the sobriquet "Riot House."

The Riot House staff were famously indulgent of the many
bands that inflicted property damage before the limos arrived
in the porte cochere for the ride back to LAX. Led Zeppelin,
particularly the band's drummer, John Bonham, and road manager, Richard Cole, thrived on bombarding pedestrians with
water balloons, pitching furniture over the balconies, or encouraging groupies to hurl bottles of Dom at the billboards across
Sunset. Cole once had a motorcycle sent up the freight elevator
to the eleventh floor, which the band and entourage took over
in its entirety, and roared up and down the halls. "The Hyatt
House was one of those places that had a rather tolerant attitude

towards groups like us," recalled Neal Doughty, pianist of REO Speedwagon, a Midwestern road band that toured virtually nonstop throughout the '70s before hitting it big in the '80s. "One night we got crazy and threw a chair out the window. Ten seconds later we got a call from the desk. All they said was, 'Did you at least look first?'" The hotel was the setting for the birth of a classic song or two. Paul Stanley and Gene Simmons of Kiss, under pressure from Casablanca Records founder Neil Bogart to write an "anthem" for the band, composed the group's signature "Rock and Roll All Nite" at the Riot House. At some point, Little Richard checked in and never left, making the Riot House his home for years.

As the Strip shifted from its psychedelic and folk-rock roots of the '60s to the harsher rhythms of the '70s, a new breed of groupie arrived on the scene. Taking up stations on the Whisky–Rainbow–Riot House axis, Morgana and her friends were altogether different from Miss Pamela's GTOs. "They were definitely our inspiration," says Morgana, "but Miss Pamela just seemed so old to me. I just thought, Well, these are has-beens, we're the new thing here. We were hot. We had every reason to think: We're here, now." Younger—she was sixteen when she first started hanging out at the Rainbow—bolder, and less whimsical, Morgana and her friends were a logical outgrowth of rock's march from cottage industry to sleek international cash machine. Record sales, fueled by the boom in rock music, were increasing so rapidly that in 1976 the Recording Industry Association of America was compelled to create the platinum record award for sales of one million albums. (Given that L.A. bands were the engine driving the industry's expansion, it was fitting that the first album certified platinum was the Eagles' *Their Greatest Hits, 1971–1975*.)

The money pouring in from record sales and increasingly lucrative tours was redefining a caste that had scarcely existed five years before: the rock star. As the counterculture that launched contemporary rock shifted from innocence to arrogance, the bands themselves, some still trading on hippie ideals of collectivism and inclusion, began to behave very much like Nero on his way to the vomitorium. Suddenly concert promoters in provincial cities were hustling to fulfill contract riders that demanded premium cognacs, limousines for the entourage, and lavish backstage spreads of macrobiotic meals for twenty-five. Creedence Clearwater Revival, a band that wore its working-class bona fides on its sleeve, traveled by Learjet. It was nothing for Deep Purple's Ritchie Blackmore, dining in the Oak Room at the Plaza Hotel in New York, to hurl his baked potato across the restaurant and calmly go back to slicing his steak.

Bob Greene, then a "youth" columnist for the *Chicago Sun-Times* who traveled with the biggest bands of the '70s and witnessed the atavism firsthand, later dubbed them "gangs of princes." Comely young women were always part of the princely contract. Although women had bestowed their favors on traveling musicians from the troubadours to the Tommy Dorsey Orchestra, in the '70s the confluence of the sexual revolution and the unprecedented sums being earned by young men barely twenty-five years old fueled a burgeoning sense of entitlement only hinted at from the front of the house, especially when it came to the girls loitering behind the amps with cloth backstage passes pasted provocatively above swelling halter-topped breasts. These new groupies, as often as not barely out of adolescence, were aware of their complicity in the contract and, at least at first, welcomed it. "We loved the decadence," says Morgana. "It was kind of a dichotomy because we knew in some ways we were very innocent, and that's where the whole sex thing came in. Being very sexual and willing to experiment sexually, there was a power in being able to provide fulfillment of fantasies of these men in power that were older than me. Sex was used as a power play. And the more you had, the more you got."

Morgana's voyages to the Strip began when she still lived with her mother. "She was horrified," Morgana says. "I would leave and not come home for days. And then come back and get grounded and then sneak out and go back to the Strip. There was just no stopping me." It was probably inevitable that as her waking hours increasingly revolved around the Strip, she would take up residence where so many of her conquests lived and recreated. When Morgana finally moved out of Beverly Hills, she shared a house just off Laurel Canyon Boulevard in the canyon; her housemates were a secretary from the Whisky and the musicians Bill Lordan and Willie Weeks, an in-demand session bassist. "Each canyon had it own ambience," she says. "Laurel Canyon was that laid-back-peace-sign-let's-get-high-let's-be-friends atmosphere." But the canyon's proximity to the Strip tempered the granola-and-granny-glasses vibe. "There was something about Laurel Canyon that was more upscale," she recalls, as opposed to the frankly hippie Topanga Canyon, miles to the west near the ocean, where Neil Young had pitched his flag. "It wasn't quite as glamorous as Coldwater or Benedict. It was more . . . rock and roll. And I think that was the charm of it for those of us who hung out there."

When not hanging out in the canyon, Morgana could usually be found at the Whisky and Rainbow by night and the Riot House by day. "If a cash transaction were taking place, the Hyatt would be labeled a bordello," she recalled. "You meet the guys in the coffee shop and then you go to their rooms and have sex with them. It was very relaxed; the hotel would never kick you out. This is long before the word got around that the coffee shop was a happening place. We were there kind of post-GTOs and between where the whole groupie thing really exploded. We just happened to be very lucky with our timing."

One afternoon Morgana was in the Riot House lobby when a stranger approached and said he had a friend who wanted to meet her. Like many of L.A.'s second-generation groupies, Morgana had her sights set on the men of Led Zeppelin. Los Angeles had been a stronghold for the band since its first tours, and by 1972, after four hugely successful albums, their visits to L.A. were legendary for stunning concerts at the Forum and sheer depravity almost everywhere else. The band was savaged by the elite rock press for its bombast and Robert Plant's caterwauling vocals, but the little girls of L.A. understood. "That was the ultimate band to try to, uh, y'know, hang out with," Morgana says.

In fact, British touring musicians of all stripes were the preferred quarry of the L.A. queens. For wretched working-class Englishmen freed from the British class system, hitting L.A. as a budding rock star could be a life-changing event, made all the more wondrous by a welcoming committee of stunningly beautiful girls who proffered their goodwill and bodies with the barest of preliminaries. "America was epitomized to me by these girls," says Michael Des Barres, who arrived in L.A. from England in 1972. "The young girls represented to me the absolute change of being in America, which after my whole life of living in this archaic, sort of regimented country where I could have been speaking Latin, I come to America and the sandwiches are this thick and the girls are this thin. They were middle-class girls who made the decision to abandon themselves to the potency of rock and roll. And that's what I fell in love with, that sense of change and newness and existentialism." Says Morgana: "There was definitely a mutual thing happening. The California-Girl-blond-hair-suntan was very appealing to them; conversely, the

English-dark-hair-never-see-the-sunshine thing was very interesting to us."

No sooner had the stranger at the Riot House made his en-
treaties than Morgana beheld a vaguely familiar-looking young
man with a distinctive glyph dangling from his neck. He was
Zeppelin's bassist, John Paul Jones, and the glyph—three ovals
interlocking a circle—was a logo that Zeppelin's guitarist and
taskmaster Jimmy Page had insisted each member of the group
adopt in lieu of names on the band's fourth album, which featured the classic-rock warhorse "Stairway to Heaven." Morgana
says Jones took her hand, led her around a corner, gently pushed
her up against a wall, and kissed her. "He said, 'What can I do to
make you happy?'" Morgana recalls. That his offer was, according
to the princely contract, more suitably her line than his was not
lost on her. "That was what was so stunning; it was actually re-
versed. I was thinking: Well, everything's perfect right now, so
what more do I need?" Soon thereafter the couple retired to a
house in Beechwood Canyon, where Jones pulled out an acoustic
guitar and played "Stairway to Heaven" while Morgana, "in
groupie heaven," lay enraptured on the bed. "He immediately
took to me and I just thought it was the most fantastic thing," she
says. "I didn't have to do anything. He was very special." The
next morning Jones gave Morgana cab fare back to the Riot
House.

In the summer of 1972, Led Zeppelin returned to L.A., and
the groupies went on high alert. "There were more girls than
usual," Morgana recalled. "Zeppelin brings them out in droves."
Soon enough, she and a lissome blond friend, Tyla, were ensconced with the band at Rodney Bingenheimer's English
Disco, another boîte on the Strip favored by British rock and
rollers, ostensibly celebrating Bonham's twenty-fifth birthday.
The party was soon besieged by the club's sizable contingent of

"little girl groupies," as the sixteen-year-old Morgana character-ized the aspirants, of whom Lori Mattix and Sable Starr were most gratingly ascendant. "We didn't like them very much," Morgana says. "They were kind of new on the scene and prob-ably thirteen or fourteen years old. They were just very oppor-tunistic."

When a photographer approached the table to shoot the band in cozy repose with Morgana and Tyla—all the musicians, save Page, were married—Sable and Lori inserted themselves into the party just as the flash went off. What the camera cap-tured is perhaps the definitive portrait of life among the Strip's rock-and-roll demimonde, circa 1972: Morgana and Tyla sit in queenly self-possession between Plant and Bonham; Morgana has just taken a puff off her cigarette. Crammed into the side-lines, Mattix, looking every inch the Lolita, sits next to Bonham, who glares malevolently at the camera. Perched next to Plant, Sable shows an incautious amount of leg and smiles disingenu-ously while Plant seems to sneer at the intrusion—he may have been thinking about the impact the photo might have on his wife. (Attending a party at the home of a club owner years later, Morgana was surprised to see herself staring out from an enor-mous blowup of the photo hanging on the living room wall.)

After the photographer was chased out of the club, Morgana—dressed in Landlubber jeans belted with a leather whip—and Tyla took the dance floor and performed for the plea-sure of the band. They were soon joined by the interloping Sable and Lori, which culminated in Tyla "kicking the shit" out of Sable's leg and delivering a withering dressing-down in the ladies' room. "[Tyla] was with Robert and she wasn't going to let Sable bulldoze her way in," Morgana says. Such catfighting was becoming increasingly common as more and more girls descended on the Strip to sample the pleasures, real and imagined, of groupiedom. "The waitresses at the Whisky were famous for that," Morgana says. "They'd scope out the bands, and if any of the waitresses had their eye on one, it was pretty cut-throat. They'd get you bounced out of the club, spill drinks on you, humiliate you. It was very territorial. These guys were big prizes."

A few weeks later, Morgana and Tyla were nursing a cup of tea in the Riot House coffee shop when they heard that Plant was entertaining upstairs. "Robert fancied Tyla," Morgana re-called, "so we knew it would not be a problem getting into his room." There they found Plant and his protégé Roy Harper, an eccentric English folksinger and part of the Zeppelin entourage. (Morgana had previously bedded Harper, during which Bon-ham and a brace of roadies broke down the hotel-room door while she frantically tried to cover up with a bedsheet.) Now Plant repaired to an adjoining room with Harper; Tyla followed. After a few minutes, according to Morgana, a naked and hugely erect Plant reentered and asked her to join the others next door, where she beheld Tyla and Harper, naked, sitting on the bed. "They asked me if I wanted to hang out with them," Morgana recalled. "I thought about it for half a second."

As the decade wore on, Morgana racked up plenty of notches on her whip: Johnny Winter, Randy California, Alice Cooper. Her days were spent in preparation for her nights, her income from sketchy part-time jobs supplemented by gifts, endless free meals, and drinks provided by the men she partied and slept with, a blanket no-cover-charge policy at her regular haunts, and, she admits, "a rich, normal boyfriend on the side who helped me out." But the fizzy decadence that she and her girl-friends had helped define as the Strip shook off the earnestness of the '60s was fading fast. There was a sense that the new, ever younger girls were lowering the level of discourse by sheer callowness. "I was very serious, very into 'You'd better take me seriously and not just as some bimbo,'" Morgana says. "My friends and I would try to have some depth about us. It wasn't just giggles and getting laid."

The rock-and-roll business was booming ever larger—1976 and 1977 would see the release of *Frampton Comes Alive!* and Fleetwood Mac's *Rumours*, unprecedented successes from formerly obscure British journeymen that sold in the tens of millions. Meanwhile, the disco craze about to burst out of New York's gay and fashion subcultures was poised to shovel ever more gigantic sums into the record company coffers. Los Angeles was by then the undisputed epicenter of the record industry, with the finest recording facilities, the best engineers and producers, and a critical mass of the world's most influential popular musicians, many of them Morgana's neighbors in Laurel Canyon. And as the record business went, so went L.A. Cocaine was suddenly everywhere. A separate and craven caste of groupie, the "coke whore" who would blandish sexual favors on any Jack or Jimmy who was holding, no matter how repellent—treat him, in other words, like a groupie treated a rock star—further devalued the scene's mystique.

By then, Morgana admits, "I was getting very disillusioned with the whole thing. It had gone from being innocent and playful, from people getting together to share common interests and fun and kind of connecting with the world. It became more and more dangerous. Big money was involved, big drug deals were going down, rather than people just exchanging a joint." Morgana herself scored pot in the parking lot of the Canyon Store and sold amphetamines to friends (she kept the Quaaludes) prescribed by corrupt Hollywood and Beverly Hills physicians in whose waiting rooms one would bump into all the regulars from the Rainbow. The new harshness of the scene was wearing. "It became people toting guns and having large quantities of money from the big drug deals," she says. "And people started dying."

One night, hitchhiking to the Strip, she was picked up by a man who drove her up into the hills and put a knife to her throat. "Somehow I talked myself out of that one, because he was ready to just slit my throat." Accepting an invitation from a man at the Riot House to travel to Las Vegas, she was mistaken for a prostitute by the vice cops when she used a house phone at the MGM Grand and was locked up in the county jail overnight. "The next day I got bailed out by this black guy who I'd never seen in my life who declared I was his now and that I was going to work the Strip for him." The pimp took her coat and money and left her under the guard of a subordinate for two days until her hysterical crying freaked him out sufficiently to abandon his post, and she made her escape back to L.A. She was seventeen. "You had to be tough to a certain degree," she says, "and I just got tired of having to put on the tough air just for self-protection."

Then, just when the record industry and the Strip seemed ready to test the absolute limits of decadence, the punk movement exploded onto the scene and seized the pop-cultural high ground. The Sex Pistols' 1977 album, *Never Mind the Bollocks Here's the Sex Pistols*, was a blistering repudiation of everything a rich, bloated band like Led Zeppelin—and with it, the Riot House–Rainbow scene—represented. Punk was an indictment of the entire rock-star ethos, which had, so the party line went, taken rock down a ruinous path; the punks, by returning rock to its dumbest, rawest essentials, were taking it back. Led Zeppelin never entirely recovered from punk. Though their catalog continued to sell and "Stairway to Heaven" year after year topped the most-requested-songs list, their post-punk albums, while competent and hugely lucrative, never approached the impact of their earlier work, and the band was finished as a modern cultural force. In 1980, Bonham, who personified the band's excesses, choked to death while sleeping after bingeing on vodka over the course of a band rehearsal and party.

The party was changing on the Strip as well. Rodney's English Disco had closed, and by 1979 the Whisky was booking a heavy rotation of seminal L.A. punk bands like X, the Germs, and Black Flag. The violence that accompanied the shows, culminating in a full-scale riot at a 1979 Black Flag concert at the Whisky, so dispirited Mario Maglieri and Elmer Valentine that they closed the club for two years.

Morgana, meanwhile, had married a singer from an L.A. band in 1976 and given birth to a daughter, effectively ending her groupie days. In any event, she says, "the whole rock-and-roll thing was almost at an end. Once punk came in, the lifestyle was very much changed." She and her husband divorced in 1981, and she briefly flirted with returning to the groupie circuit, but the bands had all changed and the scene was no longer hers to own. "I tried to pick it back up, but it was too difficult as a single mom to live that lifestyle. It's geared to if you have no responsibilities and can just party all night, and when you have a kid, that just isn't working anymore." She moved in and out of L.A., and today lives in northern Arizona, where she works as a Web-page designer and consultant.

On a cool evening in the spring of 2004, Morgana returned to the bordello red banquettes at the Rainbow for the first time in eighteen years, having organized a reunion of her cohorts from the '70s. It was a typical Saturday night at the Rainbow, which is to say it was mobbed with leather jackets and miniskirts and jaw-dropping décolletage. On the front patio, the enticing aroma of garlic mixed with cigarette smoke and impertinent perfume and the roar of motorcycles pulling in off the Strip. Mario Maglieri, white-haired and pushing eighty, watched over the scene in shirtsleeves as his fearsome-looking doormen collected the ten-dollar cover and dispensed rainbow-imprinted drink chits with the solicitousness of ticket takers at Disneyland. That's how it's always been at the Rainbow, and part of what has allowed the place to weather every trend since 1972 and seduce successive generations with veal parmigiana and the promise of being treated like stars as they come to the Strip to remake rock and roll in their own image.

Down the street, the Riot House is now the Hyatt West Hollywood, fresh from a multimillion-dollar renovation seemingly designed to hoover every last flake of cocaine, real and metaphorical, from the carpets. Still, most every night a rock-and-roll tour bus is parked out front, the hotel offers a special "band rate" for booking ten or more rooms, and the management in the '90s took the heartening step of designating the Zeppelin-defiled eleventh floor a sort of rock-and-roll shrine, outfitting the rooms with stereo equipment. It's been a while since the front desk has seen a plummeting television explode on Sunset Boulevard, but the millennium is young.

At the Rainbow, Morgana and her friends were shown to a corner banquette on the left side of the dining room's horseshoe, where she and Led Zeppelin had barricaded themselves behind bottles of Watneys and Chianti so many nights thirty years ago. Of that time and the life she led, Morgana says, "You know, there was a lot of hurt, there was a lot of vulgarity, and there were often wives or girlfriends who would chase you off, and the guys themselves would be rather crass at times. It was kind of like Babylon, and then it just kind of crashed and turned into something very different. But there was something about the lifestyle, the charisma, and it still lingers in me. It happened to capture me at an early age and it never left.

"There's no way," Morgana says, "I could do it now. But I'm so glad I did it when I was young. I wouldn't have changed a thing."

TEN

ALL THE YOUNG DUDES

★

Glam comes to the canyon, "Love 'em and Lear 'em," the Starship *is waiting, the lessons of Johnny Rotten, sex and drugs and rock and roll—a reappraisal*

Just when L.A.'s singer-songwriters and country-rock cowpokes looked as if they had a lock on Sin City in the '70s, Los Angeles and the canyon were rattled by one of those rude imports that England likes to lob at the former colonies to remind them the sun hasn't entirely set on the empire. It had been roughly ten years since the British Invasion taught L.A.'s feckless folkies and surfin' safarians how to be rock-and-roll stars; now the Brits meant to set the agenda again, this time with a superfabulous confection known as glam. Glam was rock and roll that raged with style and the slimmest soupçon of substance, the inevitable product of a rock-and-roll culture in England then suffering from a surfeit of drugs and boredom. Whereas the Eagles and Brownes and Mitchells and Kings were at that moment writing deadly earnest introspections about relationships or, in the case of the Eagles, the mythos of the American Southwest as seen from Sunset Boulevard and Laurel Canyon, English glam bands like the Sweet, T. Rex, Slade, Mott the Hoople, and Gary Glitter were singing about . . . well, it was hard to tell sometimes. T. Rex's Marc Bolan, exemplar of glam, appended these lyrics to "Bang a Gong," the group's signature song and, in America, its only real hit: "You're an untamed youth / That's the truth / With your cloak full of eagles / You're dirty sweet and you're my girl."

Glam performers gave off fuzzy sexual vibes—even though most were avowed heterosexuals—a bit of theater baffling to American rock and rollers and frightening to large swaths of the country. "I mean, nobody had seen anybody like us in Mobile, Alabama, in 1972," says Michael Des Barres, who moved to L.A. from London with his glam band, Silverhead. "I'm in a yellow dress and blue cloche hat, and these rednecks want to fuck me or kill me, they didn't know which."

Glam per se was never as big in the United States as it was in Britain, where sexual ambiguity in pop-cultural icons was and remains far less threatening. But it had a profound effect on the New York and L.A. music scenes. Glam legitimized L.A.'s Alice Cooper, whose dabbling in eye makeup and rock-as-theater heretofore had garnered only crumbs—by 1973 the band was selling out arenas with Alice appearing onstage in ripped leotards while the Trans Am–driving youth of Omaha and Indianapolis roared in full-throated approval. In New York City, Lou Reed, late of the Velvet Underground and Andy Warhol's Factory scene, began appearing in mascara, bondage leathers, and chromium dog collars and soon had his first bona fide hit with "Walk on the Wild Side," a roll call of the Max's Kansas City back room. Then there was David Bowie, who had started as a sort of pansexual folksinger, emulating Dylan, but soon appeared in drag so extreme that it made Cooper and Reed look like Pittsburgh Steelers. He famously turned himself into a character/caricature, Ziggy Stardust, with his band the

Spiders from Mars. Almost alone in the glam movement, Bowie had style *and* substance, as well as an unfailing sense of the moment. When he had wrung every last drop of glitter-flecked sweat from glam, he hung up his platform boots and remade himself into an uptown R&B crooner just in time for disco.

Glam was a hit in New York—the outrageously femme New York Dolls would have been impossible without it—but it was an even bigger hit in L.A. Drugged-out rock and rollers flaunting six-inch platforms, roosterish haircuts, and women's clothes somehow seemed right at home in Hollywood, where glamour has always been smudged with decadence. Glam didn't supplant L.A.'s singer-songwriters, who were then consolidating their market domination, or the established blues-rock giants like Led Zeppelin, but its gender-bending and celebration of the glib and glamorous were in some ways more in sync with the times than Linda Ronstadt. "A lot of it was just that, the superficiality of it," says Des Barres, "and Silverhead was way more interested in the superficiality of rock and roll."

America was at the moment in the throes of an energy crisis, a crippling recession, and Richard Nixon's wrenching, slow-motion self-destruction. Bad times have historically encouraged the creation of irresistible cultural froth; glam provided the same escapism as Nick and Nora movies had during the Depression. Glam also brought to the mainstream camp attitudes and accoutrements previously the province of gay culture, and it had the palliative effect of rejuvenating rock and roll while prefiguring the truly revolutionary punk movement that would follow close on its heels.

Glam was a signal event in the lives of many musicians then growing up in L.A. A young misfit named Frank Ferrana, at the time being raised in transience at the Sunset Towers apartment building on the Strip, was obsessed with the Sweet's vocalist,

Brian Connolly, and why, among other matters, Connolly had "bangs that curled under." Ferrana would soon change his name to Nikki Sixx and found Mötley Crüe, which at the dawn of the '80s led a brace of L.A. "hair" bands who took glam's lace-and-mascara costumes and coiffure and wed them to meat-and-potatoes rock and roll, reviving the Sunset Strip after punk imploded and selling millions of records.

Ground zero for L.A. glam was Rodney Bingenheimer's English Disco. A gnomish scenester from Mountain View, California, Bingenheimer had served as a genial aide-de-camp to Sonny and Cher and as Davy Jones's stand-in on *The Monkees* before working for several L.A. record labels. He hauled the then-unknown Bowie around to L.A. radio stations in his pre-Ziggy days and, after sampling the glam scene in London with him, opened the English Disco at 7561 Sunset in 1972. (It was briefly located next to the Chateau Marmont in what is now the Bar Marmont.) For two years the tiny club vied with the Rainbow Bar and Grill as the main watering hole for British bands, glam or not, as well as for a delirious cross section of L.A. musicians and camp followers—from Shaun Cassidy to Alice Cooper to Iggy Pop—along with neo-celebrities like Mackenzie Phillips, daughter of the Mamas and the Papas' John Phillips, then in her wild-child phase. (Silverhead's second album, *16 and Savaged*, was inspired by the ferocious, extremely young groupie scene at the club.)

Glam would barely outlast Rodney's, which closed in 1974. In the meantime, Laurel Canyon lost any semblance of being a latter-day Bloomsbury as the first wave of musicians moved out and the drug dealers moved in. The mystique from the Joni-CSN–Byrds collective played on in a sort of plaintive counterpoint as the canyon began to morph into an altogether harder and more cynical place. "Laurel Canyon" was now fixed in pop-cultural amber along with "Haight-Ashbury" and "Woodstock" as one of the ciphers of the '60s; questioning the myth was, at this juncture, out of the question. Nevertheless, what the canyon had been and what it was in fact becoming were increasingly at odds. In the post-Manson, pre-punk days, sheer hedonism began to overtake the hippie ethos that had shaped the canyon since the mid-'60s. "Now I've drunk a lot of wine and I'm feeling fine," Mott the Hoople's Ian Hunter sneered in the Bowie-penned 1972 smash "All the Young Dudes," which served as glam's unofficial manifesto and, for many in the canyon, a lifestyle mission statement. The canyon in the '70s more closely resembled a Dionysian playground with no compensating world-view beyond having a really, really good time. Of course, it couldn't—and didn't—last. Forces darker than anyone could imagine were gathering that, some would later claim in righteous retrospection, punished the revelers for their hubris. But for the moment it was fun, fun, fun of a sort Brian Wilson could have scarcely imagined when he cruised the streets of Hawthorne in 1963. And pulsing at all times behind the merriment was the exuberant rock and roll of the '70s.

Mark Belack (not his real name) lived in a cottage on Weepah Way, one of the precarious trails threading the Kirkwood Bowl. It is axiomatic that the canyon's every byway must have storied residents past and present, and Weepah was no exception. Belack's neighbors included Keith Carradine; John Paul Getty III; Patrick Reynolds, heir to the Reynolds tobacco fortune; and Susan Tyrrell, riding high on her best-supporting-actress Academy Award nomination for 1972's *Fat City*. Belack worked at the radio station KHJ, but the cost of living in the canyon was such that he and his roommate, a boyhood friend from Northridge, could afford to drive an Alfa Romeo Veloce Spider and a Porsche 911, respectively. "Our rent was nothing," Belack says. "Our landlady loved us, just loved us, so all of our money went into partying and nice clothes and nice cars."

The house itself was modest but touched, like so many structures in the canyon, with infamy—Bill Eppridge, who took the iconographic photo of Robert Kennedy sprawled on the kitchen floor of the Ambassador Hotel, was the previous tenant. The house also had the block's only swimming pool. "It was almost like a commune," Belack says. "You couldn't help not get to know just about everybody because it's like living in a hallway. Your neighbor's right there on your fence: 'Can I come over and go swimming? Who's at the Whisky? What passes did you get for tonight?' This doesn't happen in a suburban neighborhood. Laurel Canyon was special, it was rockin', it was fun. It was like: step outside your door, there's a party. Many of the people were in the music industry. Nobody had a job, like, at Macy's. Everybody was interesting, everybody was a bit of an artist no matter what, a bit bohemian and unusual."

One afternoon, in a flash of LSD-induced inspiration, it was decided that flooding Weepah Way would be an amusing diversion. "I think I started it," Belack says. "I was washing my car." Hoses were led to the steeply pitched street—a concrete drainage channel ran down the middle—followed by Belack, Reynolds, Tyrrell, and Getty careening downslope on inner tubes. "We did it over and over again," Belack recalls. And what did the neighbors say? "We *were* the neighbors."

The summers of '72 and '73 were glorious times to be young and living in Los Angeles. The Rolling Stones and Led Zeppelin were at their creative peaks and performed some of their best concerts ever at the Forum. Rodney's was in full swing. Sex was in the air, cocaine was everywhere—neither had yet been re-branded scourges. It was tequila sunrises and sunsets, hot days and warm nights, creamy thighs, bottoms, and breasts turned cocoa brown from languorous weekends at Nicholas Canyon Beach north of Malibu. (Appropriately enough, in

1972 "fuck" appeared for the first time in the *Oxford English Dictionary*.)

"The early '70s was a period of time that you could meet somebody, and you could go out and have lunch with them, and if you could make each other laugh enough by the end of lunch, you'd say, 'You want to take another hour and check into a motel?'" says Michael James Jackson. "First of all, we were young, and secondly we weren't paying much attention—my generation, I think, wasn't paying much attention—to what the rules were. And those of us in the music industry felt like we were dealing with one of the most powerful currencies that was going on. There was the smell of a lot of money around, which was very intoxicating. People were able to give themselves permission to act in certain ways and pursue certain things." Laurel Canyon, clotted with musicians, record producers, and dope dealers, was the epicenter of it all. "How does it feel to be one of the beautiful people?" John Lennon queried, in a different context, some years before. The answer was: It felt great. "There were actors, models, everybody was really good-looking," Belack recalls. "I must say there weren't any ugly people in Laurel Canyon. There really weren't."

A typical day for Belack during those summers began by ceremonially injecting a watermelon with vodka and dumping it in the pool so that it would cool by the time he and his roommate returned from work. (In winter, firewood was available from a cord in front of David Carradine's house. "He was never there, ever, but there was always a fresh stack of firewood," Belack says. "We'd fill our arms and go, 'Thank you, Grasshopper.'") The boys made ready for the night by first playing a favored musical selection. "We'd start off by listening to 'Low Spark of High-Heeled Boys,'" he says. "We primped as much as the girls." The primary fashion accoutrement was platform shoes. "That cracks me up because everybody walked all over the canyon back then—the heels on those shoes were like *that*—and if you got all the way home and forgot to get cigarettes, you'd go, fuck it, and walk down to the Canyon Store in them."

Soon the evening's guests would arrive. "The girls would drive in from the Valley or Hollywood. All the girlfriends we had were total rockers: the leopard skin, the lipstick, the giant Rod Stewart hairdos. They were always dressed to the tens." As for the attraction, Belack says, "We were young, had a pool to sit around, and lived in Laurel Canyon. We were getting free passes to the clubs. And because the labels were sending the jocks at KHJ stacks and stacks of please-play-me records, promo things with a hole punched in them, we had albums that weren't in the stores yet, so we could call the girls and say, 'Guess what we've got?'"

After the obligatory joints and cocktails, the entourage adjourned to the Strip. "We'd all pile into one or two cars so we wouldn't have as much hassle parking on Sunset," Belack says. From there it was on to Rodney's, whose proprietor, in a fit of generosity, had befriended Belack and his roommate, an endorsement that served to swell the ranks and toothsomeness of their lady friends. "Plus, we liked to dance, and not a lot of guys would, and all the girls wanted to dance. So we were really popular." One night, preparatory to hitting the Rainbow's tiny upstairs dance floor, they rigged the soles of their platforms with gun caps to facilitate satisfying explosions—Chess King–clad flamencos on the Sunset Strip. "It was a big hit," Belack says. "Everybody started doing it. For a couple of months you couldn't buy caps anywhere in town."

In addition to the vodka-infused watermelon, the beer and sangria, the occasional tab of acid, there was cocaine. "A *lot* of cocaine," Belack clarifies. "It was so available, and everybody had it. Everybody had a little spoon around their neck with the little spread wings, the angel of cocaine or whoever she was. Then of course everybody had the little amber vial with the black lid and a little chain on top so you could do a one-handed bump." Demand having a way of outstripping supply, bulk coke purchases were favored. "First of all, you wouldn't buy a gram," Belack says. "You'd buy an eight-ball. You'd go in on it with your friends." In the rare event one couldn't score, "you could always go to the Canyon Store and just stand in the parking lot for a while, say to somebody: 'Hey, I'm looking for some blow, you know anybody?' But nobody had to do that. It was just rampant; it was everywhere."

Still, as Belack points out, "this *was* Laurel Canyon. If we were out in Reseda it would be different. It was all about getting high and it was cool. Somehow, we all managed to keep our jobs."

By the mid-'70s, the sheer surfeit served up by the record industry seemed as if it would never end. The hits just kept on coming for Laurel Canyon's alumni. Carole King's *Tapestry* kicked off the decade by rocketing to No. 1 and forging the template for the enormous L.A. singer-songwriter albums to follow. Joni Mitchell's *Court and Spark*, released in 1974, would become her most successful record, reaching No. 2. Jackson Browne racked up three gold albums in the '70s before hitting *The Pretender* out of the park in 1976. The same year the Eagles, with a fistful of Top 10 hits under their belt and despite losing founding member Bernie Leadon (replaced by Joe Walsh), released *Hotel California*, which stayed at No. 1 for eight weeks and produced two No. 1 hits. Troubadour sweetheart Linda Ronstadt hit No. 1 with 1974's *Heart Like a Wheel*. The L.A. scene's

gold dust was such that it clung even to nonnatives. America, a
folk-rock trio made up of the sons of U.S. Air Force officers sta-
tioned in England, scored a string of Top 10 hits throughout the
mid-'70s with a sound strongly reminiscent of Crosby, Stills &
Nash. Fleetwood Mac was a sputtering British former blues
band before adding Lindsay Buckingham and Stevie Nicks, an
L.A.-based singer-songwriter duo. The band, reconstituted with
a sleek L.A. sound, sold 4.5 million copies of 1975's *Fleetwood
Mac* before unleashing 1977's *Rumours*, which was No. 1 for seven
months, sold nineteen million copies, and remains the sixth-
bestselling album ever recorded. These were numbers unimaginable even by Beatles standards, and they utterly changed the
record industry, reshaping the priorities of the labels and the
expectations of the talent—and, inevitably, the tenor of life in
the canyon.

"When the money came in, it was like it was pouring out a
slot machine—there was this tidal wave of success," says Jackson.
"The concert world became gigantic, the merchandise world
became gigantic. Just the enormity of putting out a record and
it selling five million units in those days was beyond anyone's
comprehension. The amount of dollars generated was just overwhelming and changed both the mentality of people in charge
of the labels as well as completely changing their focus." Before
the singer-songwriter explosion, the L.A. record business hadn't
quite jettisoned its ad hoc, hand-sewn past. "The business was
finding its way," says Colman Andrews. "I don't think at the
outset of the '70s that very many people really saw the financial
potential of the record business." The industry was still in the
hands of executives like Warner Bros.' beloved Mo Ostin and
Atlantic Records co-founder Ahmet Ertegun, men who loved
music and musicians. "They operated in a way good record producers and film directors operate, on a certain conceit," Jackson

says. "And the conceit is: if it moves me, it's gonna move you. There was a lot of serendipity involved. It wasn't until '73 and '74, when the people in charge of the labels started seeing so many millions of dollars coming in, [that] they became more focused on the dollars than being driven by their passion for the music."

While Jackson was at A&M Records, a distinguished independent L.A. label co-founded by the trumpeter Herb Alpert— it would reap a fortune in the '70s with Peter Frampton's *Frampton Comes Alive!*—he lobbied A&M's chief, Jerry Moss, to launch a spoken-word label that would document the works of people like Buckminster Fuller. It was a quixotic proposition, as Jackson well knew, but he felt compelled to push for it anyway. "I said, 'Y'know, Jerry, we're the gatekeepers,'" Jackson recalls. "'The public only gets to choose from what you decide they're gonna get. And all this other stuff, they don't even know it exists if we filter out too much. I was just thinking, we have a social responsibility to offer—'" Jackson says Moss cut him off. "He looked at me and said, 'I have no social responsibility. I'm here to make money.'"

While A&M and the rest of the music industry made money as never before, the tempo of the business and culture was accelerating, the audience fragmenting. By 1976 glam had come and gone. Disco and punk, miles apart aesthetically and in every other way, emerged simultaneously and further balkanized record business demographics. It was left to L.A.'s massively popular singer-songwriters to hold the center. By now their folk- and rock-influenced hybrid, born out of Troubadour Hoot nights and canyon jam sessions, had become the era's de facto pop music, as likely to be heard on Top 40 hit parades as on the FM rock stations that it had spawned. The popularity of the music made it a certainty that the newly flush record labels would try to score with something similar. Says Jackson, "Carole King would immediately be followed by a number of female piano-playing singers. James Taylor would show up with a guitar, and suddenly you'd have a bunch of solo guitarists." Thanks to this pandering, the originality and sheer quality of the music, which had led to its unprecedented success, would now serve, perversely, to suffocate it.

The cosseting of talent, which had started out at the beginning of the folk-rock days as naive generational hero worship, was now codified into the business plan. "We were all there—the agent, the manager, the producer, the engineer, the record label—to serve the artist, because the talent was where the money was," says Jackson. In those days there was an unspoken rule at most labels that an act had three albums to prove themselves. Today "you get one song," says Jackson. "You get signed by Sony and they put out a single, and if it doesn't happen, there's a really good chance the label's going to drop you." The first stirrings of this attitude were evident at record labels in the 1970s, but for the moment talent was the goose laying egg after platinum egg and so was courted assiduously. "The artist really had all the power," says Jackson. Add in superstardom and seven-figure royalty checks, and the "artists" quite predictably began to lose their bearings.

By the time of *Hotel California*, the Eagles' Don Henley had begun an affair with Stevie Nicks, who was on extended tours with Fleetwood Mac behind the unstoppable *Rumours* album while he and the Eagles were off on one of the band's endless odysseys. Getting the two lovers in the same city, let alone the same time zone, was proving problematic. Solution: Henley chartered a Learjet, flew Nicks to the latest stop on the Eagles' itinerary, then flew her back to the Fleetwood Mac tour. Within the Eagles' entourage, the practice became known as "Love 'em and Lear 'em." Bandmate Joe Walsh, an old hand at on-the-road outrages, took to traveling with a chain saw—a gift from the band's manager, Irving Azoff. The success of *Hotel California*, Walsh later said, "made us very paranoid. People started asking us, What are you going to do now? And we didn't know." Many artists of the '70s who experienced extreme fame and sudden wealth, says Jackson, were stalked by feelings of inadequacy. "There was a basic insecurity with all these artists, which was: 'I don't really deserve this. I just wrote a song. It took twenty minutes, and look what happened.' I think it was hard for them to accept the gifts that arrived."

Rock-star indulgences of the '70s nevertheless seemed only to get ever more indulgent. Ward Sylvester, the manager of the Monkees and teen idol Bobby Sherman, gutted a Boeing 720B—a four-engine intercontinental airliner similar in size to Air Force One—and converted it into the *Starship*, a flying pleasure dome chartered by Led Zeppelin, Elton John, Alice Cooper, and the other big bands of the day (accoutrements included a built-in organ and a master bedroom suite in the rear cabin). Mark Belack blundered into a party in Benedict Canyon held to celebrate the first album by Wings, Paul McCartney's post-Beatles band. "Everyone had been told to wear white," Belack says. "And when you got there, everyone was told to walk to a tent, where your clothes were airbrushed by these artists. It was like a Fellini movie." This and a thousand nights like it were what civilians now expected of rock stars and their retinues in Los Angeles, and the participants did their best to live up to the fantasy, even as the novelty wore off and the decadence began to feel suspiciously scripted. Michael Des Barres, accomplished student of rock-and-roll dissipation, fairly snorts in derision. "It was *faux* decadence," he says. Los Angeles and the canyon, then and now, "are about as decadent as fucking

Mister Rogers' Neighborhood. What's wonderful about Hollywood is how good you are at faking it. True decadence you never see."

Although Hollywood and the rock-and-roll crowd commingled uneasily, sex, drugs, and the canyon could be an effective leveling device. Rising in tandem with the canyon-Troubadour stars and sharing their countercultural underpinnings was a new generation of baby-boomer filmmakers and actors whose various ships came in with the same tide that lifted the Ronstadts and Brownes to stardom. A company town, Hollywood demands deference, and for years musicians, like writers, were glorified handmaidens to the moviemakers, necessary craftspeople of a lower caste who kept the business humming but didn't overstep their station. As it did so much else in the '60s, rock stardom turned this hierarchy on its head. Movie stars wished *they* were rock stars, in part for the aphrodisiacal effect on women. (It was an article of faith that Dennis Hopper's and Peter Fonda's characters in *Easy Rider* were based on David Crosby and Roger McGuinn.) That the Hollywood types sought out the musicians, and not the other way around, implied—mostly correctly—that the canyon elite were cooler than the actors.

"I didn't pal around too much with the actor people," says Henry Diltz. "They were always on the fringe, coming around because they really liked the music and the musicians. But the hard core of it—the brotherhood—was really these musicians." Says Morgana Welch: "There was a big division back then between the movie people and the rock-and-roll people. They were more establishment; the rock-and-roll crowd was very antiestablishment. We were rebels, we dressed different, and the drug use, if it was happening, which I'm sure it was, was more underground, whereas we were just blatant with it. We were more open and honest about who we were, and they were pretentious and still acting."

But it wasn't long before baby-boomer actors and directors, thanks to some undeniably great work and the beginnings of celebrity obsession in the media, were feted like rock stars themselves. "There was definitely a feeling of entitlement," says Lucretia Bingham, who came to L.A. in 1973 to film a small part in Oliver Stone's first feature, *Seizure*. "This was the period of the auteurs—Coppola, Lucas, and Spielberg. Not only were they making money, but they had huge adulation. Pauline Kael was writing about them in *The New Yorker* as if they were gods."

Bingham abandoned acting and became a writer and painter, purchasing a house on Wonderland Avenue on Lookout Mountain for $25,000. By the mid-'70s, she was enjoying the full emancipation then expected of an attractive young woman living in a cosmopolitan city—sanctioned by the feminist movement, *Ms.* magazine, and the heady atmosphere of L.A. itself. "I'd grown up in an East Coast family where you went to college, got married the day after you graduated, and became an editor at a New York publishing house," she says. "That's not what I was doing." What Bingham was doing, when not charting a successful if unconventional career path, was having multiple affairs with Hollywood's A-list and generally living like one of D. H. Lawrence's heroines, had Lawrence lived in Laurel Canyon and understood that stretch limos sometimes had difficulty negotiating the hairpin turns on Lookout Mountain.

"I did everything freely, willingly, with the full knowledge of what I was doing," she says. "I was aware that it was bad. You can't forget that about any of us at the time. We were deliberately delving into the dark side. It was not like we thought it was good. We were not hippies; we were not into, 'Oh, everything that feels good *is* good.' We were going: Here's a plate of offerings. Try all these things and you are a demigod because—we were all reading Nietzsche—we thought we were more aware, more intelligent, we could handle all this. And then, by the late '70s, we realized we really couldn't."

It was, as Bingham scarcely need point out, "a very promiscuous time." Says Andrews: "The whole period between the introduction of the Pill and the discovery of AIDS was very free sexually. There was no serious health reason not to just fuck around, in most cases. Mentally or morally or spiritually there may have been other questions, but that didn't really bother people." Bingham, and plenty of other women, indulged accordingly. "I was kind of the quintessential Laurel Canyon girl during the '70s. I would have three-week flings with people, and then discard them like Kleenex. I had a list a mile long. I basically would schedule my week around all my different lovers. You could see one famous director on Tuesday and another one on Saturday and play them against each other and have fun. We hadn't been told there was a downside to that, and the downside, of course, was sexually transmitted diseases, which I was completely innocent about. Don't forget that the 1960s, the drugs, the music, blew us all away, and we were told in the '70s we could do it all. It was the Me culture. Anything I wanted to do was fine." Says Jackson: "If it was introduced in the late '60s, we were just learning how to really enjoy it in the '70s. We had training wheels in the late '60s and were driving pretty well by the '70s."

Bingham recounts a typical afternoon at the height of the era. "At five o'clock one of my lovers would come over, we'd smoke a joint, have sex. I could have sex with somebody and then go out on the town without them, hit the parties, go home probably one drink too many, and then, at the very height of the promiscuity, before the awareness of STDs, sometimes I'd have a late-night date, too." Bingham came to understand that she may have overestimated the charms of unlimited options. "It was very empowering but also, in the final analysis, really debilitating and demoralizing. Like many of us I was going through major therapy for the first time in my life and working out all this repressed anger. So I used to break bottles in my walkway. I had forty-six steps that led up to my house. And I would stand at my front door and scream as I threw the bottles, and they would crash and break. And of course I never cleaned any of them up, so when my mother came to visit me about a year after I'd started doing this, there was probably four feet of broken glass, which I just left as a testament to my rage. She just looked at it and said, 'This is *so* neurotic.' But it was typical of the sort of thing where we all felt like we had permission to do what we wanted. And did."

Meanwhile, the compleat L.A. cocaine cowboys were having second thoughts. The peaceful, easy feelings of the Eagles' first records grew progressively dark as the decade wore on, culminating in *Hotel California*'s unsparing allegories about the soul-sucking wages of Los Angeles in the 1970s. "There was a time during 1976, 1977, when the record business went crazy," Glenn Frey later recalled. "That was when *Hotel California* came out, and *Saturday Night Fever* and *Rumours*. That was the music business at its decadent zenith. I remember Don [Henley] had a birthday party in Cincinnati, and they flew in cases of Château Lafite Rothschild. I seem to remember the wine was the best and the drugs were good and the women were beautiful, and, man, we seemed to have an endless amount of energy." Said Henley: "Those kinds of record sales were unprecedented. I guess everybody thought it was going to continue like that. Lots of money was spent on parties and champagne and limos and drugs. And then of course the bottom fell out . . . I think we knew intuitively that it would pass. I think we could sense the future. I mean, this was the dream we all had. This is why we came to California. It just got bigger than we ever expected it to. It kind of scared us, I guess."

Despite the Eagles' enthusiastic indulgence of rock-star perquisites, tucked away in their collective limo of the soul was the memory of starting out young, broke, and idealistic—although, as Henley pointed out, "it's hard to be an underdog when you're selling 12 million records." Nevertheless, he never entirely divorced himself from the shared values of his larger peer group, and lamented what had become of them. "The dream was unfulfilled," Henley recalled. "In the late Seventies greed reared its ugly head. I guess it was disillusionment that the Sixties didn't quite pan out. For all the publicity about the Baby Boom generation and how we were going to change the world, we weren't in control. The same people who had always been in control were still in control. While we were out taking drugs and preaching flower power and having rock concerts and love-ins, people were running the country."

Michael Des Barres was at that moment coming to grips with daily life in the canyon as a nominal rock star in residence. "In '72 I hadn't had time to get fucked-up and paranoid. It was all joyous, it was great: I'm twenty years old and I can stay up for a week. There's a problem?" By the time he had settled in the canyon, he was less sanguine. "Then the reality sets in. What it really was, was seedy. And wood. Lots and lots of wood. I'm not a big wood fan. I like metal and concrete and stuff. It be-came: Go to Ralphs"—the ubiquitous Southern California supermarket—"and go shopping. Then I'm not in my yellow dress and blue cloche hat and platform character shoes. The practicalities of it were something else. I didn't mind. I was so in love with Pamela that that made it great."

Des Barres's glam band, Silverhead, had dissolved after two albums. By 1977 he was lead singer of Detective, a band put together under the auspices of Led Zeppelin's Swan Song vanity label. A Zeppelin clone launched into the gathering punk explosion, the band never stood a chance, and Des Barres knew it. "I did it because of [Zeppelin manager] Peter Grant and Jimmy [Page] and because of a very interesting concept: a green card. I needed that fucking green card, and me and Pamela needed the money. [Detective] was a corporate band; this wasn't young kids coming together in the garage. I called it my green card band."

In 1978 the Sex Pistols played their first and only American tour. Des Barres was in the audience at what turned out to be their last gig, in San Francisco. "I was in this cruddy thunking metal band and I went up and saw them," he says. The experience was shattering. Des Barres, no stranger to onstage charisma, was astounded by the Pistols' singer, Johnny Rotten (né Lydon). "For me, he's the Bob Dylan of that era. It was a combination of his utter confidence, the certainty that what he was doing was completely new and completely himself: 'This is me, take it or leave it. I could give a fuck what you think.'" The audience, Des Barres says, "was in silence, unbelievably mesmerized, and Rotten just looking at them. The last thing he ever said onstage was, 'You ever feel you've been *cheated*?' And meanwhile, Sid"—Sid Vicious, the band's bassist—"is on his knees picking up the money they've thrown. Then, blackout, and they were gone."

The concert was a watershed for Des Barres. "The rock-and-roll gods would dictate that I would see John Lydon in all his *Clockwork Orange* brilliance," he says, then ticks off the Pistols' signature broadsides at the corpulent ruling class in England and, by extension, the ruling class of rock and roll as represented by bands like Led Zeppelin and the canyon's singer-songwriter elite. 'Anarchy in the U.K.,' 'God Save the Queen'—it *so* needed to be said, it really did, and he said it. I was singing about 'I want to fuck you, baby, let's have a party.'" Three years after glam peaked, the Pistols had served notice that the party—and a lot else—was over. Detective released two albums, both of them plodding failures, and was scheduled to begin recording another. After seeing the Pistols perform, Des Barres knew that it was pointless. "I was meant to go back to rehearsals with Detective for the third record, and I said, 'Fuck it, I can't do it.'"

As fate would have it, he wound up making friends with the Pistols' guitarist, Steve Jones, and in the '80s formed the band Chequered Past with Jones and former Blondie members Clem Burke and Nigel Harrison. He and Pamela were now raising a son, Nicholas, born in 1978, but Des Barres remained in the throes of traditional rock-star addictions once so grimly fashionable, now just grim. He had a moment of clarity one afternoon traversing Laurel Canyon Boulevard. "Me and Steve were totally broke; we were completely on the skids—we had one scooter, and we shared it. So here's us rock-and-roll boys, black leather, tattoos, on a fucking scooter going down Laurel Canyon. And we're waving at the girls and Steve is completely out of his head on heroin, and the scooter just very, very cinematically went and fell on us both. And I remember rolling into the gutter and thinking: Okay, so I came here in '72, this was magic, this was Jim Morrison, this is absolutely the apex of rock and roll. And here's me and Steve Jones lying in the gutter with a Lambretta on our heads. It couldn't have been more perfect, and it woke me up." Des Barres returned to acting, landing progressively larger roles in movies and on TV shows like *WKRP in Cincinnati*. In June 1980—the '70s over for him literally and in every other way—he quit drugs and drinking.

As the '70s waned, there was a palpable sense that the lush vistas that started the decade were being squeezed as if by the iris of a camera lens closing. Chris Hillman was playing in a trio with Gene Clark and Roger McGuinn, his former bandmates from the Byrds. His chief recollection of the '70s was monumental disappointment. "The whole decade I find is a complete waste in all facets of American culture," he says. "There were some good things, don't get me wrong. But that wasn't a good time for me. I lost a lot of people." Bill Graham had long since shuttered his Fillmore theaters. His San Francisco rock palace Winterland—where John Hartmann had been so astounded by the longhairs and light shows fourteen years before and where the Sex Pistols played their final gig—was used by the Band in 1976 as the venue for a farewell concert filmed by Martin Scorsese, *The Last Waltz*, which included performances by a who's who of guest stars that included Joni Mitchell, now in her thirties and performing free-ranging jazz excursions that bore little resemblance to her dulcimer-strumming Lookout Mountain repertoire. (Graham closed Winterland after a final concert featuring the Grateful Dead on New Year's Eve, 1978.)

If punk had punctured the mystique of bloated rock stars in the late '70s, disco dealt a mortal blow to the canyon country rockers. Whereas punk sold sporadically in the United States, disco was racking up numbers that sometimes eclipsed even the biggest singer-songwriters. The soundtrack to *Saturday Night Fever* sold thirty million copies worldwide. Casablanca Records, home of disco queen Donna Summer, briefly became L.A.'s hottest label. Its chaotic *Arabian Nights*–themed headquarters on the Strip sported a parking lot full of Mercedes-Benz convertibles, mirrored executive suites, and throbbing disco punctuated by the sound of staffers hoovering hectares of cocaine. "When disco came in, that was the end of it," says Sally Stevens, then working at RCA Records, weak sister of the major labels. "You can't dance to country rock."

One morning in 1979 Stevens walked into her office and beheld a young man she didn't know standing there. "He said, 'Hi, my name is Vince Gill and I was told to come see you.'" Gill was the lead singer of Pure Prairie League, a country-rock band that had scored a hit, "Amie," in 1975. RCA was slashing its roster, and Pure Prairie League was among the bands to be let go. Stevens had been delegated to give Gill the bad news, which she ascertained only after excusing herself and buttonholing her superiors. "So I had to go in and say to Vince: 'Gee, I'm awfully sorry. I really apologize. This is a horrible way to treat you. I don't know who you are, and you don't know who I am, and that should give you a good idea of what you've walked into. But the bottom line is they're not going to support Pure Prairie League. Country rock is over.'" Stevens then told the stunned young musician, with remarkable prescience, what the future held. "'Right now they want disco; they don't want this stuff anymore. And I'm sure ten years from now you'll have the last laugh on this label.' And he said, 'Thank you very much for being honest.' I said, 'I'm sure I'm not far behind you,' and that turned out to be the truth because they laid all of us off." It didn't take long for Gill to have the last laugh. Within the year, the bottom fell out of disco and took the record business with it. PolyGram Records, corporate parent of Casablanca, didn't return to profitability until 1985. Gill reemerged in the '90s as a gigantic country-music star with a string of Top 10 hits and multiplatinum albums.

As disco pumped up and then decimated the record labels,

punk was tearing its way through the L.A. scene. On and off the Strip, the clubs that had catered to the Byrds and the Doors and then to glam were booking soon-to-become-Los-Angeles-punk-legends X and the Germs. Outside the Whisky, where flower children formerly gathered in at least a pretext of peaceful good vibes, the sidewalks were clotted with loutish punks harassing passersby. "They would just stand there in front of cars or fall across the hood and stare at the people inside," says David Strick. "You'd see the beginnings of this kind of free-floating hooliganism." The punk shows were becoming dangerously violent. Derf Scratch, bassist in Fear—John Belushi's favorite band during his final, sodden days in L.A.—was badly beaten after the band came offstage one night.

Amid the punk Götterdämmerung it seemed inconceivable that ten years earlier the Eagles could have defined the L.A. scene with paeans to Carlos Castaneda and the southwestern desert; they closed the decade with *The Long Run*, an album reeking of exhaustion and resignation. During its recording Henley visited the Troubadour for a night of reminiscing and had to shout over a punk band playing covers of "Pretty Vacant" and "God Save the Queen." "Did you do it for money?" Henley prodded the party-palsied heroine in "The Long Run," his and Frey's final, withering chronicle of Southern California hedonism gone wrong. Poisoned by their success and at each other's throats, the Eagles broke up after a dispiriting tour in support of the album. Hillman, having lived through the protracted disintegration of the Byrds ten years before, was bitterly amused. "The last days of the Eagles I was howling because I had already been around the block with this, right? They're all going to the gigs in separate limousines because they hate each other's guts." The Eagles wouldn't play together again for fourteen years.

In the canyon, grinding indulgence was replacing the frothy high spirits of the mid-'70s. A house on the back side of Lookout Mountain hosted weekend sex parties, the rooms crammed with bunks proffering straight and gay sex, bowls of Quaaludes and poppers, and scores of naked bodies groping, licking, snorting, fucking. Now in addition to cocaine there were the first sightings of freebase, the purified form of street cocaine several magnitudes stronger and even more fiendishly reinforcing. (Converting regular cocaine to base requires volatile solvents; Richard Pryor famously set himself ablaze while mixing up a batch in 1980.) "We used to have—forgive me, God—parties where the women, we'd all get in bed, we're all loaded on base," says one well-traveled canyon scenester. "We would take Bic pens, pull the ink out, take a hit, and then blow it into their vaginas, and then make love because it would numb the vagina. There's like six of us on the bed. You'd sit there going through withdrawal while somebody makes the next batch, like being in a Turkish opium den. Very ritualistic." Soon a subculture of beautiful young women emerged around town whose pimps were base dealers who used the girls as pushers of both sex and drugs.

In 1978 Bingham was working on a magazine story about women on the extreme fringes of the L.A. party circuit. "I was titillated by the whole scene of it—it was like watching ancient Rome. These girls were really further out on the edge than I was. A lot of these parties ended up in orgies. I remember being at the Playboy Mansion when Hefner sent his pimp around to tap certain people on the shoulder, to move the party into the grotto, which is where the late-night orgies went on. This guy tapped me and I said, 'No, thank you,' and he goes, 'What! No one says, no, thank you!'"

The boundaries were blurring between decadence and

seediness, glamour and the grotesque. Finally, says Bingham, "there was one of those defining moments where you realize it has gone from fun into something bizarre." One night she found herself at yet another party hosted by a movie producer, this time in Coldwater Canyon. "I remember a perfectly dressed young woman being there, really exquisitely dressed in a kind of tuxedo suit, with a Vidal Sassoon haircut. She was very pale, before pale was chic. She looked at me across this plate of cocaine, and she had one perfect little drop of blood on her nostril. And I thought: There's something *really* wrong with this picture." The next day Bingham received a phone call from a man she'd met at the party. "It turned out he was kind of like a pimp for musicians. He said, 'You know, George Harrison would like to ask you to come to Palm Springs with him this weekend. I'll pick you up in the limo tomorrow.'" Bingham, appalled at the presumption, turned him down.

On the Rainbow-Whisky circuit, Morgana Welch received a similar proposition from two of the other three Beatles. "A friend of mine who was a pretty well known photographer called me up at 2:30 in the morning and said, 'I'm sitting here with John Lennon, Ringo, Harry Nilsson, and Keith Moon, and we'll send a limo for you, will you come?'" She demurred, although admitted in hindsight she might have considered accepting if the notoriously wild Moon were not involved. "He called me back and said, 'Please, please,' and I just said no, leave me alone. It was nonspecific, and it could have been some kind of gang-bang situation, which I wasn't going to risk."

Bingham, in any event, had had enough. "All of us were just kind of living an extended adolescence and thinking that it was just going to continue. But all of us were beginning to get wakeup calls. Just the level of seediness, the kind of fringe people who were beginning to show up. It began to get spooky. People either pulled themselves out of it or went further downhill. There were a lot of casualties."

Strick, on a magazine assignment, spent a night at the mansion of Gary Kellgren, a prominent recording engineer and producer who'd co-founded the Record Plant studios in New York and L.A. "The reason the magazine was doing a story on him was because he'd become sort of a casualty of the scene, even though he had a ton of money. He'd become just completely dissolute and fucked-up." Strick hung around Kellgren's faux-Norman castle above the Strip for a single night. "He had this sicko entourage that just kind of came by and brought him drugs. All kinds of music-fringy people. He was still working—he took us to a Frank Zappa session at the Record Plant that he was supervising at five in the morning. Around midnight a couple of long-haired Samoan guys came to the castle and dropped off a pretty large amount of cocaine, which as I remember was wrapped in condoms, because Gary Kellgren put one through his belt loop for the rest of the night."

Soon one of the entourage delivered to the door a striking blonde, who disappeared with Kellgren for an hour. "They came out, and she had nothing on; she'd wrapped a big piece of drapery around herself. They'd clearly just had sex and something else, I'm not sure what, and were half-stumbling, half-dancing around in this 'aren't we having fun' sort of way." Months later, when Strick's photos were about to run, he got a call from the *New York Post*. Kellgren had just been found floating dead in his swimming pool, and the newspaper wanted Strick's pictures. "It was this sense of one of those typical Brian Jones endings to one of these '60s people's lives in the '70s, when his string got played out in that scene. It was a very intense, one-night exposure that I got to it."

Boomers in the vanguard of L.A.'s recording and movie

industries were already beginning to pull back. "We had long since given up the sort of hippie side," says Andrews. "We didn't necessarily have any money, but by the mid-'70s we were certainly aware of the good things in life, I would say. We were working real jobs, thinking about getting married, or buying houses." The beer- and tequila-soaked clubs and restaurants like Dan Tana's were joined by smart places serving sophisticated cuisine in settings more reminiscent of Soho or the Left Bank. The boomers' culinary revolution was just around the corner; a host of young West Coast chefs would soon remake the restaurant industry as thoroughly as their peers had transformed movies and music. Michael McCarty's Michael's in Santa Monica and Alice Waters's Chez Panisse in Berkeley led the charge. There was a lively scene at Ports, a tiny bar and restaurant far off the Strip on Santa Monica Boulevard. "It had been a place called the Sports Inn—they took off the 'Inn' and one *S*," says Andrews. "I was probably there every night for five or six years, mid- to late '70s. There was a small front room that had five tables. One night I came in, and at three of the tables was Claes Oldenburg, Milton Glaser, and Antonioni. So it was that kind of place."

Rolling Stone's founder, Jann Wenner, who'd always had an uneasy relationship with the magazine's hippie image, pulled the magazine out of San Francisco in 1977 and relocated to a suite of offices on Fifth Avenue in New York with a view of Central Park. Across L.A. there was among boomers a real sense that the train was leaving the station. Jim Morrison, whose ramblings were starting to look increasingly prophetic, called it back in '68 in the Doors' "Five to One": "Your ballroom days are over, baby, night is drawing near." Morrison was not given to explaining himself, but the couplet sounded a lot like a warning shot for a generation fired ten years too early. Not everyone was ready to hear it. "There were those who just couldn't grow up, who just got stuck in Laurel Canyon and 'L.A. is my candy store and it'll always be my candy store,'" says Bingham. "And the rest of us had moved on, going, 'The candy has turned sour.'"

ELEVEN

EVE OF DESTRUCTION

The peace-and-love generation grows up and out of the canyon, punishment for the inebriates and fornicators, Johnny "Wadd" Holmes and the bloodbath on Wonderland, the road to paradise is paradise

September 16, 1979, dawned hot and smoggy in Los Angeles, a Sunday like a hundred others during the fall, when L.A.'s true summer begins. It's possible during the rest of the year to pretend that the city is a vast oasis pitched between the Pacific on the west and the San Gabriel and San Bernardino mountain ranges to the north and east. In fact, Los Angeles receives only fifteen inches of rain annually and usually no rain at all between April and November. In early autumn hot, dry winds—the fabled Santa Anas—come howling out of the Mojave Desert. Canyons funnel the superheated air, often at gale force, straight into the L.A. basin. The humidity plunges and the temperature soars: 102, 104, 107. Chaparral and eucalyptus, with resinous, highly flammable foliage, heave and rustle in the winds, wicks waiting for the flame. When it comes—and it always does, because this is the natural order of things—the fires burn ferociously, the wind acting like a blowtorch. One-hundred-foot eucalyptus with trunks as thick as water mains simply explode;

at night moist air from the ocean drifts over the inferno, trig-
gering hellish tornadoes of flame that whirl through the ruined
hillsides. The fire wishes only to burn all the way to the sea, as
it has done for millennia; and so Los Angeles, having been built
in its path, burns, too. On September 16, 1979, as if directed by
some biblical fiat to punish the fornicators and inebriates, fire
came to Laurel Canyon as never before.

It started at around two in the afternoon on the canyon's
southwestern flank. Almost immediately huge flames were
menacing Grandview Drive, built shoulder to shoulder with
homes possessing some of the best views in the city. The fire
came so suddenly that most escaped only with the clothes on
their backs. Some gamely hurled whatever possessions they
could grab—Waterford crystal, a porcelain statue—into swimming pools. Within minutes twenty-three houses on Grandview
and adjoining Colecrest Drive were burning out of control. At
8353 Grandview, John Mayall and his guests were watching a
movie in the screening room of his beloved three-story house.
That the house had earned the sobriquet "The Brain Damage
Club" was testament to the style and substance of Mayall's entertaining. (A highlight for especially spirited revelers was leap-
ing off the third story into the swimming pool terraced into the
hillside.) The house held Mayall's two thousand hours of video-
taped movies, his sixteenth-century antiques, a vast collection of
pornography dating to the nineteenth century, as well as the di-
aries of his travels around the world with Eric Clapton, Mick
Taylor, and the other British guitar legends who passed through
his bands in a sort of finishing school.

Mayall had been so taken by the canyon before he moved
there he recorded a song cycle, *Blues from Laurel Canyon*; the
centerpiece was "Laurel Canyon Home," with the lyric: "Now
the sun is sinking, it's time to reminisce / Here's a way of living,
that I will sorely miss." Now, within minutes, it was all gone,

save the foundation and swimming pool. Mayall and his guests escaped just before the house was engulfed. The fire was so intense it melted his nineteen-year-old son Jason's 1958 Volvo sedan. As with Chris Hillman's house just up the hill on Magnolia, which burned on a similarly hot, witchy day in the '60s, Mayall's house seemed to have succumbed to the canyon's rock-and-roll curse: the fire mowed down nearly every house on Grandview that overlooked L.A. but spared all those on the canyon side save his. (Mayall would rebuild on the same lot and live there until the mid-'90s.)

And so it went. Mayall's neighbor on Grandview, Elmer Valentine, co-founder of the Whisky, was spotted the day after the fire poking through the ruins, grief-stricken not about his palatial house but about the fate of his bull terriers, Bo and Annie. How many nights had Valentine stood on his deck and listened to the sounds of revelry wafting up from the Strip, knowing it was as much his creation as anyone's? All that was left of the house was the pristine, mocking stone fireplace, a burned-out Porsche 924, and four wine bottles on the front step with blackened labels. For days afterward, it was said, Valentine waited, heartbroken, for Bo and Annie to somehow find their way home—not to the charred hulk on Grandview, but to the Whisky. In a final bit of degradation, for months after the fire skate rats with gravity-defying Mohawks and safety-pinned cheeks congregated on Grandview late at night to smoke herb and 'board in the empty swimming pools in a sort of post-apocalyptic performance art. Far below, the lights of L.A. winked and seduced as ever.

Occurring just three months before the end of the '70s, the fire was the prescribed metaphorical finale for Laurel Canyon's salad days: darkness replacing light, despair trouncing hope, a burnt offering to whatever gods watched over what many had considered paradise, destroyed by hubris, greed, carnal overindulgence, and now, quite literally, flame. In this point of view there was the baby-boomer conceit that the generation in fact controlled its destiny and thus the destiny of its pop-cultural creations, that whatever it embraced, and now rejected, would be rendered, no questions asked. "We are stardust," Joni Mitchell sang on the eve of the '70s, "we are golden," the "we" it could and did go without saying being the royal we of the boomers, so flush with entitlement that they could unironically anoint themselves in popular song. Now, with the '70s finished and the best and brightest boomers eager to colonize new lifestyle frontiers, Laurel Canyon, still smoldering, could safely be consigned to the used-up artifacts of an era being repudiated by its creators: Adam and Eve and Crosby, Stills, and Nash—cast out of the garden forever. Lucretia Bingham, for one, wasn't buying it.

"There were wonderful movies made and wonderful music made," she says. "It was an era of amazing creativity. I became a true artist and writer in those years. I worked extremely hard, produced the best paintings I'd done, wrote some of the best articles I've ever written, the best short stories. It was a truly furious artistic time. I might talk about the nights I was out partying, but in the days I was working very hard." Besides, she knew the canyon idyll was finished. She sold her house on Lookout Mountain in 1980.

But the denouement of Laurel Canyon had not reached its finale. Epochs end when they feel like it, and Laurel Canyon's had far too much momentum to be stopped by a mere fire. What would finally kill off the canyon mythos, ironically, would be sex and drugs, though in the context of illicit commerce and sadistic revenge. It was July 1, 1981, and Laurel Canyon was about to rejoin the real world.

———

Michael James Jackson was driving down Lookout Mountain on his way to work when he saw the police tape in front of the dreary stucco house at 8763 Wonderland Avenue. By chance, it was directly across the street from Bingham's old house, with its four feet of shattered bottles on the stairway. "That was always kind of the slum side of the street," Bingham says. "The three houses in a row there. They were slums when they were built. Awful houses." The house at 8763 had the usual Laurel Canyon rock-and-roll pedigree; Paul Revere and the Raiders were said to have lived there in the good old "Mr. Tambourine Man" days. Now it was occupied by an assortment of cokeheads, dealers, and ham-fisted thieves known as the Wonderland Gang. Their arrival at the house was symptomatic of the hard-core drug scene spreading through the canyon in the late '70s and early '80s. The house was leased to Joy Audrey Miller, a forty-six-year-old heroin addict. Two ex-cons, Billy DeVerell—Miller's boyfriend—and Ronald Launius, the gang's nominal leader, rounded out the household.

As Jackson approached the house on July 1, he beheld the yellow police tape and a swarm of LAPD black-and-white cruisers. Then he looked closer and could scarcely believe what he saw. "There was blood spatter on the windows," he says. Bingham, meanwhile, received a frantic phone call from the man who'd bought her house. "He was totally freaked-out because he'd heard screams"—the night previous—"but it was so typical to hear screaming in Laurel Canyon he didn't think anything of it." Says Jackson, "In the middle of the night you would hear some woman screaming, and you would be concerned until you figured out she was getting laid."

What happened at 8763 Wonderland, sometime in the hours between dusk and dawn, would shock Los Angeles as thoroughly as the Manson murders twelve years earlier. Police entering the house, hardened by the medieval cruelties meted out by Manson's girls, were stunned at the tableau. Miller, De-Verell, Launius, and Barbara Richardson, a houseguest, had been bludgeoned to death with such force that their blood, flesh, bone, and cartilage covered the walls, ceiling, and floors in a gruesome fresco. A fifth victim, as badly beaten as the rest and left for dead, miraculously survived. Thanks to a bloody palm print, it was soon deduced that John Holmes, the porn star, possessed of a twelve-and-a-half-inch penis and, at the time of the murders, a coke habit that was killing his day job while fueling an escalating life of crime, had been present during the butchery. Porn stars, moldy drug misanthropes, and murder were about as far as you could get from peace, love, and understanding. And with that, Laurel Canyon lost whatever pretext of innocence it clung to as the '80s bore down.

"Nothing as violent in terms of its aggression had ever happened in that canyon since I had been there," says Jackson. "It wasn't like somebody shot somebody in the midst of a passionate argument; somebody intentionally went in and brutally massacred a group of people. That was beyond comprehension—there was no frame of reference for that. That somehow suddenly tainted the vibe in the canyon."

There had been reprobates floating around the canyon before, of course, and the Manson scare had demonstrated that not all longhairs could be trusted implicitly. But Wonderland was truly something else, the end of an era. "A lot of weird people were attracted to the canyon," Jackson acknowledges. "You'd stop at the Canyon Store and there'd be guys staggering out of there you just couldn't imagine. But they still could fall under the heading of a kind of hippie generation that had absolutely made the canyon its home. And within that enclave, it had felt the same way that the late '60s had."

In the aftermath of the murders, it was necessary to look no further than the canyon's fellow hippie utopia to the north to see that it would come to this. The Haight took all of one year to fall apart, as hard drugs and vicious, predatory dealers took over the streets. "When dope murders happened in the Haight in '68, suddenly people realized it was not the paradise we'd all thought it was," says Colman Andrews. There was no small irony that Los Angeles, slandered by San Francisco's rock elite as a soul-sucking Gomorrah, should surrender its last vestige of '60s atmospherics a full fourteen years after the Summer of Love. But the Wonderland murders, just up the road from the house where Graham Nash and Joni Mitchell composed their hippie pastorals, were more than anyone could take. "There was the overall sense that the innocence was gone," says Bingham. "Don't forget that this was also the beginning of awareness of AIDS. Now we were getting the message: drugs kill, sex kills, and there are people out there who are really ugly and bad. It was like, boom, this is not safe anymore."

The alleged motive for the murders was nearly as repellent as the crime. John Holmes, on the skids after "starring" in hundreds of porn productions and, by his estimate, penetrating fourteen thousand women with his prodigious member, had taken to snatching luggage at LAX to pay for his coke habit. In the course of these travels he fell in with Eddie Nash—the former Adel Gharib Nasrallah—a Lebanese immigrant and proprietor of a string of Hollywood clubs, including the Starwood, a glam stronghold in the '70s now overrun with punk bands. Nash was also involved in a constellation of criminal activities, including drug trafficking and money laundering. Nash was in thrall to Holmes's porn-star cred, Holmes to Nash's coke supplies. To feed his $1,500-a-day habit, Holmes at one point traded sex with his twenty-year-old girlfriend for as much rock as Nash would give him. He was also frequently in residence at the Wonderland house, scoring and running up a considerable debt.

In the scenario laid out by police after the murders, to pay off the Wonderlanders, Holmes set up Nash to be robbed by the gang by leaving a sliding door unlocked at Nash's house in Studio City. On June 29, the gang burst in on Nash and his bodyguard at gunpoint and made off with quantities of illegal drugs, guns, jewels, and cash. Nash allegedly summoned Holmes to his house and, after threatening his life and those of his family, wrung a confession about his involvement in the robbery. Two nights later, the bloodbath began on Wonderland.

The actual assailants were never arrested, but police knew Holmes was present and questioned him relentlessly. They were particularly interested in knowing whether he had in fact planned the murders with Nash and, since he was clearly at the house during the butchery, if he participated of his own volition or as punishment. Holmes never gave up anything meaningful to the cops and was forced to stand trial in connection with the murders. He was acquitted in 1982. In 2001, Nash pleaded guilty to federal racketeering charges and paying a $50,000 bribe to a juror in a 1991 trial for the Wonderland murders that ended in a hung jury—he was acquitted in a subsequent trial—and was sentenced to thirty-seven months in prison.

The "Four on the Floor" murders, as they were dubbed by L.A.'s ever-empathetic police, were the inspiration for the director Paul Thomas Anderson's 1997 *Boogie Nights* and for *Wonderland*, released in 2003 and starring Val Kilmer as Holmes. After spending three months in prison on a contempt charge related to a grand jury investigation of the murders, Holmes was released in 1982 and resumed his porn career. After a brief flurry of activity, he began a long slide, as drugs made him an unreliable performer. He contracted AIDS in 1986 but continued working, not telling his partners of his disease, before dying of complications related to the virus in 1988.

The Wonderland Murders were unquestionably a watershed for Laurel Canyon, but they alone didn't kill off the canyon's parsley-sage-rosemary-and-thyme pseudo-mysticism; that was dying an entirely natural death, from attrition, long before John Holmes started hitting the pipe on Wonderland. In fact, the diaspora of musicians began for reasons as predictable as love and money. Joni Mitchell was one of the first to go, forsaking her house on Lookout Mountain for Bel-Air. She and Nash had separated—Nash wanted to marry, she didn't. "It was not a happy time for me," Nash says. "I was deeply in love with Joan, more than I would have admitted to her. I don't know why that is, but men are strange sometimes. When we parted I went to San Francisco, bought the first house I saw, and moved in. It was hard."

Mitchell leased the house to Ron Stone, her neighbor and co-manager. Although he soon became successful enough himself to move to gaudier quarters, he didn't, even after "everybody I knew with the exception of Mark Volman had moved out. I could have afforded better. I didn't want better. I stayed for romantic reasons." Stone ended up leasing the house from Mitchell for the next twenty-seven years—"she was a good landlady"—and raising his children there. "There was a mystical kind of atmosphere in the house," he says. Stone now presides over Gold Mountain Management—the name is a holdover from the canyon's original hippie managers, Lookout Management—whose clients have included Nirvana and Bonnie Raitt. Which is to say Stone is not typically consumed by flights of whimsy. He freely admits that actually living in the house "was a nightmare. When it rained, it leaked. Cold air came through the cracks. I never really noticed until I lived in a proper house."

Still, he found it irresistible, and not necessarily for its very, very, very fine pedigree, though there was an undeniable kick in knowing Mitchell's watercolor on the cover of *Ladies of the Canyon* depicted the view out his dining room window. The house, says Stone, "was somehow blessed. A lot of bad things happened in that neighborhood, but nothing happened to the house." There was the time, when Mitchell still lived there, that the house next door—shared by Canned Heat—burned in a furious blaze that somehow spared hers. "By all rights it should have burned the house to the ground, but for whatever reason it blackened the back door and stopped," Stone says. Years later he and his family were home when a giant eucalyptus tree came crashing down. "It fell backwards, defying the laws of nature, up the hill instead of downhill, which would have crushed the house." Stone ultimately renovated the house. "I went to the bank, took out a loan, even though I never actually owned it. Very bizarre. It was a weird relationship. It never occurred to me that it wasn't mine."

The memory of the house where Nash and Mitchell composed their most enduring songs continues to reverberate for both. Says Nash: "Did you ever see that movie about this enchanted cottage, and this couple were terribly scarred in an accident but every time they went to the cottage they were beautiful again? The house reminded me of that house. Once you walked through that front door, everything disappeared." On January 17, 2005, Nash answered his phone in Hawaii, his home for the past thirty years. It was Mitchell, calling from L.A. "She said, 'Do you want to go to the house?' I said, 'What?' She said, 'I'm thinking of selling it.' I said, 'Really? Why?' She said the people renting it, three guys came over the fence and tried to rob them. And Joni thinks that those things are signs, and so she thought it was a sign that she should give it up. She wasn't there to protect it. So she wanted to to know if I wanted to go back and reminisce for a few minutes." Nash, about to leave on a world tour with Stills and Crosby, declined.

In any event, the practicalities of canyon living, or lack thereof, demanded a reappraisal once one's income increased by several thousand percent in the course of a year. "As people made money, they found they could upgrade their lives," says Volman. "The forty-thousand-dollar home Joni Mitchell lived in in Laurel Canyon was a nice place but really small. The minute you're having some platinum records, as she did, I'm sure she wanted to invest her money, and it was the natural thing to do. Living in Laurel Canyon was great for starting out." Sally Stevens was living in a tiny cottage nearby at the time. "No one was planning on staying in Laurel Canyon for the rest of their lives," she says. "Everyone was heading west. There was a lot of talk about that, about wanting to be a success." Says Stone: "If you were unsuccessful, you lived in Laurel Canyon. And the minute you got successful you went to Coldwater or Benedict Canyon."

Volman held on until 1989. But before that, he says, "we had outgrown that house. Huge yard. Really small house. Also, Laurel Canyon is not that kid-friendly. It's all hills and mountains and trees and really nowhere for the kids to go, so when they want to get together, it really had to be planned out. My daughter, when she got her car, none of her best friends lived in Laurel Canyon; they all lived down in the flatlands." Henry Diltz bought his house across the street from Volman in 1967. He became a father in 1977. By 1979 he had moved to the Valley. "Here's the thing," he says, "we needed a lawn." Pushing a pram down Lookout Mountain Boulevard, with its incredible pitches, multiple blind corners, and blasé locals who drive as if it were the Hollywood Freeway, can be lethal for both father and baby. "Plus, you get tired of driving up and down to birth-days parties, shopping," Diltz says. "If you're making four trips a day up and down the hill, finally you say, What the hell, I might as well just live down there."

Diltz dreaded the move. "I thought that it would be the worst day—the thing I would regret most in my entire life—the day that I moved out of Laurel Canyon. I could see the sense of it, and my wife really instigated it. I went along with it, thinking: Boy, am I going to regret this." To his surprise, he didn't. "I never did, never regretted it at all. It was great moving down." For one thing, the days were finished when Diltz could wander over to Mickey Dolenz's house, just across the street from Alice Cooper's and up the road from Mitchell's, where "Harry Nilsson, John Lennon, and Ringo Starr would come over because Mickey had a great lit-tle record room downstairs, all carpeted, and they would hang out at all hours." All of that, a memory as fresh as yesterday, now be-longed to another era. It was as if Wendy and the Lost Boys had abandoned Neverland and moved to Sherman Oaks.

Diltz, like Volman and the rest of the Lookout Mountain fra-ternity, was simply growing up, and out of Laurel Canyon. "It was traumatic," Diltz says. But it also wasn't, because the canyon's past fifteen years had yet to pass into legend. "I never thought of it like, Wow, here we are, this is a cool place, this is the musician's hang-out," Diltz says. "It didn't seem like a magical place at the time. It was just kind of a place to live." Says Nash: "When I wrote 'Teach Your Children' and 'Our House,' we didn't know what we were doing." 'This sounds pretty fun, we can sing this, let's do this!' And then all of a sudden people are singing it back to me forty years later?"

The Jazz Age probably looked that way to Scott Fitzgerald even as he was drowning in gin rickies and contemplating dia-monds as big as the Ritz. As he lamented in *Tales of the Jazz Age*,

"I have tried, unsuccessfully I fear, to weave . . . a pattern which would give the effect of those months in New York as they appeared to at least one member of what was then the younger generation." Which is another way of saying it's a bitch to parse a revolution while you are living it. James Thurber wrote of the "candied incandescence" with which nostalgia colors the true character of places and things. The American 1950s, whence the canyonites sprang with so many awful memories, were in the 1970s refurbished by the boomers themselves, whipsawed by the tumult they had unleashed, into a sort of lost suburban utopia in movies like *Grease*. And so Laurel Canyon's golden age—if that is in fact what it was, and the hyperbole seems more appropriate with each passing year—would become evident only in hindsight.

"I don't think I've ever lost my feelings for those times," says Nash. "It's different for David and Stephen because they lived here. But I was imported from England, which was an incredibly different culture, even in the music business, and I was immersed in this whole other scene. It was liberating: people want to know what I *think*? Wow! It was so freeing; as an artist and a writer, there wasn't an existence that wasn't better for me then. There was a freedom and a sense of hope in the air and a sense that we could really change the world. We were optimistic and full of piss and vinegar, and we were writing these great songs. I never wanted to go back to England. And I never did."

"The road to paradise," goes an old Spanish proverb, "is paradise." When told of it, Diltz seized pencil and paper in his cottage in the San Fernando Valley—hemmed in by neatly arranged files holding the thousands of photographs he took in and around the canyon in the '60s and '70s—and immediately wrote it down. Then he put down the pencil. "It's true," he said.

EPILOGUE

Laurel Canyon will probably never again witness the perfect cultural storm that formed over it in the mid-'60s and raged through most of the '70s. The confluence of a huge generation hitting their early twenties simultaneously, a monolithic popular culture left over from the '50s that invited scorn and reinvention, and a recording industry coming of age along with its gigantic new constituency was unprecedented and perhaps unrepeatable.

In the early '80s, a new generation of post-punk L.A. bands began hitting the boards up and down the Strip, revitalizing the Whisky (which had closed for several years) and Gazzari's—launching pads for the Doors, the Byrds, and the Buffalo Springfield. The music was the hard rock of Led Zeppelin shot through, in the early days, with fresh energy and irreverence, though the message was a dreary litany of sex and party escapades. It was loud, uncomplicated, and blatantly commercial, and it fit right in with a country swinging violently toward social conservatism and unfettered capitalism. Ronald Reagan, despised by the canyon elite during his scolding-father reign as California governor in the 1960s, was now, unbelievably, president. The National Endowment for the Arts emerged as the favorite whipping boy of freelance cultural censors for trickling out grants to artists whose cultural and sexual orientation varied from that of pious and punishing middle-American white males. MTV arrived in 1981, favoring bands as much for their telegenics as for their musicianship, which suited the boys now pummeling the Strip just fine. Mötley Crüe, Poison, Ratt, and the rest jacked their hair into towering roosterish bouffants and blackened their eyes with mascara—a holdover from glam minus the androgyny that held no interest for the studly "hair" bands.

Some of the new breed took their places in Laurel Canyon—Mötley Crüe's bassist, Nikki Sixx, among them—but a second coming of the canyon as a collective for musicians and their retinues to share ideas, dope, and generational solidarity was not to be. For one thing, the careerist streak that the '60s canyonites had managed to keep nominally in check was now out in the open. There was brutal competition to succeed, to rack up platinum albums almost immediately. The coke, heroin, booze, and partying, despite the dire warnings of AIDS and high-profile death and debilitation, were out of control from the start. Finally, there was no unifying subtext to the music beyond exhortations to party till you puked. Even at their commercial zenith in the '70s, when their self-absorption was at its most annoying, the canyon singer-songwriters had a nodding acquaintance with emotional intimacy and, in the Eagles, a journalist-like fetish for chronicling the times in which they were living.

The metal lite coming out of L.A. in the early '80s, while selling millions upon millions of albums, was mostly mindless party music, as enlightening as a shot of Jägermeister and a bump of coke. Only the "hair" bands that survived the first rush of success and stupidity and allowed themselves to mature, notably Mötley Crüe, made music of any consequence. Not until the rise of post-punk alternative rock late in the decade, including the Red Hot Chili Peppers and Jane's Addiction, would yet another wave of bands from L.A. have any real impact. Meanwhile, Guns N' Roses, who claimed the Rainbow Bar and Grill on the Strip as their spiritual home, led a separate charge with chiseled rock that, briefly, held promise for an aggressive new form for the musician.

It can be argued that many of the conditions that allowed Laurel Canyon to become such a hothouse of creativity exist again today. Generation Y, spawn of the baby boomers, is statistically a larger generation and is hitting young adulthood in a massive demographic bulge. There is even an unpopular and desultory war steadily picking off its cannon fodder in a manner eerily reminiscent of Vietnam. Yet Gen Y has yet to show an inclination for speaking with one voice, or rallying behind a single band, as the Boomers did around the Beatles and then the L.A. bands of the '60s and '70s. Unlike their parents, who seized the moment and, with narcissistic glee, bent the world to their will, Gen Yers are balkanized as a cultural force and exert their influence piecemeal. Thus far their only truly huge music stars have been the Britneys and Christinas and J.Los, manufactured by boomer-age record company executives for maximum market penetration in the same manner as the Brill Building machine of the '60s, only with far more cynicism and far fewer good records. Even the notion of chops and paying one's dues has gone out the window in an era when everybody is a star. "Look at what we're dealing with now," grouses Chris Hillman, "the end game: *American Idol.*"

More promising is hip-hop, Gen Y's one universal cultural obsession. Hip-hop's deconstructed riffs and postmodern pastiche have resulted in intriguing compositions that reach across decades but still sound fresh, such as Eminem's rap over Aerosmith's 1973 chestnut "Dream On." It is a testament to the sturdiness of the era's music that it can be recycled in this fashion. And while it's true that bands from the '60s and '70s reinterpreted older musical forms, especially folk and blues—the Doors went so far as to record Kurt Weill's "Alabama Song" from Weill's and Bertolt Brecht's modernist opera, *The Rise and Fall of the City of Mahagonny*—Gen Y may be the first generation of twenty-year-olds to venerate and personalize the hits of their parents' salad days, the equivalent in 1976 of Jackson Browne covering Perry Como.

The musicians of the canyon in the 1960s and '70s wanted to create music first and foremost for themselves. "You gotta remember one thing from my era," says Hillman; "we got into music because we liked to play." Part of the mission was also building a culture their parents didn't—and couldn't—understand. Yet hip-hop unquestionably fulfills those criteria. It's been twenty-seven years since the first hip-hop Top 40 hit, the Sugarhill Gang's "Rapper's Delight," and the recordings of hip-hop's first generation of stars such as Grandmaster Flash, Run-D.M.C., Ice Cube, and Public Enemy retain their cultural relevance—indeed, have become "classics" played on radio stations devoted expressly to old-school hip-hop just as there are classic rock stations devoted to Led Zeppelin and Eric Clapton.

Whether Gen Y's best and brightest will ever coalesce in a particular place and time, as their elders did in Laurel Canyon, remains to be seen. The evidence would suggest not. Despite their great numbers, Gen Y is far more diverse racially, ethnically, and demographically than the boomers; hip-hop notwithstanding, it is hard to imagine a single issue or cultural trend that could unite them as thoroughly as their parents bonded over the Vietnam War or rock and roll. They are also able, thanks to the Web, digital file sharing, and powerful recording software, to consume and create music without the intervention of the recording industry. While there will always be scenes where young musicians inspire one another—New York City's Williamsburg neighborhood is a recent example—it's just as likely the modern equivalent of Stephen Stills running into Neil Young on the Strip will take place within the Web's virtual Laurel Canyon. The potential is tremendous. Because of the Web, young artists are exposed to an arsenal of ideas unimaginable in the '60s, at warp speed. And maybe that's the point. A constant refrain, invariably posed by smug boomers, asks when the new generation will create "their Beatles." The answers are: never, and, they already have. Marshall McLuhan's prophecy in the '60s was right: the medium and media have reached parity. The Web is Generation Y's Beatlemania.

Every year—sometimes in July and sometimes in August, you never know until the last moment—the people of Laurel Canyon come down from the hills to get their picture taken in front of the Canyon Country Store. They come from the Kirkwood Bowl and Lookout Mountain, from Grandview and Colecrest and Ridpath and Jewett and Yucca and Willow Glen and Wonderland. There's undoubtedly a good reason for this tradition, which involves lots of drinking of Red Bull while the photographer, on a teetering ladder across Laurel Canyon Boulevard, waits for a break in the traffic, but nobody remembers what it is. Most canyonesque, nobody cares. As soon as the picture is taken—and everyone conspires to delay this moment as long as possible—the subjects melt back into the hills. There's something affirming about this ritual, as organic and inevitable as the waxy yellow flowers that bloom every winter and fill the canyon with jasmine musk. It's as if once a year the "creatures," as Jim Morrison immortalized them in the Doors' "Love Street," are driven to renew their neighborhood vows.

Forty years have passed since the folk rockers first arrived, but Laurel Canyon carries on as ever. Since then it has survived attempts to ram an eight-lane freeway through its heart, two major earthquakes, and countless mudslides and fires without losing its essential character. Of all the L.A. city canyons—Benedict, Beverly Glen, Coldwater, Nichols, Beechwood, and the rest—Laurel Canyon stands apart for reasons, like the fabled marijuana high, that tend to defy explication. Lisa Cholodenko, who wrote and directed *Laurel Canyon*, about an aging record producer's fumblingly chaotic life on Lookout Mountain, gets close when she describes the canyon as "kind of lazy and kind of dirty and kind of earthy and sort of reckless. That you can tuck yourself in a canyon in the middle of Los Angeles—that's extraordinary."

Even locals' attempts to codify the canyon's bona fides tend to fail. A proposed sign at the intersection of Laurel Canyon Boulevard and Mulholland Highway "welcoming" motorists to the canyon inspired a half hour of contentious debate at a community board meeting. Serendipity—like the wild fennel that pokes up through the canyon's crumbling granite walls—is tenacious here. "People like to preserve a certain kind of quality of their lifestyle," says Gail Zappa. "They aren't so anxious to develop it so that it loses its charm. I think it's something very vigilant and very aware—like, 'Don't fuck with this, because we're not gonna let you in here to mess with it.'" Several years ago little gravity-defying rock sculptures appeared along Laurel

Canyon Boulevard. They just materialized, like crop circles. No one seemed to know where they had come from, but they looked cool and were therefore subsumed into the canyon's free-ranging aesthetic. Word later got around that the chef at the pizza joint underneath the Canyon Store had put them up as a freelance beautification project, because he felt like it. That, everyone agreed, was very cool.

The nexus for all of the above, the Canyon Country Store, opened in 1919. The original foundations that survived its 1929 fire form the grotto-like walls of Pace, the funky-chic restaurant downstairs, which has successfully imbibed the canyon's esprit right down to pizza-box graphics that wouldn't look out of place on a poster promoting a Buffalo Springfield concert at the Kaleidoscope. Over the years the building has housed a combination art gallery–restaurant, while the parking lot has served as a clearinghouse for untold volumes of contraband. Glenn Frey, then a callow folkie fresh from Michigan, later said that when he happened to glimpse David Crosby sitting on the steps of the store, he knew he had made the right decision to come to L.A. "The Country Store was like the lobby of the Laurel Canyon hotel, and therefore was a fabulous fucking place," says Michael Des Barres. "The residents of this crumbling establishment would gather for their milk and cookies. We used to go there at all hours of the day and night. It was lovely, just catching up with the dealers."

By all that is logical, the store, with its old-timey Coca-Cola sign and twirling ceiling fans, ought to have been gentrified years ago into a merry market like the famed Oakville Grocery in Napa Valley, with pots of pesto and aioli on the sandwich board and the sort of staff that could step into a Ralph Lauren ad. Instead, it remains deeply idiosyncratic and utterly unpretentious, its only concession to trendiness being the addition of an espresso bar that hosts a daily gathering of goldbricking locals who smoke and talk while their dogs slumber in the morning sun. The Canyon Store is where ashen locals instinctively massed at daybreak the morning of the 1994 Northridge earthquake, shopping for reassurance as much as for what they could buy from the toppled stock. And where bottles of Johnnie Walker and Ketel One were cinched into sacks amid stunned silence on the evening of September 11, 2001.

Celebrities of all stripes continue to treat the store as a sort of demented commissary. While he was renting on Lookout Mountain, Liam Neeson would stop by for his morning orange juice, towering over the starstruck girl at the checkout. One night it would be a Beastie Boy by the beer cooler; another, Keanu Reeves by the magazine racks; still another, Renée Zellweger, Renée Zellweger's sister, Renée Zellweger's mom and dad, and George Clooney around a table at Pace (Clooney paid), while Matthew Broderick wandered the aisles upstairs.

Tommy Bina, the genial Iranian expat who's owned the store since 1982, modestly allows, "I don't think there is any store in the entire world that has so many celebrities come through." With little prodding, Bina names a few. "Sophia Loren, she still comes in every once in a while. Everybody from *Beverly Hills 90210*, Ben Kingsley—he was Gandhi—Sofia Coppola, Johnny Depp—he always was thinking—Don Henley, Bruce Springsteen." Bina pauses. "Robbin Crosby from Ratt." The canyon's omnipresent Brit faction has its own aisle marked with a miniature Union Jack stocked with HP Sauce, Weetabix, Oxo cubes, and other delights from the empire, started when David Bowie sheepishly prevailed upon Bina to order Cadbury Flake bars. Mick Jagger thereafter suggested U.K.-style Kit Kats. Before his incarceration in the Bonny Bakley murder case and subsequent acquittal in its criminal trial, Robert Blake, who was

trying to quit smoking, kept an open pack of Parliaments behind the register and asked that the staff dole them out to him,
one per visit. Blake later extended privileges to other jonesing
smokers.

Regulars make piecemeal contributions to the decor.
Christina Applegate, raised on Lookout Mountain, donated an
American flag bearing a likeness of the ubiquitous Morrison,
which hung over the front doors before shredding during an El
Niño. The psychedelic art-nouveau exteriors were painted in
1968 by Spike Stewart, now a film director. The walls and coun-
ters are cluttered with totems: the sleeve from Jackie DeShannon's *Laurel Canyon* album, a grainy photograph of the canyon
dusted in snow from a freak storm in the '40s, hand-tied incense
smudges made from locally picked wild sage, and, over the front
door, enormous blowups from Photo Days past. And it is here,
finally, that Bina clears up the origins of the tradition.

In 1994, when Stewart touched up his paint job on the
store's facade, he concurrently designed a T-shirt, the proceeds
from which were to be applied toward local animal-welfare
causes. Somebody got the idea of taking a group photo of
T-shirt owners wearing their purchases in front of the store on,
say, the Fourth of July. This was a success. The T-shirts kept
right on selling, however, so the next year another picture was
taken, and the next year, and so on. Before long Photo Day was
augmented with corn dogs and balloon hats and live music from
unsigned canyon bands. Residents proudly display their live-
stock, from pit bulls to, one year, a brace of billy goats.

To happen upon these events in the middle of a Saturday
afternoon—part English country fete, part founders-day celebration, part honorary love-in—is to witness the various inscrutable personalities of Laurel Canyon finally made flesh. In
this city famous for having no psychic center and paltry tradi-

tions, once a year the canyon faithful jockey for position on the store's front porch as the traffic on Laurel Canyon Boulevard slows to gawk, just as it did thirty years before when the hippies gathered with their joints and apple wine on the concrete traffic triangle across the street, now occupied by a photographer screaming at everyone to *shove over,* he can't get everyone in the frame. The impulse, then and now, is the same: Behold, the tribe has gathered. Make of us what you will, but you will know that we are here, now, in this canyon. There's even a freak flag, flying high, as everyone flashes peace signs, hoists dogs and children and over-caffeinated beverages skyward, and cheers madly, waiting for the photographer to signal that he's got the shot.

And then, having reminded themselves why they live here, everyone drifts back up the hill to their Laurel Canyon homes.

NOTES

All quotations in this book are from interviews conducted by the author except as noted.

PREFACE

xiv "There was amazing tribal life": Jackson Browne, in Holzman and Daws, *Follow the Music*, p. 224.

xvi "This is God speaking": Barry Friedman, ibid., p. 226.

1. SO YOU WANT TO BE A ROCK-AND-ROLL STAR?

5 "In the strictest sense": Gene Shay, in "Folk Music," http://www.humanitiesweb.org.

8 "I can remember": David Crosby, in Crosby and Gottlieb, *Long Time Gone*, p. 85.

13 "standing in front of a mirror": Ibid.

14 "It was like winning": Gene Clark, ibid., p. 111.

2. UNCLE FRANK'S CABIN

24 "The rent was seven hundred dollars": Zappa with Occhiogrosso, *The Real Frank Zappa Book*, p. 101.

28 "except for plastic clip-on curlers": Des Barres, *I'm with the Band*, p. 40.

36 "there were 6,000 people": Alice Cooper, in Cooper and Gaines, *Me, Alice*.

36 "He was our hero": Ibid.

36 "All right, all right": Ibid.

36 "Even hippies hated us": Ibid.

38 "He handed me a bottle": Zappa, in Zappa with Occhiogrosso, *The Real Frank Zappa Book*, p. 102.

3. LADY OF THE CANYON

41　"powerful white middle-class matriarch": Ann Douglas, in *Terrible Honesty*, p. 6.

41　"aimed to ridicule and overturn everything": Ibid.

42　"Christian beliefs and middle-class values": Ibid., p. 8.

42　"Plumpness [would] never again": Ibid.

42　"her notions of middle-class piety": Ibid.

42　"modern America, led by New York": Ibid.

43　"[Elvis] won over the children": Bobbie Ann Mason, in Dugan, *Picturing the South*, p. 142.

44　"absolutely certain that no matter which way": Thompson, *Hell's Angels*.

46　"There was a place for women": Dalton, *Piece of My Heart*, p. 44.

47　"It's true, honest to God": Cass Elliot, in Jerry Hopkins, "The Rolling Stone Interview," *Rolling Stone*, Oct. 26, 1968, p. 20.

47　"That's when Harvey showed up": Denny Doherty, *Dream a Little Dream: The Nearly True Story of the Mamas and the Papas*, http://www.dennydoherty.com.

47　"When I heard us sing together": Elliot, in Hopkins, "Rolling Stone Interview," p. 20.

49　"My house is a very free house": Ibid.

50　"I said, 'Cass, I don't know'": Gary Burden, in "Mama Cass," *Under the Covers*, DVD (Triptych Pictures, Lightyear Entertainment, 2002).

52　"before any of us were anybody": Stephen Stills, in "Crosby, Stills & Nash," Ibid.

53　"David and I were messing around": Ibid.

54　"Cass called me": Graham Nash, ibid.

54　"That was a moment,": Ibid.

55　"My role in the Mamas and Papas": Elliot, in Hopkins, "Rolling Stone Interview," p. 20.

56　"I was told": Ibid.

56　"They're paying me an outrageous amount": Ibid.

57　"Cass Elliot is the only fat person": Phillips, *You'll Never Eat Lunch in This Town Again*, p. 153.

57　"I wonder . . . how they knew": Ibid., p. 154.

57　"Cass had started it all": Ibid., p. 155.

57　"I'm not," she thought to herself: Ibid., p. 156.

4. EVERYDAY PEOPLE

66　"The band sounds really good": Waddy Wachtel, "The Penguin Biographies," http://www.fleetwoodmac.net/penguin/waddy.htm.

5. BUSINESSMEN, THEY DRINK MY WINE

107 "She had a backlog": Elliot Roberts, in *Joni Mitchell: Woman of Heart and Mind*, DVD (Eagle Rock Entertainment, 2003).

108 "Elliot became wildly excited": David Geffen, ibid.

109 "I took her around to people": David Crosby, ibid.

109 "David set it up": Roberts, ibid.

111 "There was a camaraderie": Ibid.

113 "Don't be stupid": Geffen, in Crosby and Gottlieb, *Long Time Gone*, p. 145.

116 "Wait until they make some money": Joni Mitchell, radio interview by Jim Ladd, *Inner View*, Dec. 29, 1980.

6. 1969

130 "sitting there, taking a long hit": Taylor, *Prisoner of Woodstock*, p. 34.

132 "It's creating a sort of microcosmic society": Mick Jagger, quoted in *Gimme Shelter*, directed by Albert and David Mayles, 1970.

137 "Tens of thousands of people": Stan Goldstein, quoted in Michael Sragow, "*Gimme Shelter*: The True Story," *Salon*, Aug. 10, 2000.

7. TROUBADOURS

142 "The Troubadour was the first place": Don Henley, in Joe Smith and Mitchell Fink, *Off the Record* (New York: Warner Books, 1990).

147 "I really didn't know anybody": Ibid.

147 "I said my group's not": Ibid.

150 "The Troubadour has been a gold mine": Doug Weston, in Robert Hilburn, "A Man Who Had a Passion for Art of the Troubadour," *Los Angeles Times*, Feb. 16, 1999, p. 1.

153 "My whole life came alive": Elton John, in Myrna Oliver, "Doug Weston, Troubadour Founder, Dies," *Los Angeles Times*, Feb. 15, 1999, p. 1.

8. SHE DON'T LIE

155 "A little snow": Shapiro, *Waiting for the Man*, p. 229.

160 "My senses were lit up": *The Vaults of Erowid*, http://www.erowid.org.

160 "In less than five minutes": Ibid.

161 "Some of my dearest friends": Cab Calloway, in Shapiro, *Waiting for the Man*, p. 91.

172 "At first it seemed OK": Paul McCartney, in Jon Wilde, adapted by David Edwards, "McCartney: I Have Tried Heroin," *Mirror*, June 2, 2004.

176 "You know, I didn't write this song": Jackson Browne, in Ralph Bowling
     and Rick Bowen, *FrontRowNews*, http://www.frontrownews.com.

177 "Look at me now": Ibid.

9. THE L.A. QUEENS

183 "The waitresses were known": Stuart-Ware, *Behind the Scenes on the Pegasus
     Carousel,* p. 40.

183 "Keep walking hippie": Ibid.

184 "The Hyatt House was one of those places": Neal Doughty, *A Decade of
     Rock and Roll—Liner Notes,* http://www.speedwagon.com.

187 "If a cash transaction": Morgana Welch, *Shameless Archives,* http://www.
     hollywooddiaries.com.

189 "There were more girls": Ibid.

191 "Robert fancied Tyla": Ibid.

191 "They asked me if I wanted": Ibid.

10. ALL THE YOUNG DUDES

200 "bangs that curled under": Nikki Sixx, in Lee et al., *The Dirt: Mötley Crüe,*
     p. 27.

209 "made us very paranoid": Joe Walsh, in Robert Hilburn, "The Eagles: The
     Long Run Is Over," *Los Angeles Times,* May 23, 1982.

213 "There was a time": Glenn Frey, in Anthony DeCurtis, "The Rolling Stone
     Interview," *Rolling Stone,* Sept. 20, 1990.

213 "Those kinds of record sales": Don Henley, ibid.

214 "it's hard to be an underdog": Ibid.

214 "The dream was unfulfilled": Ibid.

11. EVE OF DESTRUCTION

225 September 16, 1979: Details of the 1979 Laurel Canyon fire were taken
     from a report in the Sept. 24, 1979, *Los Angeles Herald Examiner.* Staff writ-
     ers Rudy Aversa, Ellen Futterman, Carol Gulotta, Andrew Jaffe, Robert
     Knowles, Sarai Ribicoff, and Joel Sappell spent five days hiking through the
     ruins assembling a house-by-house reconstruction of the fire.

237 "I have tried, unsuccessfully I fear": F. Scott Fitzgerald, in *Tales of the Jazz
     Age,* p. viii.

BIBLIOGRAPHY

Berg, A. Scott. *Goldwyn: A Biography*. New York: Alfred A. Knopf, 1989.

Cogan, Jim, and William Clark. *Temples of Sound: Inside the Great Recording Studios*. San Francisco: Chronicle Books, 2003.

Cooper, Alice, and Steven Gaines. *Me, Alice*. New York: Putnam, 1976.

Crosby, David, and Carl Gottlieb. *Long Time Gone: The Autobiography of David Crosby*. New York: Doubleday, 1988.

Dalton, David. *Piece of My Heart: A Portrait of Janis Joplin*. New York: St. Martin's Press, 1985.

Dannen, Fredric. *Hit Men: Power Brokers and Fast Money Inside the Music Business*. New York: Times Books, 1990.

Davis, Stephen. *Hammer of the Gods: The Led Zeppelin Saga*. New York: William Morrow, 1985.

Des Barres, Pamela. *I'm with the Band: Confessions of a Groupie*. New York: William Morrow, 1987.

Douglas, Ann. *Terrible Honesty: Mongrel Manhattan in the 1920s*. New York: Farrar, Straus and Giroux, 1995.

Dugan, Ellen. *Picturing the South: 1860 to the Present*. San Francisco: Chronicle Books, 1996.

Fiegel, Eddi. *Dream a Little Dream of Me: The Life of Cass Elliot*. Chicago: Chicago Review Press, 2005.

Gaines, Steven. *Heroes & Villains: The True Story of the Beach Boys*. New York: Dutton/Signet, 1986.

Goodman, Fred. *The Mansion on the Hill: Dylan, Young, Geffen, Springsteen, and the Head-On Collision of Rock and Commerce*. New York: Random House, 1997.

Gray, Michael. *Mother! The Frank Zappa Story*. London: Plexus, 1993.

Greene, Bob. *American Beat*. New York: Atheneum, 1983.

———. *Billion Dollar Baby*. New York: Atheneum, 1974.

Hajdu, David. *Positively 4th Street: The Lives and Times of Joan Baez, Bob Dylan, Mimi Baez Fariña, and Richard Fariña*. New York: North Point Press, 2002.

Holzman, Jac, and Gavan Daws. *Follow the Music: The Life and High Times of Elektra Records in the Great Years of American Popular Culture*. Santa Monica, Calif.: FirstMedia Books, 1998.

Hopkins, Jerry, and Danny Sugarman. *No One Here Gets Out Alive*. New York: Warner Books, 1980.

Lecaro, Lina. "Have You Ever Been Teen?" *L.A. Weekly*, Nov. 6–12, 1998.

Lee, Tommy, Mick Mars, Vince Neil, Nikki Sixx, and Neil Strauss. *The Dirt: Mötley Crüe: Confessions of the World's Most Notorious Rock Band*. New York: HarperCollins, 2001.

MacDonnell, Allan. "In Too Deep," *L.A. Weekly*, Oct. 3–8, 2003.

Meade, Marion. *Dorothy Parker: What Fresh Hell Is This?* New York: Villard Books, 1988.

Norman, Philip. *Shout! The Beatles in Their Generation*. New York: Simon & Schuster, 1981.

Phillips, Julia. *You'll Never Eat Lunch in This Town Again*. New York: Random House, 1991.

Quisling, Erik, and Austin Williams. *Straight Whisky: A Living History of Sex, Drugs, and Rock 'n' Roll on the Sunset Strip*. Chicago: Bonus Books, 2003.

Seireeni, Richard. "Early Canyon History," www.laurelcanyon.org.

Shapiro, Harry. *Waiting for the Man: The Story of Drugs and Popular Music*. London: Quartet Books, 1988.

Stuart-Ware, Michael. *Behind the Scenes on the Pegasus Carousel with the Legendary Rock Group Love*. London: Helter Skelter, 2003.

Taylor, Dallas. *Prisoner of Woodstock*. New York: Thunder's Mouth Press, 1994.

Thompson, Hunter S. *Hell's Angels: A Strange and Terrible Saga*. New York: Random House, 1966.

————. *Songs of the Doomed: More Notes on the Death of the American Dream: Gonzo Papers, Vol. 3*. New York: Summit Books, 1990.

Webb, Jimmy. *Tunesmith: Inside the Art of Songwriting*. New York: Hyperion, 1998.

Zappa, Frank, with Peter Occhiogrosso. *The Real Frank Zappa Book*. New York: Touchstone, 1989.

Zimmer, Dave. *4 Way Street: The Crosby, Stills, Nash & Young Reader*. Cambridge, Mass.: Da Capo Press, 2004.

DISCOGRAPHY

A selection of albums with Laurel Canyon roots.

Alice Cooper
Pretties for You (Straight, 1969)
Easy Action (Straight, 1970)

Jackson Browne
Jackson Browne (Asylum, 1972)

The Byrds
Mr. Tambourine Man (Columbia, 1965)
Turn! Turn! Turn! (Columbia, 1966)

Crosby, Stills & Nash
Crosby, Stills & Nash (Atlantic, 1969)

Crosby, Stills, Nash & Young
Déjà Vu (Atlantic, 1970)

Jackie DeShannon
Laurel Canyon (Imperial, 1968)

The Doors
Waiting for the Sun (Elektra, 1968)

The Eagles
The Eagles (Asylum, 1972)

Cyrus Faryar
Islands (Elektra, 1973)

Fraternity of Man
Fraternity of Man (ABC, 1968)

The GTOs
Permanent Damage (Straight, 1969)

Carole King
Tapestry (Ode, 1971)

Love
Da Capo (Elektra, 1967)
Forever Changes (Elektra, 1967)

The Mamas and the Papas
If You Can Believe Your Eyes and Ears (Dunhill, 1966)

John Mayall
Blues from Laurel Canyon (Polydor, 1968)

Joni Mitchell
Ladies of the Canyon (Reprise, 1970)

Modern Folk Quartet
Changes (Warner Bros., 1964)

The Monkees
The Essentials (Rhino, 2002)

The Mothers
Fillmore East: June 1971 (Bizarre, 1971)

The Mothers of Invention
Freak Out! (MGM/Verve, 1966)

The Turtles
It Ain't Me Babe (White Whale, 1965)

ACKNOWLEDGMENTS

Special thanks to Brian DeFiore, Denise Oswald, Tommy Bina and all at the Canyon Country Store, Brian Kend, Tiger Michiels, Mary Michiels, Jim Roup, Cary Baker, Todd Everett, David Rensin, Nancy Seaman, Steve Randall, Sally Stevens, Henry Diltz, Steve Pond, Michael James Jackson, Merle Ginsberg, Kate Garrick, Colman Andrews, and everyone who so generously contributed to the writing of this book.

INDEX